Planning Better Programs

The Adult Education Association Professional Development Series

CONSULTING EDITORS

Don F. Seaman, *Texas A&M University*

Alan R. Pardoen, *Mankato State University*

BUILDING THE LITERATURE OF A PROFESSION

About twenty-five years ago, between 1955 and 1959, the Adult Education Association developed a popular series of pamphlets to provide guidance to practitioners responsible for designing and delivering educational services to adults. At that time, it was recognized that many teachers, group leaders, and administrators working directly with adults had no training in the field of adult education, and few even knew that such training was available.

Rapid expansion has occurred in adult education since the inception of the old series. Institutions have responded enthusiastically and imaginatively to adults' increasing demands for programs. In addition, there has been significant development of the literature on the needs and interests of adults and on programming techniques to meet the needs of the adult student.

The expansion of the literature, the new clientele groups, and the increased number of participants created the need for a new series of publications which would be of value to those who serve on the firing line, working directly with adult learners on a day-to-day basis.

Although training programs in adult education have increased, they have not kept pace with the expanding field. Many of those employed in adult education are not aware that there is a growing body of knowledge and techniques which can help them perform their role better. Many are not even aware that they are functioning as "adult educators."

The AEA Professional Development Series is a cooperative effort of the Adult Education Association and the McGraw-Hill Book Company. The first titles were released in the fall of 1980. Each publication takes a practical, "how to," approach, with philosophical and theoretical considerations enhancing and lending support to the practical side of the content. Frequent examples, case studies, and critical incidents demonstrate the application of information, enabling the reader to perceive how an idea may be put to use in an on-the-job situational context.

The intended audience for the series is the administrator, teacher, or counselor who is faced with the day-to-day responsibility of providing educational services to an adult population, and the aspiring adult educator currently engaged in a formal training program in preparation for assuming a role as an adult education leader.

The Series

Boyle: Planning Better Programs
Seaman: Working Effectively with Task-Oriented Groups
Ilsley and Niemi: Recruiting and Training Volunteers

Planning Better Programs

Patrick G. Boyle, Ph.D.
Professor
University of Wisconsin-Extension
Madison

McGraw-Hill Book Company

New York   St. Louis   San Francisco   Auckland   Bogotá   Hamburg
Johannesburg   London   Madrid   Mexico   Montreal   New Delhi
Panama   Paris   São Paulo   Singapore   Sydney   Tokyo   Toronto

This book was set in Times Roman by David Seham Associates.
The editor was Donald W. Burden;
the production supervisor was Dominick Petrellese.
The drawings were done by VIP Graphics.
R. R. Donnelley & Sons Company was printer and binder.

PLANNING BETTER PROGRAMS

1234567890 DODO 8987654321

Library of Congress Cataloging in Publication Data

Boyle, Patrick Gerald, date
    Planning better programs.

    (Adult Education Association professional
development series)
    Includes index.
    1. Adult education. 2. Continuing education.
I. Title. II. Series: Adult Education
Association. Adult Education Association
professional development series.
LC5219.B6   374   80-18643
ISBN 0-07-000552-4

Contents

Preface   vii
Acknowledgments   ix

SECTION I CONTINUING EDUCATION PROGRAMMING

1 Programs and Programming Processes   3
2 Philosophical Concerns of the
   Continuing Education Programmer   18
3 Change as an Assumption of Program
   Development   35
4 Approaches to Program Development   42

SECTION II THE ORGANIZATION AND PROGRAM DEVELOPMENT

5 Institutional Concerns in Program
   Development   63
6 The Role of the Programmer in
   Program Development   69

SECTION **III** **INVOLVEMENT OF PEOPLE IN PROGRAM DEVELOPMENT**

7   A Rationale for Involvement of
    People   91
8   Methods and Procedures for
    Involvement   109
9   Advisory Committees   120

SECTION **IV** **IDENTIFICATION OF PROBLEMS AND NEEDS**

10 Situational Analysis   139
11 Approaches to Clientele Analysis   155
12 Approaches to Community
    Analysis   165
13 A Framework for Establishing
    Priorities   172

SECTION **V** **PROVIDING LEARNING OPPORTUNITIES**

14 Program Development and
    Instructional Design   183
15 The Concept of Educational
    Objectives   194
16 Planning Learning Opportunities   206

SECTION **VI** **DETERMINING AND COMMUNICATING PROGRAM VALUE**

17 Determining Program
    Effectiveness   225
18 Communicating Program Value   236

Index   241

Preface

There is a crucial need for lifelong learning. Many people are seeking opportunities from continuing education to expand their intellectual horizons and gain new knowledge in order to cope with rapid change. Others, confronted by the growing complexity of technology, seek retraining to upgrade their skills or prepare for entirely new careers. Groups and individuals pressing for new options in society—blacks, women, the poor—look increasingly to education as their only door to greater opportunity and fulfillment. And many young people who drifted through or dropped out of high school are realizing their mistake and recognize higher education as a crucial second chance to gain much needed skills.

These people—from all socioeconomic levels and of all ages—are turning to continuing education institutions for lifelong learning opportunities. With the changing population structure, this trend will continue. It is up to the leadership of such institutions to provide these opportunities if we are to avoid the prospect of large numbers of citizens permanently restricted in their ability to function and grow.

This textbook is designed to focus on the development of effective programs to meet the great challenge of lifelong learning. It presents a comprehensive review of program development concentrating on fifteen relevant concepts, with practical suggestions for application. The text does not offer a precise prescription for development of a program for a specific agency or institution, nor is it designed for personnel of a specific agency or institution. In fact, it is as applicable to the county agricultural agent as to the coordinator of business programs, the Community Change Agent, or the director of a continuing education center. The book includes descriptions, discussions, theory, analysis, and practical suggestions for the programmer or student of program development.

Although there are many periodicals and published papers about issues, problems, and applications of programming and curriculum building, this is the only general textbook that presents a total picture for the continuing education programmer or the student of program development. It provides a perspective of problem-solving programming as a major focus in continuing education today.

Patrick G. Boyle

Acknowledgments

My interest in program development emerged during doctoral research with my major adviser, Professor Walter T. Bjoraker. It has continued throughout my professional career at Wisconsin.

Students and colleagues with whom I have worked on program development represent a variety of professional areas, organizations, and agencies. Many students have been associated with Extension and its various program areas—agriculture, business, pharmacy, library sciences, and family living. Several social action, educational, and church-affiliated organizations and agencies have been represented by students. As a result of these varied experiences, I have prepared this book for continuing education programmers interested in developing or advising others on planning programs.

Graduate students at Wisconsin who have challenged and influenced my perceptions are Oscar W. Norby, M. P. Lacy, James M. Kincaid, Mohammad Douglah, Irwin R. Jahns, Richard F. Heard, Thomas E. O'Connell, Wilbur Voorhees, Brock Whale, Donald J. Blackburn, Glen M. Farrell, Sahir Sudad, Gwenna Moss, Michael C. Shannon, Joe Donaldson, Joy Dohr, and Cathleen Finley. In addition, colleagues at Wisconsin who have had a significant influence on my understanding of program development include Gale VandeBerg, Jerold Apps, Sara Steele, Laverne Forest, Robert Rieck, and Harold Montross.

I would like to thank Rita Sears, Ellen Segalla, and Sheila Mulcahy for their efforts in typing, editing, and processing the materials for this book; and my wife, Mary, and sons, Steve and Jim, for their patience and support.

Patrick G. Boyle

Planning Better Programs

Section I

Continuing Education Programming

We must prepare for the challenges ahead as a nation, as communities, and as individuals. In the process of preparing for the future, we must understand the interdependence of our environment, our values, our economy, our work patterns, our family structures, our traditional concepts of education, and our ways of life. Thus, as we look to the future, there is a need for continuing education. People in every walk of life and leaders in both the public and private sectors need access to knowledge and research and opportunities to grow and develop. They need to reach their full potential as citizens of society.

This first section focuses on the basis for continuing education programming. A concept of program is developed in Chapter 1. Emphasis is given to three types of programs that are identified as developmental, institutional, and informational. Also, the concept of program is examined from the view of levels of programs, the programmer's role, and the function of the organization.

In Chapter 2, a framework is presented for the continuing education programmer to use in developing a working philosophy. Programmers must identify their beliefs about education, learning, the learner, the pro-

1

grammer, and program development. This identification is often a challenging effort but extremely important. Beliefs will greatly influence the actions we take and the procedures we follow in program development.

The concept that change is the basic assumption we make when developing programs with adults is presented in Chapter 3. As defined here, the term "change" means preserving and maintaining the present situations as well as growth and development. It also may include reversing the present trends. This definition and assumption about change provides the ultimate goal for effective program development.

Fifteen concepts considered relevant for effective program development are identified in Chapter 4. These concepts will have to be implemented by following a planned set of procedures that depends upon the programming situation. For example, need identification procedures are probably different in development than in institutional programming. A suggested program development model or framework is presented for each type of program. There are similarities and many differences in the three approaches.

Chapter 1

Programs and Programming Processes

Today, there is a crucial need for lifelong learning. More and more people, many well beyond traditional college age, are seeking opportunities for continuing education to expand their intellectual horizons, to develop a better understanding of society and its institutions, and to gain new knowledge to enable them to cope with rapid change. Others, confronted by the growing complexity of technology, seek retraining to upgrade their skills or prepare for entirely new careers. Groups and individuals pressing for new options in society—blacks, women, the poor—look increasingly to education as their only door to greater opportunity and fulfillment. And many young people who drifted through or dropped out of high school are perceiving their action as a mistake and see education as a crucial second chance to gain much-needed skills.

These people—from all socioeconomic levels and of all ages—are turning to continuing education agencies for lifelong learning opportunities. This trend will continue. It is up to the professional leadership of continuing education to provide these opportunities; otherwise, we face the prospect of having large numbers of citizens permanently restricted in their ability to function and grow. A broad interpretation is being used for continuing education agencies so as to include a variety of private and public organizations, such as extension organizations, continuing education centers, churches, and mass media. This book is designed to focus on the development of effective programs to meet this great challenge of lifelong learning.

Program plans of educational institutions for the 1980s will likely include a wide variety of programs using modern technology and many instructional approaches. Some examples will be educational programs to:

• Help citizens identify, prevent, and solve family crises, such as family violence, child abuse and neglect, divorce, teen-age pregnancy, alcoholism, and drug abuse.
• Provide in-depth counseling and management assistance, financial analysis, market and feasibility studies, cash flow and business planning, and industrial engineering help to small business owners and managers.
• Update the competence of professional architects in areas of new technology, designs, materials, and energy, social, and natural resource issues.
• Help women and minorities understand equal opportunity and social security laws, welfare rights, community property and divorce law revisions, and the legal problems of the displaced homemaker.
• Utilize a computerized retrieval system for farmers, agribusiness personnel, and state and federal agency personnel on diagnosis of plant and crop and animal-pest problems, and proper identification of recommended treatments.
• Use mediated instruction to update pharmacists on drug information.
• Help citizen leaders, neighborhood organizations, and municipal and county governments to improve their problem-solving skills, build linkages between community, state, and federal agencies, identify priority problems, and expand their ability to make action decisions to improve the quality of community life.

The challenge for the continuing education programmer is to understand and utilize effective program development approaches. This first chapter initiates this process by exploring the concept of program.

A CONCEPT OF PROGRAM AND PROGRAM DEVELOPMENT

The term "program" is perplexing because it is consistently used to communicate many divergent thoughts, ideas, and practices. "Program" is often equated with "curriculum" as used in references focusing on formal school situations. Definitions of "curriculum" usually express the concept of structured learning opportunities to achieve specified objectives.

Johnson said, "[C]urriculum is a structured series of intended learning outcomes."[1]

The definition of "program" as used in this book is much broader than this definition of curriculum. *Program* is the product resulting from all the programming activities in which the professional educator and learner are involved. For example, it would include need analysis, planning, instruction, promotion, evaluation, and reporting.

Program development is defined as a deliberate series of actions and decisions through which representatives of the people affected by the potential program are involved with a programmer to:

• Develop an organizational structure for analyzing, interpreting, and making decisions about problems or situations that should be changed or improved.
• Effectively utilize resources in the study and analysis of the people and their communities.
• Establish priorities on the problems and situations for which desirable changes should be identified in the plan of action.
• Identify desired outcomes to be attained through the program with people and communities.
• Identify resources and support for effective promotion and implementation of the program.
• Design an instructional plan that provides for extensive involvement of the learners in appropriate learning experiences.
• Implement the plan of action that is designed to provide appropriate learning opportunities such as conferences, meetings, workshops, individual consultations, and radio and television programs.
• Develop appropriate accountability approaches so as to make effective judgments about the value of the program.
• Communicate the value of program to financial decision makers, the participants, and other interested individuals and groups.

Program development is really an attempt to plan an educational program that will contribute to improving the health of the people and their community. *Health* is defined here as the state of being, the condition, the situation. It may be the economic health (for example, levels of per capita income) or the social health (housing conditions for the aged) or the environmental health (levels of phosphates in lakes) or cultural health (the number and scope of leisure activities available). The changes needed to improve these situations must be identified and described. The knowledge, attitudes, and skills that people need in order to change these situa-

[1]Mauritz Johnson, "Definitions and Models in Curriculum Theory," in Arno Bellack and Herbert Kliebard (eds.), *Curriculum and Evaluation,* McCutchan Publishing Corporation, Berkeley, Calif., 1977, p. 6.

tions must be described. These needed changes become the central and critical challenge in effective program development.

In this text the terms "need" and "problem" are used interchangeably. It is also recognized that the term "need" may apply more appropriately to the individual, while "problem" may be more meaningful in reference to community or group situations. However, to avoid a confusing distinction, the terms are used interchangeably.

In order to avoid confusion, the term "programming" is used synonymously with "program development." The concept of program can be most effectively understood when we explore several dimensions or ideas relating to it. These dimensions provide an interpretation of program as it relates to types of programming activities and events, the organization, the programmer, and the different clientele and levels of programming. A *programmer* is an individual who provides leadership and performs tasks related to planning, organizing, teaching, and evaluating continuing education programs.

PROGRAM TYPES

One approach to understanding the concept of program is to attempt to classify or categorize all the different types of programs. In adult or continuing education there are many different types of programs. As was illustrated at the start of this chapter, the continuing educator may design (1) programs to help teachers, nurses, lawyers, or pharmacists maintain certification standards; (2) programs to help a community change certain economic or social situations, such as developing housing for elderly, revitalizing the downtown of a small town, building a recreational facility for youth, or changing attitudes about equality; (3) programs to distribute information that is new or is needed by professionals, individuals, families, or communities for immediate use. In addition, there are national programs in such areas as energy conservation, health care, and economic stability.

Understanding the different types of programs is significant because the type of p ogram and its goals have implications for the nature and design of the learning opportunities to be provided, the resources necessary to achieve the goals, and the role of the programmer in the programming process. In order to assist in the development of the concept of program, three different types of programs have been identified and described. They are:

- Developmental
- Institutional
- Informational

Figure 1.1 Comparative Analysis of Program Types

	Program types		
Factors	Developmental	Institutional	Informational
Primary goal	Define and solve individual, group, or community problems.	Growth and improvement of an individual's basic abilities, skills, knowledge, competencies.	Exchange of information.
Source of objectives	Developed primarily out of needs or problems of the clients.	Developed primarily from the discipline or field of knowledge and from the educator.	Derived primarily from new information available from research findings, new laws, or new regulations.
Use of knowledge	Knowledge or content is used to aid in the solution of the problem; it is a means to an end.	Mastery of content or knowledge is the focus. Programs are focused on how to achieve this end.	Content is transferred to the client for immediate use.
Involvement of the learner	Involved in determining problem or need and the scope and nature of the program.	Involved in implementing the learning experiences.	Involved primarily as a recipient of the information.
Role of the programmer	Facilitating the entire educational process from need identification through the evaluative process. Other roles will include promotion, legitimation, and communicating the results.	Disseminates knowledge through instructional process.	Provides answers to requests for information.
Standards of effectiveness	Effectiveness is determined on the quality of the problem solution and the degree to which individuals, groups, and communities developed problem-solving skills.	Effectiveness determined on how well the client mastered the content or desired competencies.	Effectiveness determined by the number of persons reached, and how much information was distributed.

The three types are summarized in Figure 1.1 on the basis of several differentiating factors. For example, the objectives for a developmental program will evolve from the interests and needs of the people and communities involved. If a community is concerned about the problems of the aged, the program objectives will be identified by several different groups and individuals through a series of analytical and legislative experiences. In the institutional type of program the objectives are based primarily on the field of knowledge or discipline. New research on drug use and its effect on the human cardiovascular system would provide the source for a program for pharmacists. Newly enacted legislation affecting the social security benefits for the elderly would provide the basis for objectives of informational programs for groups of the elderly as well as for administrators of social security programs. The difference is that, in the drug example, it would be necessary to draw from several basic disciplines or fields of knowledge. In the informational example, new regulations important to the aged have to be shared. Similar examples are appropriate for the other differentiating factors.

Following are more detailed descriptions of the different types of programs.

Developmental Programs

This type of program identifies major problems of clientele, communities, or segments of society, after which an educational program to help people successfully solve or cope with the problems can be developed. This type of program has become increasingly significant as the rate of change in society has increased. We must continually adapt to the world around us, and as the rate of change in the world increases, so must the rate of adaptation. Developmental programs have the need for continual direction and adaptation of change as their basis. The individual, the group, the community, and the society are faced with a seemingly never-ending series of problems that involve change of some type:

- A group of youths in a community gets involved in the use of drugs. They become very active and involve a large portion of the youth of a community. The youths, parents, and community have a major problem. A solution must be found for this situation since the drug abuse situation is leading to many other community problems.
- A church might find that their program, which had worked well in the past, no longer appeals to a new generation of churchgoers. They decide that the program must be more relevant to problems in society to attract younger members. They meet opposition to change from the older people in the church. The educational program must provide for a solution to this dilemma.
- A community might be faced with a new mineral discovery in their area. A mining company would like to come in and develop the in-

dustry. But what about the social, health, economic, and environmental impact of such a move on the area? What will be all the consequences of this developmental effort? What will happen to the town when the minerals are gone? The people feel they must face such problems before the mining company is allowed to start developmental operations.

• An individual has an intensive interest in classical jazz as a part-time vocation. A series of varied educational opportunities over a period of time would be necessary in order to develop competence and satisfaction.

• The society is faced with the problem of a dwindling energy supply and an ever-increasing demand for energy. How are conservation measures to be implemented? Can education help people understand what needs to be done and how to do it, before the society runs out of energy resources?

• A community and its people want to determine the orderly and effective use of all the land, but particularly land for agriculture, housing, and natural habitat.

These are but a few of the many problem types for which developmental programming must design educational approaches that can make a significant contribution.

Several significant aspects distinguish developmental programs from other types of programs. Developmental programs often begin in very ambiguous situations. Although there may be recognition of a need, the problem is often not well defined nor are priorities established. Because these programming efforts begin in open, undelineated situations, the full range of programming activities must be carried out. With only the recognition that a situation should be more desirable, the developmental programmer must decide on the process to use, exactly what the problem or aspect of the problem is to be focused on, and what goal is to be attained. Thus, the objectives are developed out of an extensive analysis of the situation. The situation may be a community, a professional association, a church, or a section of a state. This analysis usually requires the involvement of several potential clientele groups from the very beginning. They are usually the most valuable resource in this type of programming, since their recognition of the problem, their actions to solve the problem, and their satisfaction with the solution determine the success or failure of the program.

Another significant aspect of developmental programming is that knowledge is used as a means for contributing to the solution of the need or problem. Knowledge is useful mainly to the extent that it helps achieve the goal. So, while transfer of knowledge and mastery of skills often take place in developmental programming and are important for its effectiveness, they are generally a means for obtaining the main goal—that of finding solutions to problems.

Related to this point is the manner in which such programming efforts are evaluated. As mentioned, a developmental program can be considered successful if solutions to the problems can be found. This is the usual way of evaluating the effectiveness of developmental programs. However, many continuing education programmers would consider programming efforts successful if the individuals, group, and/or communities develop in some way as a result of the problem-solving efforts. This would be considered a valuable outcome regardless of whether a good problem solution was achieved or not. At this point, developmental programming overlaps with institutional programming. This overlap will be discussed further, following a review of each major type of program.

Institutional Programs

The focus of institutional programming is to bring about growth and improvement in an individual's basic abilities, such as thinking and communicating. The focus of this type of program is to teach the content of a discipline or the parts of several disciplines to further the development of an individual. The term "institutional" is used to reflect a close relationship between the mission of the institution and the focus of the program. In this type, program development decisions are often based on the logical organization of a body of knowledge, and the continuing educator attempts to help participants master the discipline. Learning opportunities in institutional-centered programs are structured and carefully designed to achieve specific objectives. Some examples are:

- People whose skills become obsolete because of new technology enroll in technical schools to learn new trades. They are now participating in developmental programs designed to help them master new skills. Enrollment of professionals in developmental-type programs is an attempt to help them keep up with new research and technology.
- Many professionals, such as teachers, lawyers, nurses, are required to earn a certain number of units per year to update their knowledge in their field. They enroll in courses or workshops designed to develop or improve their understanding of new information and research as well as techniques.
- Likewise, a group of volunteer 4-H or Girl Scout leaders participate in a week-long workshop to learn leadership techniques and receive human relations training so that they can become more effective as leaders. These programs are all designed to help individuals develop skills, knowledge, and/or abilities in a certain area, which reflects the major goal of institutional programming.

Unlike developmental programming, in institutional programs objectives are not developed primarily from the needs recognized by the client. Objectives are generally developed from the knowledge within a field or discipline. The level of development and the needs of the student have an important effect on objectives and usually establish the level at which the program begins. For example, professional development programs for engineers might be developed mainly from needs identified through reviews of professional journals related to the field. If the needs were solely identified by practicing engineers, much new information in the discipline might be overlooked.

In evaluating institutional programs, mastery of content by the client is the main criterion used to determine results. While the focus is on the development of individuals, institutional programs are often a part of a larger problem-solving effort. For instance, in the earlier example the parents, youth, law enforcement officers, and medical professionals may need institutional programs on many aspects of drugs before the community-youth drug problem can be solved.

Informational Programs

This form of programming is often found in adult or continuing education. Essentially, it is an exchange of information between the educator or programmer and the student. The student approaches the educator, asks a question, obtains an answer, and departs. Some examples are a biologist in a national park, a home economist in a large fabric or appliance store, a dial-access system on health or gardening questions.

Informational programs have a goal of delivering information to students. The objectives for informational programs are derived from new information that is essential or desired by people. For example, new research findings related to health, new restrictions on the use of chemical pesticides, new laws regulating land use and water quality all become objectives for new informational programs. The focus in this type of programming is on identifying new information that should be disseminated. The success of informational programs is determined by evaluating the degree to which information has been available to people and the degree to which they have used it.

Informational programs differ from the other two types in that there are few feedback mechanisms. Generally, a student will request information and the programmer will provide it. Or a programmer might use a variety of means (mass media, brochures, and the like) to make information easily available to people. For example, the needs of the handicapped or the need to conserve energy and what can be done about each. Since there is less direct interaction with the client than in developmental or institutional programming, the program's effectiveness is difficult to measure. Usually, quantitative measures such as the number of student contact hours or the number of people contacted are the means used to determine effectiveness.

Informational programs are often a significant aspect of developmental and institutional programming. They stand out as distinct from developmental programs, however, in that the need or problem is known, and the continuing educator has decided to provide answers and is confident that he or she can provide the right ones. The remaining task is to get the information to the clients. The need for the information is very specific and clear.

Informational programming differs from developmental programming in that the information or answer is provided to the client. There is no attempt to help individuals gain an understanding of the concepts or the background that produced the information, only an understanding of the specific facts and how to use them in their life situation.

Although three types of continuing education programs have been described, it is important to understand that in most major programs there is considerable overlap. A student in my program development course developed a model for a proposed rape crisis center. She employed all three types of programs as integral parts of the proposed program of the center. The rape crisis center itself is an example of a "problem-solving or developmental approach" having developed a direct response to a real problem. But the center also functioned as an informational outlet, concerned with the legal aspects of rape. Further, the center offered an institutional-oriented course on the techniques of self-defense. Thus, we see that while one can conceptualize the three types separately, in a practical and pragmatic sense they can be interrelated and often are combined in a major program.

The three basic program types just described obviously do have important implications for all aspects of successful programming. The challenge is for the continuing educator to determine the types of programs to be developed and then to plan the program development approach.

PROGRAM AND THE ORGANIZATION

One way to think about the concept of program is to relate it to an organization. The program might be viewed as including all the activities of the educational organization. Some of these activities are directed toward the attainment of more or less explicit educational ends. Others are directed toward maintaining the viability of the organization or institution as a social entity. Figure 1.2 illustrates this idea.

Some educational efforts are directed toward target populations external to the immediate, organizational structure. They may be single activities (meetings, workshops, radio tapes, or lectures) and may have little or no relationship to the organization's other educational offerings; they may be organized into more systematic, sequential, integrated units, such as grade-level sequences, curricular or course units, and the like; or they may include the three types of programs previously described.

Figure 1.2 Program as Related to Organization

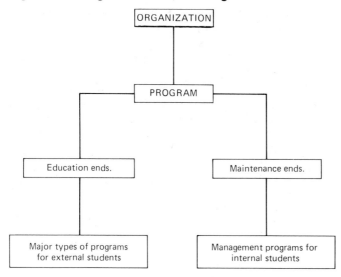

Other educational functions are internally oriented and provide programs to members of the organization. The staff development function of an organization is an example of an internal program.

Maintenance activities are less concerned with educational ends and more concerned with promoting and maintaining the organization as a viable social unit so it can continue to fulfill its educational functions. Such activities are generally referred to as administrative management and administrative leadership.

Although various maintenance functions are central to the operation of educational institutions, they are important only insofar as they contribute to the development and implementation of the primary task of the organization—education. If they are ends in themselves, then educational ends become secondary and maintenance takes precedence. Ideally, most activities and resources are directed toward institutional ends or goals rather than toward institutional maintenance, but this is not always the case.

PROGRAM AND PROGRAMMER RESPONSIBILITIES

Another way to describe the concept of program is to categorize the workload of the professional programmer by major responsibilities: (1) major change or developmental programs, (2) routine programming and informational activities, and (3) organizational and maintenance responsibilities. The following descriptions illustrate these three types of responsibilities in the programmer's total workload.

Major Change Programs[2]

The major change program is a programming effort in which resources are focused on an important need or problem, and in which valuable results are provided for many people through education. A major program is a total, concentrated effort that the professional programmer initiates to deal with a major problem that needs attention, and it is usually developmental in nature. One requirement is that a series of specific decisions be made as the program develops. Though the development of a major change program proceeds systematically, each phase in its development depends on those that went before. With the key problem or focus as a guide, one event or activity leads to another, one action creates follow-up action.

Most major programs require an interdisciplinary approach, since most serious problems today are complex and interrelated with other problems. They need the efforts of many professionals and resources from various disciplines, agencies, and organizations. They also need to be focused on over a period of time. Change does not happen immediately or easily, but takes time and extensive contact.

Many activities and events are not major programs even though they take considerable time and effort. These activities and events are important and should be considered a part of the total responsibilities of a professional continuing educator. In some situations they are traditional and occur each year. Those who are reached benefit from the experience a great deal, but the various benefits seldom add up to impressive results on serious problems that affect many people.

A major program is not an isolated workshop, event, institute, or course. It is not a single activity. It is not a variety of different educational offerings available cafeteria style. It is not individualized response to the continuous and urgent request from individuals for information.

A major program has the following characteristics:

- Intensive professional staff effort is devoted for a specific period of time.
- Extensive resources are focused on a serious need or problem.
- Many people see important results that affect them.
- Various activities are conducted in planned sequence and aimed at a common goal.

Routine Programming and Informational Activities

The pressure within any organization and from outside groups and individuals is often for the "individual activity or event" approach to pro-

[2]A major educational program is also referred to as a major project, major staff effort, major program emphasis, or major focus. Understanding and using the concept is more important than the words used to define it.

gramming. There are weekly news columns, radio or television programs, office calls, and individual consultations. Many people want one-shot meetings on many different topics. The telephone is always ringing. The continuing education programmer must speak at meetings, plan single events, and participate in other traditional or ongoing activities.

Major programs will not replace all these program activities, but as many of these traditional, ongoing activities as possible should be used to carry out the major program. A fair exhibit can be developed and passed on to different communities later; some radio time can be given; or a speech for a civic or community group can use some content from the major program.

Also, enough time, energy, and resources should be projected each year so activities and planning time specifically for the major program will not get slighted by routine or informational activities.

Organizational and Maintenance Responsibilities

Every professional must perform certain organizational and maintenance tasks for the vitality and effectiveness of the organization. Activities such as staff meetings, association conferences, faculty or staff committees, professional improvement workshops, program promotion, and informing the public are necessary for the organization to function effectively. They take time and should be planned for in advance.

PROGRAM LEVELS

The level of a program is an interesting and useful way of further developing an understanding of program. A program can be conceptualized at various levels, including national, state, community, organizational, and individual. The levels are relative, but each lower level should contribute to the program and goals of the higher levels. A national energy program can be seen as a composite of everything done by members of all the affiliated state organizations. A useful way of categorizing levels of programs is to use statements of objectives. General levels have broader statements with more specific statements for an individual program or even one workshop, meeting, or newsletter. Figure 1.3 illustrates levels of programs as applied to an economic agricultural situation. The continuing educator has a program focusing on individual farmers, which if successful would contribute to achieving the county-level objective.

If the county-level objective is achieved, then the state will have more efficiently managed dairy farms. This achievement in turn should contribute to improving the economic conditions of the state.

This example of program levels could be applied to any problem or program area. The basic idea is that program is used to define educational

Figure 1.3 Program Levels

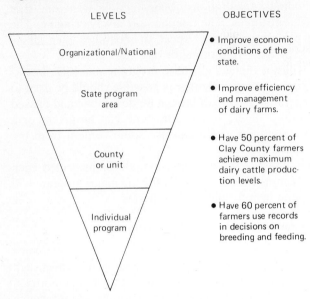

efforts that are very specific and individualized and also very broad and general goals, such as improving the general economic conditions of a state.

SUMMARY

The focus of this first chapter has been on developing a concept of program and program development. It has been emphasized that program as used in this book is much broader than curriculum as used in formal school situations. Three types of programs were described: developmental, institutional, and informational. The purpose in describing different types of programs is to provide a basis or focus for selecting procedures and approaches for program development. It is important to recognize that each type of program is not mutually exclusive. Some programs overlap and utilize two or even all three types. Subsequent chapters in this book will focus on specific concepts that are applicable to all three types of programs. A discussion of the different types of program development frameworks is presented in Chapter 4. Examples will be given that illustrate some of the activities or actions necessary for the effective development of a program.

DISCUSSION QUESTIONS

1 What is a program?
2 Identify what you consider the unique characteristics of programs for adults.
3 How would you describe the types of programs that you have developed?
4 Identify specific roles for the programmer in each of the three types of programs.
5 What unique characteristics would an organization or institution need to develop each type of program described?

Chapter 2

Philosophical Concerns of the Continuing Education Programmer

Many new and different social, economic, and environmental problems have come sharply into focus in recent years. Both the causes and the solutions of such problems appear to rest with the continuing growth of human technology and information. On the one hand, expansion of knowledge continues to change our environment and lives by creating new and complex problems; on the other, our increasing knowledge better prepares us to deal with such problems.

From both the public and the governmental point of view, education is being increasingly recognized as an effective means for solving the problems of society. The result has been an increased expectancy that continuing education efforts across the nation will provide the leadership and knowledge required for effective need or problem resolution.

The above statement reflects a philosophical belief about education and its role in helping people find a higher quality life. Our beliefs, values, and attitudes provide the basis for many of our actions in developing continuing education programs. Thus, continuing education programmers need to identify and utilize a set of beliefs about such things as education, continuing education, continuing education agencies, the learner, the programmer, and the program development process.

There is a distinction between a personal philosophy and other analytical tools for understanding or conceptualizing continuing education. Whereas the latter deals with what is and why it is, the former deals with what should be. Tyler noted the importance of philosophy and its part in giving meaning to the development of educational programs:

> It is certainly true that in the final analysis objectives are matters of choice, and they must therefore be the considered value judgments of those responsible for the school. A comprehensive philosophy of education is necessary to guide in making these judgments.[1]

Whenever we view a continuing education program, our view is under the influence of our personal beliefs. Efforts to construct a philosophy will help us to better understand the gaps between the reality of problems, clientele, and programs and the way we want things to be. A well-developed program in continuing education, then, is one in which there is consistency between the beliefs of those involved and the actual program.

A FRAMEWORK FOR DEVELOPING A WORKING PHILOSOPHY

Developing a working philosophy of continuing education programming is a complex task. Due to this complexity, we believe that it becomes necessary to develop a framework or system by which we can organize our beliefs. The ideal philosophical framework will allow us to systematize our considerations while at the same time retaining flexibility for change. A good working philosophy must be constantly revised and adapted to meet new situations in programming. A framework must not substitute order for flexibility. The following framework is designed so programmers can begin to order their beliefs:

- Beliefs about the purpose(s) of education and continuing education
- Beliefs about learning and the learner
- Beliefs about teaching and the programmer
- Beliefs about the process of program development

The beliefs, attitudes, and values that the programmer has are very important in developing a conceptual framework for program development. They provide the basis or foundation for a variety of decisions for

---

[1]Ralph Tyler, *Basic Principles of Curriculum and Instruction,* University of Chicago Press, Chicago, 1974, p. 4.

all phases of the total programming effort. The following sections are not intended to provide answers for what your definitions and beliefs should be, but rather to present ideas about what could be. The challenge is for each programmer to identify and clearly articulate her or his own beliefs, attitudes, and values about education, the educator, and the educational process.

Beliefs about the Purpose(s) of Education and Continuing Education

The traditional view of education has been long centered upon the subject matter as a body of information that has been worked out in the past and should now be transmitted to the learner. The main purpose of education in this view is to prepare people for certain tasks and responsibilities that have been identified well in advance. The major shortcoming of such an approach is that it does not allow for active participation by the learner in the development of the educational process. Moreover, the body of information that is taught is seen as essentially static, and yet we are in an age characterized by rapid change in every realm.

In contrast, the second view of education is the cultivation of individual experiences and maximum potentials, the free interaction between the learner and the environment, and the continued attempt to change and improve this environment. But the problem in education goes far beyond merely choosing between different views, for there is always the danger that in rejecting one set of principles, one may develop another set of principles that is equally sterile and rigid. As Dewey has aptly observed:

> When external control is rejected, the problem becomes that of finding the factors of control that are inherent within experience. When external authority is rejected, it does not follow that all authority should be rejected, but rather that there is need to search for a more effective source of authority.[2]

Thus, Dewey makes it clear that it may be easy to escape one form of external control only to find oneself under another and perhaps more dangerous form of control. To Dewey, "freedom resides in the operations of intelligent observation and judgment by which a purpose is developed."[3] As far as education is concerned, the question really becomes one of cultivating this very basic freedom of thought in the individual.

The behaviorists have attempted to represent human conduct as a set of actions, each of which is a response to a particular situation. But any situation confronting an individual at any particular moment is indeed

[2]John Dewey, *Experience and Education,* Collier Books, New York, 1967, p. 21. Material was used by permission of Kappa Delta Pi, An Honor Society in Education, West Lafayette, Ind.
[3]Ibid., p. 71.

susceptible to an indefinite set of alternatives. Furthermore, we cannot represent human conduct as something separate and distinct from the thought that directs it. It is in this sense that education has failed when educators have not allowed either a place for inquiry or the practical thought that explores new possibilities and new opportunities within their framework:

> A man may be enslaved to his own behavior not because he has failed to do that which he knew to be right, but because he is enclosed within a system of habit that does not present the varied possibilities of action available to him. The freedom that he lacks is not freedom of the will, but rather freedom of thought; a wider range of perception and discrimination, a larger possibility of his asking himself the questions that might have been asked, a greater likelihood of his realizing that there were further ends to be achieved other than the obvious ones.[4]

Such a view is totally opposed to the individualist's view that events are simply sequences of causes and effects. But a cause is not merely a preceding state of affairs; it is a state of affairs as known or understood by an individual. In like manner, an effect is not merely a later state of affairs; it is people who make things happen or intend them. Thus, the primary function of education becomes one of redirecting the course of an individual's evolution and controlling it. In Dewey's terms, education must see to two things:

> First, that the problem grows out of the condition of the experience being had in the present . . . and secondly, that it is such that it arouses in the learner an active question for new information and the production of new ideas. The new facts and new ideas thus obtained become the ground for further experiences. . . .[5]

In view of this, one may conclude that the old view has really failed to consider questions relevant to human choice. The nature of the transactional process emerging from a stimulus-response model is one of a process leading from empty spaces to spaces filled with "intellectual substance." The image of humans that here begins to emerge is one "of a man whose consciousness is 'spatialized,'"[6] to use Paolo Freire's expression. One is a passive being, the object of the process of growth, not its subject.

---

[4]Stuart Hampshire, *Thought and Action,* Chatto and Windus, London, 1959, pp. 67–68.

[5]Dewey, op. cit., p. 79.

[6]Paolo Freire, "The Adult Literacy Process as Cultural Action for Freedom," Loretta Stover (trans.), in Helene Castel (ed.), *World Development: An Introductory Reader,* The Macmillan Company, New York, 1971, pp. 250–251.

Continuing education by its very nature seems to be synonymous with diversity. Given the vast diversity of adults in any population, and given the diversity of their needs and interests, it is not so unusual to find this diversity reflected in programs in continuing education. For example, one might wonder what a job training program shares with an information center at a national park; what a class in Adult Basic Education shares with a sensitivity group; what an agricultural extension program shares with a Great Books club; what a learning center at the library shares with a first-aid class; and on and on. All of the above examples are considered to be continuing education; yet what do they really have in common? Perhaps a personal philosophy about the purpose of continuing education can begin to shed light on such questions as this.

Apps[7] has identified four basic purposes of adult or continuing education. Taken as a whole, they represent critical choices for the programmer as to the direction she or he would like the programming efforts to take. Thus, one poses the question: What is the purpose of adult or continuing education?

1   To help people cope with the objective conditions of their world?   This point of view flows naturally from the humanist perspective. It is essentially a coping orientation to adult education. Life is full of the unexpected and the insensitive, and this view asserts that we must learn how to bend so we will not break. The fact that many things in life happen without any regard to our existence or desires is not something that can be changed but rather something that we must each face and come to understand. In brief, the purpose of this view of continuing education is to help us to cope.

2   To equip adults with problem-solving skills?   This purpose, which is often termed problem-solving programming, is based upon the backdrop of a rapidly changing social environment. The time has long passed when a person, as a child, could know what life would be like as a parent simply by viewing one's own parents, and in turn, know what life would be like as a grandparent simply by viewing one's own grandparents. This view asserts that we cannot teach people a set of skills or knowledge that will last them a lifetime, but rather the purpose of continuing education should be to teach them the skills of problem solving. As Apps puts it: "What is important is that the learner learn how to think, learn how to identify his problems, and then through a problem-solving process, using knowledge as a tool, solve these problems."[8]

[7]Jerold W. Apps, *Toward a Working Philosophy of Adult Education*, Syracuse University Publications in Continuing Education, Syracuse, N.Y., 1973.

[8]Ibid., p. 37.

3 To help people change their social conditions? This purpose corresponds to a collective view of human nature. It does not put emphasis on the individual coping or adjusting, but rather has it that the problem is an oppressive society. It is only by working for the liberation of the society as a whole, that the individual obtains liberation. Thus, in this view, the continuing education programmer must plan programs for collective action to help bring about societal change.

4 To help people acquire the content and information necessary to live complete lives? This approach assumes that there is a basic, yet ever-expanding body of knowledge, both cultural and social, that is passed from generation to generation, and is necessary if a person is to live a fully functioning life. This approach has been for many years the overall purpose of childhood-youth education, and as such, continuing education was given the task of doing the remedial programming necessary to bring all adults up to standard. Probably the best example of the above belief is the traditional conception of Adult Basic Education, which concentrated on reading, writing, and arithmetic skills.

Continuing education is a field in its own right and thus, being separate from childhood-youth education, has expanded the content acquisition approach considerably. Herein, society is seen as a tremendously complex and changing system that requires continual educational input on the part of the learner in order to stay abreast.

The purpose of continuing education then becomes to provide programs to meet this end. Good examples of this approach are the new attempts at a second career and staff development on the job. Many people find their old skills outmoded by "advances" in technology, and education then becomes a way for them to continue as a functioning part of the work force.

In viewing the above purposes of adult or continuing education, we must ask ourselves what direction we would like to see continuing education take, or, conversely, whether we are satisfied with the diversity as it exists. The process of answering this question must be a part of our working philosophy.

Beliefs about Learning and the Learner

The adoption of a realistic view of human nature requires a theory that is based on reality. But what is this reality? We may proceed to define *reality* in the educational sphere as being mutual; that is, it neither lies in the learner alone nor in the instructional environment alone. This definition stems from the fact that every individual faces life with a mind and a spirit that are molded by all sorts of conceptions and predispositions. The degree to which a person's own predispositions are, in the encounter with other people, recognized, controlled, or altered, varies a great deal from one situation to another. If we say that education must begin with the needs and interests of the learner, it does not follow that we, as partners in the transaction, should not attempt to deal with issues and problems we perceive within the instructional environment.

This way of relating to the learner goes beyond merely accepting the learner. It means, as Buber[9] defined it, confirmation. While Carl Rogers[10] emphasized an unqualified acceptance of the person, Buber emphasized a confirmation which, while it accepts the other as a person, may also pit the person against herself or himself.

The concept of person that we are expounding here emphasizes the fact that, although one exists as an individual among many, one is nevertheless different from all others:

> To be aware of a man, therefore, means in particular to perceive his wholeness as a person determined by the spirit; it means to perceive the dynamic center which stamps his every utterance, action, and attitude with the recognizable sign of uniqueness.[11]

Recognizing this basic truth, we may now proceed to ask the question: How do we as educators relate to people? There are two basic ways in which one may influence others in their views and attitudes. In the first way, one imposes oneself on the other, while in the second way, one is related to the other "in such a way that he does not regard and use him as his object, but as his partner in a living event."[12]

This is, then, the essential difference between the concept of a free person in the sense that one is free to "unfold" and the concept of freedom that is merely defined in extraneous terms. It is the difference between whether one is merely a means to an end or whether, at the same time, one is an independent end in oneself.

This relationship between people can only be grasped in reciprocity. Asch explains this notion in the following words:

> [The] decisive psychological fact about society is the capacity of individuals to comprehend and respond to each other's experiences and actions. This fact, which permits individuals to become mutually related, becomes the basis of every social process and of the most crucial changes occurring in persons. It brings within the sphere of the individual the thoughts, emotions, and purpose of others extending his world vastly beyond what his unaided efforts could achieve.[13]

[9]Martin Buber, *The Knowledge of Man,* M. Friedman and R. G. Smith (trans.), Allen and Unwin, London, 1965.

[10]Carl Rogers, *Freedom to Learn,* Charles E. Merrill Publishing Company, Columbus, Ohio, 1969.

[11]Buber, op. cit., p. 80.

[12]Ibid., p. 74.

[13]Solomon E. Asch, *Social Psychology,* Prentice-Hall, Inc., Englewood Cliffs, N.J., 1959, p. 127.

Translating this to the educational sphere, we see learners enriching the world of each other. The educator's role in this exchange has often been obscured under all kinds of labels. However, within the present framework, it is clear that what the educator does is simply create the orderly development and organization of subject matter through relevant educative experiences. Dewey has strongly stressed that the principle of continuity of educative experience requires this type of organization by the educator: "Above all, they should know how to utilize the surroundings . . . that exist so as to extract from them all that they have to contribute to building up experiences that are worthwhile."[14]

On the other hand, involving the learner in choosing and designing learning experiences is important if such experiences are to be of any consequence. One's needs and thoughts are the focus of growth, and unless these needs are met, education becomes a futile exercise of control. The learner must therefore be involved in decisions concerning the content and structure of learning experiences.

Fundamentally, here we are concerned about "the nature of human nature." As stated in *The Idea of Man,* "the meaning of 'man' to man—the definition of the term, the explanation of the fact, the answer to the question—depends crucially upon the ideas we hold."[15] It is this internalized conception of human nature that often dictates our choices in continuing education programming. In the past, educators have tended to fall into one of three groups with regard to their beliefs about the adult learner. These groups are in a very real sense three separate working philosophies of the adult learner.

The first view assumes that a person is a reactive creature, who changes primarily as a result of changes in the environment. Thus, for example, in the case of an agricultural extension agent, who is assigned the task of trying to persuade farmers to reduce their energy consumption, success would be realized only if the farmers themselves felt the effects of their overuse of energy. This could happen if the price of gasoline and heating oil kept rising (a negative incentive) or if an alternative were offered that proved to be more cost-effective (a positive incentive). Simply put, this view holds that our behavior is determined by the results of previous behavior. If an action that we take results in a consequence that we like, then we will be more likely to act in a similar manner in the future, and vice versa. If the agricultural agent teaches energy-saving strategies to the farmer, and the adoption of those strategies results in lower gas and oil bills (an action, presumably, the farmer likes), the farmer will then be more likely to continue energy-saving strategies in the future.

The second view of human nature has generally been subsumed under the category of "humanism." Each person is treated as a unique hu-

[14]Dewey, op. cit., p. 40.

[15]Floyd Matson, *The Idea of Man,* Delta Books, New York, 1976, p. XIV.

man being capable of achieving her or his own unique potential. The concept of human nature that is being expounded here emphasizes the fact that although one exists as an individual among many, one is nevertheless different from all others. Thus, it is the primary responsibility of the programmer to effect programs that will help individuals achieve their own unique potential. Since this view would pertain to our example of the agricultural agent, the agent would be working with farmers on a continual basis and not as a result of a particular crisis, such as energy. If the work were effective, the farmers themselves would anticipate the need to conserve energy, rather than waiting until farming became a losing proposition because of astronomical gas and oil prices.

The third model of human nature, whose primary proponent in education is Paolo Freire,[16] is similar to the humanist point of view, but is much more active in its implications. The model branches off from the humanists in that it concentrates upon societal problems and collective rather than individualistic ways of dealing with those problems. To return to our example, the agricultural agent would work with farmers to show them the relationship of their rising energy costs to the energy crisis in the society as a whole. The farmers could then work together to make sure that conservation measures taken by society were equitable and did not favor certain special-interest groups. Also, they could work together to adopt conservation practices.

These are but a few of the questions that may be raised regarding the basis of human nature. The important point is, however, that each of us as continuing education programmers must begin to work out our own beliefs. Such beliefs need to be used in one's program development efforts.

Beliefs about Teaching and the Programmer

Growth is the process by which individuals, groups, and society progress toward the realization of their potentialities. It is a process that requires differing learning experiences, the particular type being dictated by the specific growth needs of the individual, group, and/or society at a particular time. Growth exists on a continuum, and depends upon the prior satisfaction of the individual's basic needs and ability to function with some degree of effectiveness within the particular circumstances. The necessity of these two achievements before growth can proceed in any meaningful way is what requires educational institutions to meet the immediate learning needs of their clientele.

Because short-range learning needs and growth needs differ for each individual, group, and part of society, and because unlimited resources are available to no single institution, diversity within the educational community is necessary. Only through the concerted efforts of all types of

[16]Freire, op. cit.

agencies and institutions can the growth of all be realized. Today, the occurrence of lacks and voids far outnumbers the duplicative efforts of institutions.

If growth is indeed the long-range and underlying purpose of adult education agencies and institutions, then what type of teaching-learning transaction is required to foster that growth? Four factors have a direct influence on the direction and amount of movement that will occur on the growth continuum. These factors are teaching, learning, the affective aspect of teaching-learning, and the life space of the individual.

Teaching is an activity that can assume many forms. We see it as a process that is neither student nor teacher centered, and aims at the discovery of beliefs, knowledge, and truths through higher thought processes. Intelligent behavior, the result of training, also depends upon that knowledge and beliefs of the individual. Thus, the difference between the technician and the professional lies in the professional's knowledge of why a certain task is performed, as well as the ability of the professional to discover the reason why a particular method does not work. Also, learning as the result of instruction may result in a change in behavior.

The second factor, *learning,* is a process that occurs on different levels and depends upon the type of teaching employed. Learning does not necessarily change behavior, but it does change the potential for behavior. It is a process that is unique for each person, and the quality of learning largely depends upon the degree to which the learning experience is meaningful to that individual.

Rote memory, recall, is at the lower level of learning. One is able to learn those things that have little or no personal meaning, and for which no immediate application to life situations is seen. Facts, behaviors, generalizations, and understandings can be learned in this way. The higher levels of learning require active thought processes. Through these processes one is able to reflect upon current situations and previous learnings, and gain insight and understanding into the various relationships one experiences. It is this type of learning that enables people to solve problems, to move from dependent to interdependent relationships, to gain a fuller understanding of self, and to accept responsibility for one's actions.

This type of learning is also more personally meaningful because it deals directly with one's life situation. What Whitehead[17] has termed inert ideas are inert because they have no meaning for the learner. Although we believe there are eternal truths and virtues, we also believe that unless learned in a meaningful way, these truths and virtues will not perform an important role in determining the behavior potential of the individual. With this type of learning and its stress on meaning, process becomes as

[17]Alfred North Whitehead, *The Aims of Education and Other Essays,* The Macmillan Company, New York, 1967.

important as subject matter. One must have opportunities to reflect upon personal experiences and previous learning in order to gain new insights and to discover, for oneself, what is good and what is truth. Since one learns as one is taught, the learned processes will enable independent and interdependent progress toward one's maximum potential. In short, it is this type of learning that enables the individual to grow.

The third factor is the *affective aspect* of the teaching-learning transaction. All learning has an emotional counterpart, and this counterpart either facilitates, neutralizes, or impedes learning. In considering this factor, the fourth factor must also be considered. This is the *life space of the individual*. The first three factors are very much under the control of the educator, while the fourth is not. Thus, the first three must be so arranged as to meet the needs of the individual. This is particularly true of the affective aspect of the transaction. Experiences (e.g., exams) that have negative emotional connotations for one individual and cause regression on the growth continuum, may also have positive connotations for another individual and promote that individual's growth. The learning experience must be designed, then, to be supportive of the learner's efforts and to meet the learner's growth needs at that particular time. This points out the need for involving learners in planning their learning experiences. They must be involved to ensure that the learning experience relates to their life experiences; that what they learn from the program content is relevant to their life situation; and that their particular experiences can be brought into the teaching-learning transaction to be discussed and explored. One other responsibility should be noted—the learner has personal responsibility for learning as well as for the quantity and quality of that learning.

The other types of teaching, learning, and affective aspects can, however, contribute to growth, if used properly. Here it is necessary that individual, group, and societal life spaces be considered to effect the proper mixture that will aid progress toward one's unrealized potential. Coinquiry and learning by reflective thinking contribute most to this growth, but other forms of teaching-learning transactions must be used at times to ensure that one's satisfaction of basic needs and effective functioning are maintained. It is not uncommon, then, for a learning experience to result in progression through multiple stages of growth, or to emphasize growth in one area and adaptation in another. It is important that institutions and educators alike ensure a steady progression toward the unknown and unrealized potentialities of people.

Beliefs about the continuing educator vary as to her or his centrality in the educational process. We might look at this question in one of three ways.

On the first extreme, one places the continuing educator at the center of the education process. The educator is viewed as an expert or specialist in a field, with responsibility to communicate this knowledge to the learners. The paradigm of this viewpoint is, of course, the continuing educator *lecturing at* a large adult group. It is essentially what Freire terms a "banking approach" to education.

On the other extreme, the continuing educator's role coincides with that of the clientele. Thus, if there is to be an educational process at all, the learners must take the full responsibility in creating it. In this approach, one often finds the continuing educator's normal roles of organizer and facilitator being rotated within the group.

I see a compromise between the above two extremes in the continuing educator approach. Variations on this role have been suggested by such writers as Lippitt, Thelen, Freire, and Bennis.[18] In this approach one can certainly identify the continuing educator. However, this person is not the sole giver of knowledge, but rather the facilitator of the client's search for understanding.

Beliefs about the Process of Program Development

Many questions and issues must be dealt with in the development of effective programs. Following is a discussion of some of these issues.

1 Involvement The question is essentially, How involved should the learner be in the program development process? Does one believe that the learner can benefit from such participation, or is this involvement more or less a waste of time? Some would assert that adults have a set of needs, and a program is designed to fulfill those needs. It is felt that the development of this program is best left to experts, and that the learner is most benefited by the interaction with the completed program sequence. This model often can be applied at the university level where the professor or expert develops the course curriculum and the students or learner use the curriculum as the basis for their studies. On the other hand, there are those who assert that the learner should be actively involved in the program development process. In essence, the learner is not learning an answer to a specific problem to meet a specific need, but rather what is learned is a problem-solving process that will help the learner to meet needs long after the programmer has gone elsewhere.

2 Needs and interests A continuing educator is faced with several levels of needs and goals that she or he feels responsibility to meet. Many

[18]This point has been cited by Gordon H. Lippitt (ed.), *Leadership in Action,* National Training Laboratories, National Education Association, Washington, D.C., 1961; Herbert A. Thelen, "The Educational Trialogue," paper presented at the Adult Education Conference, Madison, Wis., June 24, 1970; Paolo Freire, op. cit.; and Warren Bennis, Kenneth Benne, Robert Chin, and Kenneth Corey (eds.), *The Planning of Change,* 3d ed., Holt, Rinehart and Winston, Inc., New York, 1976.

times, however, these needs conflict with one another. Needs originate in many places. First, the learner has a unique set of needs. For example, a group of farmers might wish to set up a dairy cooperative, so they approach the educator with the need to learn more about this venture. Their need would be to learn more about cooperatives, in general, and dairy cooperatives, specifically. Second, the educator has a set of needs. To continue the above example, the educator might have a need to teach the social and interpersonal aspects of cooperatives. This need would conflict with the purely business interests of the farmers. Third, the continuing education institution has a set of needs. In this case, the county extension office might have a major program on its agenda, the time requirements of which might, for the educator, conflict with those time requirements given to the farmers. Finally, the society itself has a set of needs. It might be important for farmers, in general, if each small dairy cooperative were to federate into one giant dairy cooperative, thereby increasing their bargaining position. Yet, in attempting to meet this need, the educator will be in conflict with the clientele's wish to have a cooperative independent of outside interests. In brief, which set of needs should be given the greatest weight? What criteria should be devised to facilitate a sound decision?

3 Balanced programs It becomes obvious to the continuing educator that programs are not equally available to all persons. Studies by Johnstone and Rivera[19] and later surveys by the Educational Testing Service[20] have shown that by and large, it is the middle class who use continuing education services. Some would argue that this is fundamentally sound. The institution of continuing education is here to meet people's expressed needs. Since learners are adults, they are the ones who are best qualified to understand and communicate their own personal needs. It then becomes the responsibility of the institution to respond. It is seen as harmful to the basic integrity of the adult to create needs where none have been expressed. Thus, we develop continuing education programs for the middle class because they are the ones that ask for them. On the other hand, there are those who argue that the institution of adult education must reach out to as many subgroups in the society as possible. Ultimately, the institutions must be a true reflection of the society itself. If certain minorities, certain economic classes, are not using the service of continuing education, it is because those services are not speaking to their needs. It becomes incumbent upon continuing education to fully understand those needs, and then to effectively program to meet them. In this

[19]John W. C. Johnstone and Ramon Rivera, *Volunteers for Learning,* Aldine Publishing Company, Chicago, 1965.

[20]Abraham Carp et al., *Learning Interests and Experiences of Adult Americans,* Educational Testing Service, Berkeley, Calif., 1974.

view, there is much more of an active outreach of the organization to the people.

4 Evaluation Evaluation is always a challenge in continuing education programming. Some feel that evaluation should be done by an outside expert, using previously stated objectives as specific criteria for judgment. It is felt that those who developed and carried out the program are too emotionally involved to evaluate impartially. Thus, evaluation should be left to an unbiased outsider. Opposed to this view are those who feel that one cannot really know the complexities of a continuing education program unless one has been fully involved with it. This view asserts that written objectives or any other formalized criteria an outside expert might use for the purpose of evaluation are an incomplete representation of what has transpired. Thus, the people involved in the program should also be involved in its evaluation.

5 Decision making A basic question to continuing education programming is whether the programmer has the right to impose her or his values, attitudes, and beliefs on the clientele. Some would suggest that it is the goal of continuing education to enable the clientele to develop their own values, attitudes, and beliefs through the educational process. Imposition of the programmer's values onto the educational process will not foster independent, mature adult learners but rather dependent, passive receptacles for the ideas of others. In this view, the programmer must remain as impartial as possible in the development of the curriculum and presentation of materials. On the other side of the continuum, there are those who assert that impartiality is a myth. Each continuing educator has certain biases, and these biases emerge in programming even if the educator is not overtly aware of them. This view has been cogently described by Apple et al.[21] in what they termed "the hidden curriculum." Since we cannot escape our biases, it is best to be as open and honest about them as possible. Thus, if we believe that women should be treated equally with men, and we discover that the female students are discriminated against in the class, then we should work to change this situation. In short, this view states that we should be an advocate for what we think is right.

6 Support The question often arises whether continuing education should require fees. Some would say definitely no. Continuing education should try to serve the greatest number of people possible, and fees would arbitrarily exclude a certain proportion of the population who could not afford them. On the other hand, there are those who assert that the fee

[21]Michael W. Apple, M. J. Swokoviak, and H. S. Lufter, Jr. (eds.), *Educational Evaluation: Analysis and Responsibility*, McCutchan Publishing Corporation, Berkeley, Calif., 1974.

system makes for much higher quality in the program. It is felt that both teacher and student expect higher quality when there is a fee involved. The old saying "you get what you pay for" still has many adherents in our society, and a continuing program offered for nothing will be judged accordingly. This is even true of the poor, it is believed, because a fee, even if it is a heavily subsidized one, will give them a sense of self-worth that a "welfare" program cannot. In some situations the question is raised as to whether programs in one subject area should support programs in another area; for example, programs for business executives who can afford to pay high fees to support programs in the arts.

7 Focus The question of what level the programs should focus on is an interesting one. There are those who believe that the program should focus upon the individual in the form of highly personalized one-to-one instruction. It is argued that this personalized contact gives learners the greatest chance to develop their fullest potential. The continuing educator can take into account the full uniqueness of each adult learner and can plan and execute the educational program accordingly. This approach has been most fully utilized in the counseling profession, but one might suggest that upon reflection each of us would be surprised at how great a percentage of our continuing education efforts take place on the one-to-one level.

Second, there are those who believe that the best program in continuing education takes place with the group as the instructional unit. In the first place, it is asserted that the group is a more basic social unit in our culture than the individual. Thus, the learner will not only be learning but will also be undergoing a great deal of incidental learning from others in the group as well. Furthermore, it is believed that programming for the group gives a greater cost/benefit ratio than individual instruction. This fact is obvious when one considers the differences in the learner/teacher ratio.

Finally, there are those who argue that the best programming is neither with the individual nor the group, but rather with the whole community. Community-based programming can take into account the broader economic, political, and social considerations that the other two forms overlook. It is believed that specific problems can best be solved if they are approached with full knowledge of their interrelationship with other problems in the community. Although this approach has become very popular recently, it is important to realize that it is a complex method, and that the bigger the community, the greater the complexity.

8 Differences The question arises: Is the style and approach to programming different for minorities than the so-called mainstream of American culture? Some would argue that minorities are really like the rest of our society—it is only discrimination and prejudice that make them different. Therefore, the programmer should treat minorities as other learners are treated; that is, as adults, as individuals with a unique potential to grow and develop. They will then respond in kind. On the other side, there are those who assert that there is something truly different about each minority and it is this difference that must be stressed. The United States is not the melting pot it is sometimes believed to be, and the only way earlier minorities and ethnic groups—the Irish, the Italians, the Jews, and so on—have gained entry into the mainstream is by banding tightly together with their own particular group. Thus, continuing education should treat each minority as a separate entity. Our programs should stress the uniqueness of each culture, and work to create a sense of culture, racial pride, and self-worth in the individual. It is believed that the individual acting alone, no matter how strong, cannot survive the discrimination intrinsic in our society, but that the individual banded together with others of that minority can.

9 Accreditation The question arises: Should any of our continuing education programs be mandatory? There is a long-cherished view in continuing education that we must respect the "adultness" of each participant. This view asserts that, as much as possible, decisions should be in the control of the learner. Of course, the primary decision is that of attendance. In line with this viewpoint, many of our adult education programs have been voluntary in nature. In Adult Basic Education, for example, the frequency of attendance is determined by the student. The choice is the student's, reflecting integrity as a mature adult. More recently, another trend has emerged in continuing education. Our society has always trained and educated many professional groups—teachers, lawyers, doctors, nurses, pharmacists, and so on. These people complete the necessary requirements, and then are certified to practice their profession for the rest of their working years. While this system worked fine in earlier times, in today's fast-paced existence, where the increase in knowledge and new technology is geometric, one "shot" of education is no longer adequate. Thus, there is now a trend to establish continuing education programs for professionals. Since certain skills that these professional groups must master are necessary for the well-being of society, these continuing education programs are mandatory. This requirement would assure a greater confidence in our reliance upon these professions; for example, the correct use of novocaine by a nurse. At the same time, it contradicts some of the basic principles of continuing education.

10 Quality A very difficult question in continuing education programming is, How does one define or describe quality in that program? Quality has always been difficult to define. Some programs have avoided the question of quality and have substituted the term quantity in its stead. Thus, they test the success of their programs by such means as attendance figures, scores on tests given prior to training and after training, percentage of students who pass an external certification test after training, student contact hours, and so on. This approach has become increasingly popular as the whole issue of accountability has surfaced in education. For example, is the high school responsible for the fact that an individual who received a diploma later tests at a sixth-grade reading level? Even more recently, there has been a growing reaction to the perceived extreme reliance upon accountability and quantification in continuing education. This group has again brought words like quality to the forefront. How can a feeling that a continuing education program has worth—is one of quality—be used in evaluation? One method that has been advocated is the use of informal subjective interviews with participants, rather than structured quantifiable questionnaires. This method is based on the assumption that program quality is best judged in terms of both the emotional and intellectual aspects of the participants, and that quality is a relative, abstract term that is best left unquantified.

SUMMARY

This chapter was designed to help the programmer develop a working philosophy useful in program development. The concept presented was that our beliefs, values, and attitudes provide the basis for many of our decisions and actions in programming. The framework for identifying the programmer's working philosophy included beliefs about the purpose of education, beliefs about learning and the learner, beliefs about teaching and the programmer, and beliefs about the process of program development. Each individual programmer was encouraged to continually reexamine her or his philosophy so that it might remain dynamic and relevant.

DISCUSSION QUESTIONS

1 How do you define the purpose of continuing education?
2 What is your philosophy on planning programs for adults?
3 What is your philosophical basis for making decisions about involvement of people in program development?
4 Illustrate how your philosophy about learning could influence decisions in providing learning experiences.
5 Identify three controversial issues in program development. Take a position on the issue and support it.

Chapter 3

Change as
an Assumption of
Program Development

Society constantly encounters phenomenal changes. The rate and pace of change lend urgency to the notion that crisis is the ordinary state of affairs. It is important to recognize that change is not a uniquely modern phenomenon. Some kinds and degrees of change are universal to human existence.

We can make certain assumptions about the years ahead to help us detect the broad outlines of what is likely to happen. One is that people will continue to aspire to a fuller, better, and more rewarding life. Another is that technology will advance at a rapid rate. We can also say with some certainty that the future will be shaped by a person's aspirations interacting with technology.

In the past decade, change has accelerated in all aspects of our lives. Change will likely continue to dominate our future lives, institutions, and society. Change has helped form a better and more efficient society, but also has created very complex social and economic problems for people and our communities. It is the responsibility of continuing educators and educational agencies to help people understand change as it affects their total lives.

Change of some type constantly affects people. One constantly acts as either a target of change or as an agent of change—often both at the same time. How far one gets as agent or target and the level of change involved depends on one's position in a social system. The person who programs with adults is said to have the professional role of "change agent."

Many continuing education programs are designed to help individuals adjust to change. Much less attention has been devoted to preparing individuals or groups to plan for change. Certainly, the latter is more desirable; people should control their environment as much as possible rather than be continually adjusting to an environment imposed upon them. But this control is not always possible. Changes outside the control of a particular social system still may affect that system. The energy situation today is an excellent example. Energy and control over its costs are affected by many national and world issues and policies. Adjusting to change often becomes necessary. Under these circumstances, the programmer's role is to facilitate clients' understandings through education.

CHANGE AND PROGRAM DEVELOPMENT

Programming in continuing education is done to bring about some change in individuals and/or the social system of which they are part. The social system may be defined as a family, a community, a professional association, a state, or a nation. Change within a system can occur at many different levels and in many different forms. The concept of change, as used in this book, does not necessarily imply progress, development, or modernization, or any other evaluative term.[1] Destruction of the natural environment in some communities, for instance, has prompted many groups to organize and plan for preserving and protecting their environments. In this instance, planning is a deliberate action to change a course of events even though the result is no change.

Following is a discussion of the various types of change on which educational programs might focus:

Individual change. The most basic units of change in any system are the individuals who make up the system. Individual changes include cognitive, affective, and psychomotor within the life cycle of individual members of the social system.

Group change. This type of change refers to changes in person-to-person relationships. These affect group patterns as individuals develop new ways of relating to each other as members of groups and communities.

---

[1]Don Martindale, *Social Life and Cultural Change,* D. Van Nostrand Company, Inc., Princeton, N.J., 1962.

Cultural change. This type involves changes in values, norms, traditions, and mores of a social system. Some change theorists argue that changes of this type will occur much more slowly than changes in technology.

Political change. This type primarily concerns changes in legislation that influence the elements of a social system. An example is the possibility of legislation governing the use of certain pesticides—a technological change that has been widely accepted, but now appears to violate the values of certain members of the system. This confrontation may well lead to legislation (political change) restricting the use of such materials.

Technological change. This type is designed to improve efficiency and productivity in a social system. Generally, such changes are quite visible and alter ways of doing things. Consider, as examples, the effect of computers on accounting procedures; commercial fertilizer on crop production; the automobile on travel.

Economic change. This type affects the ability of a system to achieve its goals; indeed, the nature of the goals themselves. Inflation and sudden recession are examples of economic change that can drastically affect the nature of the elements of a social system.

This brief review of types of change that can occur within a social sytem indicates the all-encompassing nature of the term "social change." It is also apparent that change of one type is closely related to the other types. For example, Sorokin[2] views personality, society, and culture as three successively more comprehensive systems of human existence. The cultural system consists of symbolic constructs: meanings, values, norms, and their interaction and relationships through overt action. The social system consists of the interaction of individuals as they operate collectively toward the needs. Finally, the personality system consists of biological and psychological drives operating toward the satisfaction of the individual's needs.

At the personality level the focus is on the individual, but this level cannot be separated from the level of the social system. Mead saw both levels, social and individual, as arising from human interaction:

> The self is something which has a development; it is not initially there at birth but arises in the process of social experience and activity; that is, develops in the given individual as a result of his relations to that process as a whole and to other individuals within that process.[3]

[2]Pitirim Sorokin, *Society, Culture, and Personality,* Cooper Square Publishers, Inc., New York, 1962.
[3]George H. Mead, *On Social Psychology,* University of Chicago Press, Chicago, 1964, p. 199.

Both these levels (individual and social system) are also related to what Parsons has termed the cultural component of human interaction:

Human action is "cultural" in that meanings and intentions concerning acts are formed in terms of *symbolic* systems (including the codes through which they operate in patterns) that focus most generally about the universal of human society, language.[4]

Likewise, Lewis and Grable[5] hold that a change in group norms is a key variable in the total process of change, but that reeducation can only be realized with a change in the "culture" of the individual who must internalize her or his group's value system.

From this we may conclude that larger systems are, in fact, aggregates of smaller systems, which in turn are composed of various subsystems. This complexity points up the very important need to carefully identify the system to be analyzed.

Economic and technological change are often equated with the social system itself. They can be viewed as subsystems within the social system. The economic subsystem consists of the productive and distributive activities of the social system; the major processes involved are specialization and exchange. The technological subsystem consists of innovative activities in the realm of material resources, and the major processes involved are discovery and invention. Though these two subsystems can be viewed as distinct, they are nevertheless closely related to the three levels—personality, society, and culture. This is why there is so much vagueness in the literature as to what constitutes social or cultural change and what constitutes economic or technological change. Ogburn's[6] use of the term "culture," for instance, includes both the social and the cultural; his "material" culture includes all that is cultural and social.

In general, social change involves some modification in either structure or the functioning of the social system, or both whether the system is defined in terms of a unit as small as a family or as large as a nation. Thus, change in a social system may be seen as an "agent of disturbance to the established and organizationally referred structure and processes of life." The elements of change, however, are supported only by how well they serve human needs and by reciprocity in social interaction. This is the social expression of the reinforcement principle of psychology according to Homans's exchange theory of social interaction:

[4]Talcott Parsons, *Societies: Evolutionary and Comparative Perspectives,* Prentice-Hall, Inc., Englewood Cliffs, N.J., 1966, p. 5.

[5]K. Lewis and P. Grable, "Principles of Re-Education," in Kenneth D. Benne and Bozidar Muntyan (eds.), *Human Relations in Curriculum Change,* Dryden Press, New York, 1951, pp. 23–33.

[6]William F. Ogburn, *On Culture and Social Change,* Selected Papers edited by Otis Dudley Duncan, University of Chicago Press, Chicago, 1964.

The open secret of human exchange is to give the other man behavior that is more valuable to him than it is costly to you and to get from him behavior that is more valuable to you than it is costly to him.[7]

PLANNED SOCIAL CHANGE

Within any social system, change may be caused either by forces inside the system or by forces brought to bear on the system from without. Change resulting from internal forces may be described as "imminent change," while that resulting from external forces is "contact change." Change may be either planned or unplanned. Planned change is defined by Bennis et al. as a "conscious, deliberate, and collaborative effort to improve the operations of a human system, whether it be a self-system, social system, or cultural system, through the utilization of valid knowledge."[8] Lippitt similarly defined planned change as the process of making "a deliberate effort to improve the system and to obtain the help of an outside agent in making this improvement."[9] These definitions of planned change are very similar to our definition of program development as identified in the first and second chapters.

At this point we should note an important factor pertinent to the planning of change; that is, the importance of the clientele's notions concerning their own problems. The clientele and the programmer must together examine, analyze, and incorporate these notions. Bennis et al. state that "planned change is distinguished from other types of change in that it entails mutual goal setting, and equal power ration (eventually), and deliberateness on both sides."[10] Psychological and social change emerge from this angle. As Thelen puts it: "The core of the person is partially revealed through his performance in roles, and it is through these roles—and his need to find integration among them—that the private person is 'reached.'"[11] The process of planned change thus becomes one of education for change.

A continuous challenge for the educator is to effectively and realistically identify what change is needed in the present situation. When we analyze any situation, we are constantly faced with the task of under-

[7]George C. Homans, *Social Behavior: Its Elementary Forms,* Harcourt, Brace & World, Inc., New York, 1961, p. 62.

[8]Warren Bennis, Kenneth Benne, Robert Chin, and Kenneth Corey (eds.), *The Planning of Change,* 3d ed., Holt, Rinehart and Winston, Inc., New York, 1976, p. 4. Reprinted by permission.

[9]Ronald Lippitt, *The Dynamics of Planned Change,* Harcourt, Brace & World, Inc., 1958, p. 10.

[10]Warren Bennis et al., *The Planning of Change,* Holt, Rinehart and Winston, Inc., New York, 1969, p. 154.

[11]Herbert A. Thelen, "The Educational Trialogue," paper presented at the Adult Education Conference, Madison, Wis., June 24, 1970.

standing how a complex situation is created and developed and how important are the various components relative in time and space. Bloch and Prince[12] observe that the individual has to cope with conflicting standards from multiple components of family life, politics, economics, and religious, cultural, and educational behavior modes. Social experience is not analyzed from such separate systems in daily living. However, the complexity and the need to study this multiplicity becomes more apparent when scientifically considering problems such as alcoholism or crime.

Another question is raised in relation to the technical progress that has created an enormous rift in our social life. The question of whether to alter other significant aspects of society to suit those changes or to redirect technical processes to meet the interests of our social lives is one we must resolve before we even attempt solving the problems of others.

While resistance to change is a fact of our existence, it is imperative that we understand the forces at work in a given situation. The psychological aspect of this resistance is particularly important when we view the attitudes of groups and individuals who have defined their condition in a particular way. These patterns of behavior give rise to what Mannheim[13] has referred to as the "ideologies," or the systems of thought that attempt to change the situation. Mannheim says such divisions constitute a fundamental dynamic of social change.

In this way and similar ways, the concept of social change can provide a frame of reference from which a certain social problem or issue is perceived, appraised, and analyzed. On the other hand, one of the far-reaching consequences of social change in our time has been that we, as individuals and as groups, have become more "future-oriented," and thus sense the need for more intelligent and systematic planning.

This discussion of planned change implies a major role for the continuing educator in program development. This role must be active and prescriptive rather than passive and merely reactive to inquiry or request. In assuming the role, the programmer makes general assumptions about society. These assumptions provide the philosophical base for the policies and procedures necessary for role fulfillment. These assumptions are:

1   That planned change is a necessary prerequisite to effective economic and social progress for people and communities.
2   That the most desirable change is predetermined and democratically achieved.
3   That continuing educational programs, if properly planned and implemented, can make a significant contribution to planned change.
4   That educational changes in knowledge, skills, and attitudes of

[12]Herbert Bloch and M. Prince, *Social Crisis and Deviance: Theoretical Foundations,* Random House, New York, 1967.
[13]Karl Mannheim, *Ideology and Utopia,* L. Wirth and E. Shils (trans.), Harcourt, Brace and Company, Inc., Harvest Books, New York, 1959.

people are necessary to achieve economic, environmental, and social change.

5   That it is possible to select, organize, and administer a continuing education program that will contribute to the social and economic progress of people and communities.

6   That people and communities need the guidance and leadership of a continuing educator to help them solve their problems and achieve more desirable ways of living and of making a living.

If these assumptions are accepted, then planned change becomes the focus or basis for the development of continuing education programs. Accepting these assumptions has serious implications for the continuing education programmer and the program development process utilized. We must develop procedures for implementing the process of program development so that a deliberate attempt is made to plan an educational program that will contribute to systematic changes in society. Thus, the desired changes must be identified and described. The necessary change or need becomes a description of a condition that exists between what is and what should be, or between what is and that which is more desirable. A person, then, is motivated through education to fulfill the need or find a substitute so that the equilibrium between what is and what should be is restored.

SUMMARY

This chapter focused specifically on planned change and its relationship to program development. We make a basic assumption in program development—that change is the basis or the ultimate goal for utilizing a program development process. Change was defined so that the action or program did not always result in something new or different. Maintaining or preserving the present was included in the definition of change.

Change as it relates to a social system was discussed. Different types of change were identified and related to program development. The chapter concluded by indicating that if change is accepted as the basic assumption of program development, then it has serious implications for the programmer and the program development process.

DISCUSSION QUESTIONS

1   How do you define change?
2   In your judgment, what factors contribute to achieving change?
3   What factors prohibit effective change?
4   The basis for identification of problems and opportunities in program development is change. Agree or disagree, and state why.
5   What assumptions about change do you make in meeting your responsibilities as a continuing education programmer?

Chapter 4

Approaches to Program Development

The philosophy of programming with adults is based on the belief that active participation by people in the process is essential for effective educational programs to evolve. It is only through this approach that the continuing educator is able to provide people with educational opportunities that relate to their needs and interests and contribute to resolving problems pertinent to their economic and social well-being.

Program development is essentially the art of designing and implementing a course of action to achieve an effective educational program. This simple definition implies that the continuing educator is involved in reaching decisions through the implementation of a rational planning or developmental model. However, it should be recognized that a completely rational model is rarely, if ever, achieved in the practical world of planning with people. The challenge is to achieve the most effective effort possible. This achievement is made possible by following the most appropriate practices and procedures that allow for utilization of the concepts implied in an acceptable program development framework. Several concepts relevant to program development are introduced in this chapter. Although these concepts are important for all program development frameworks, the procedures and practices used for implementation will vary, depending on the type of program, the people involved, and the past traditions. Three different frameworks are presented to illustrate the necessary variation, depending on the type of program.

PROGRAM DEVELOPMENT CONCEPTS

The understanding a person has of the essential concepts inherent in program development obviously establishes the basis for selecting and following appropriate procedures. Figure 4.1 illustrates the alternative procedures that a programmer has when using the concept of involvement in need or problem identification. The specific programming situation would

Figure 4.1 Relationship of Concepts and Procedures

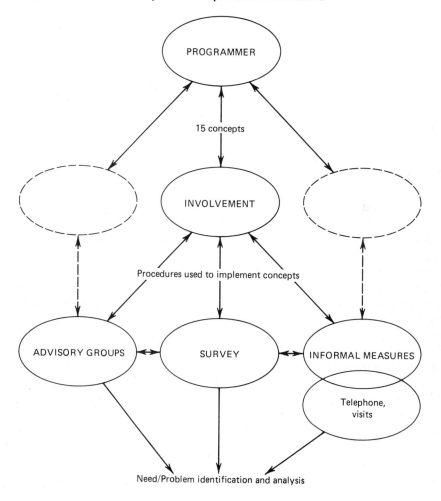

be the basis for determination of the procedure. Following is a brief review of fifteen concepts considered important for program development.

1 Establishing a Philosophical Basis for Programming

Developing a working philosophy of continuing education programming is a challenging and difficult responsibility. However, we need to recognize that our procedures and actions in program development are greatly influenced by our personal beliefs. The continuing education programmer should clearly identify her or his beliefs about education, the learner, the programmer, and the program development process. For example, the programmer's beliefs about the rights and responsibilities of the learner will influence her or his actions when involving the learner in identification of needs or designing specific learning experiences.

An important goal of program development is not merely to design better programs for present clientele but also to reach people who are not sharing in the efforts or the benefits of the programs. If a programmer accepts this goal for program development, then the procedures followed will be greatly affected.

2 Situational Analysis of Problems and Needs or Concerns of People and Communities

The ultimate goal of any continuing educational program is helping people accomplish something that will benefit them. Identification of the problems, issues, situations, or concerns that need changing or improving are the critical challenges of program development. Situational analysis, as a program development concept, emphasizes the study, analysis, interpretation, and judgments about the community and clientele.

Program development often will begin in a very ambiguous situation. There may not be a specific need identified when programming efforts begin. Even if needs have been identified, they might not represent the "real" problems and may need to be delineated, selected, and to have priorities established according to the capabilities and resources available. Through situational analysis the programmer needs to gain a thorough understanding of the situation before attempting to develop a program. While situational analysis leads to an examination of sources for objectives, it begins at a more basic level, focusing simply on getting to know the situation.

A series of decisions must be made about the structure and approach to be used in situational analysis. Decisions must be made on: Who will be involved? What will be their roles and responsibilities? How should those involved be structured? How should the clientele and communities affected be studied and analyzed? How should need or problem areas be broken down for study and analysis?

3 Involvement of Potential Clientele

Few continuing education programmers would disagree with the idea of involving the potential clientele in the program development process. Clientele involvement means including citizens in the process, connecting them to the process, or establishing situations that occupy their attention. It is a process that encourages the involvement of individuals in relation to groups and affects the persons involved in various ways. Involvement thus includes a wide spectrum of activities.

The concept of involvement is important to all types of programs. It is essential that the purposes or reasons for involvement are in congruence with the methods and resources utilized.

4 Levels of Intellectual and Social Development of Potential Clientele

Learning is an active process and the action must focus primarily on the clientele rather than the teacher. If the learning process is to be a truly living, active process, it is imperative that the programmer recognize that individual differences exist among clientele.

The programmer needs to recognize that the adult is different than the child. The adult is likely more mature with a variety of different background experiences over an extended period of time. A programmer may assume that groups of farmers, nurses, social workers, or homemakers are quite homogeneous. However, based on further study the programmer finds that the individuals are very different in attitudes about learning, social-economic background, ethnic origins, and previous professional experiences. These differences have significant implications for the program development process. For example, if the intent was to involve the group in need identification, the previous experiences of the group members would affect the procedures used by the programmer. A person with limited experiences working in group situations might find it a very threatening experience.

In identifying an acceptable program development process, the programmer must understand and provide for differences in the social and educational background experiences of clientele. Efforts will have to be identified to determine the present levels and the factors contributing to them.

5 Sources to Investigate and Analyze in Determining Program Objectives

The challenge for the continuing educator is to adequately study and analyze various sources in the development of objectives for the educational program. The sources of information that are commonly used are the potential learners themselves, contemporary society or the social and economic environment of the learner, and the subject matter area. It should be recognized that no single source of information is adequate to provide a basis for wise and comprehensive decisions about educational objectives. Each of the above mentioned sources has its own part to contribute in providing potential educational objectives. Involving the potential learner often requires the programmer to help the learner develop skill in recognizing needs.

The type of program being developed is important in deciding on the kinds and sources of information to use in developing objectives. A developmental program may require a high degree of flexibility in the level and nature of objectives. It is quite possible, for example, that a group of elderly people would first decide to get together monthly to study something. The specific objectives would evolve as the group developed some cohesiveness and structure. In most institutional- and information-type programs, it is possible to clearly establish objectives prior to most program implementation activities. The value judgments that continuing educators make about the objectives to be attained are basic in their overriding significance to the total scope of educational programs. Since objectives serve as the overall guide to the planned educational activity, these fundamental decisions must be made with care and precision.

6 Recognition of Institutional and Individual Constraints

The continuing education programmer must recognize that institutional and individual constraints inhibit the development of ideal programs. In many cases, these constraints are not obvious and enter into the program development process at various stages and in various ways. Some of the constraints would include (1) organizational philosophy about programming related to certain controversial issues, subjects, or with particular client groups; (2) financial and other resources unavailable to programs with certain socioeconomic groups; (3) beliefs of external financial decision makers about program priorities; (4) assumptions of certain programs by the community or the clientele; (5) beliefs of administrators within the organizations about program priorities; and (6) beliefs of the programmer about program priorities.

In many cases, these constraints can be avoided through effective program development procedures. However, in other situations, the constraints must be recognized and accepted as a part of the program development framework.

7 Criteria for Establishing Program Priorities

Continuing educators are often faced with the problem of too many good program needs and too many clientele groups to reach with the time and resources available. As a result, decisions have to be made to identify program priorities. Priority setting is a continuous process of decision making that takes place during all phases of programming, including delineating needs, specifying goals, identifying target audiences, defining available resources, and determining necessary actions. The first major task in priority setting is to identify criteria that will be used as the basis for decision making. Effective criteria will help make the decision-making process more rational and acceptable. The potential program clientele must be involved in identifying the criteria to be used in making priority decisions.

8 Degree of Rigidity or Flexibility of Planned Programs

A concept especially important in developmental programs is that they remain flexible and dynamic. It is difficult to effectively determine and control all objectives and procedures. Programs are often problem-oriented and developmental in nature. The program must be allowed to develop in order to meet the specific needs and to utilize the most appropriate educational experiences and resources. It is suggested that a given approach should be revised to fit different programs with stages skipped or telescoped. Constant evaluation of both objectives and methods, exploration of alternative means, and the reconsideration implicit in the involvement process all require a high degree of flexibility.

9 Legitimation and Support with Formal and Informal Power Situation

The concept of legitimation may need to be applied at many different times in the program development process. It also may need to occur at several levels. For example, programmers may have to establish themselves with the client group, the programming agency may have to establish itself in the community, and the program itself may need support in order to be successful.

Reactions from legitimizers range from a flat refusal to go along with ideas to wanting to become the center of the promotional activity. One other important caution should be mentioned. Often legitimizers will put forth no effort to help initiate or carry on the program, but they are not an important resource of subject matter, competence, time, or energy. However, if legitimization is not obtained from them, they may throw all of their resources into the blocking of the program. An oversimplified reason for such action on their part can be stated in terms of their feeling that if they are bypassed on legitimation often enough, they cease to be legitimizers, a status and role they highly prize. In some cases, the same power structure legitimizes all programs within the community or association. More often in communities there may be more specialized legitimation structures for specific kinds of programs—industrial development, health, recreation, minorities, schools, and so forth. The legitimization structure may be difficult to determine for new types of programs or during periods of change.

10   Selecting and Organizing Learning Experiences

The most widely accepted definition of learning is acquiring new patterns of behavior through experience. In this definition, behavior includes ways of thinking and feeling as well as of acting. Clientele do not learn as the result of what teachers do, but as a result of what clientele do. This basic principle is as important for clientele to understand as it is for the programmer. The client who expects to learn by simply sitting back and listening is likely to be disappointed. The programmer, on the other hand, who relies solely on the "I'll lecture, you listen" type of instruction is not likely to see much learning take place. The learner, in short, must be involved in the process of learning. The programmer, therefore, has a real challenge in selecting and organizing experiences through which the learner can be involved. A variety of participating activities for the learner—observing, listening, thinking, writing, questioning, and discussing—is necessary. Thus, a learning experience is the mental and/or physical interaction between the learner and the content of the things to be learned. In the selection and organization of learning experiences for an eight-session class, a three-day conference or a two-hour meeting, the programmer must focus on the learner and what the learner will experience.

In Chapter 16, we emphasize the necessity of using a systematic approach to determine whether all the effective dimensions of learning are included in the selected experiences. For example, assume we accept the following four ideas:

Adults learn best when they have a strong desire to learn.
Adults learn best when they have clear goals.
Adults learn best when they put into practice what they have learned.
Adults learn best when they experience satisfaction from what they have learned.

If the programmer, or whoever is responsible for teaching, is designing a three-day conference on drug abuse or water quality, the challenge is to make sure that each of these factors are provided for in the experiences of the learners.

11   Identifying Instructional Design with Appropriate Methods, Techniques, and Devices

The continuing education programmer is responsible for designing learning activities to bring about appropriate efforts on the part of the learner.

Also, the programmer might be facilitating the identification of learning activities in which other continuing educators would do the teaching. Identification of an appropriate instructional design involves the selection of the method, the techniques, and the devices. The potential clientele should again be involved by their assistance in identifying the most appropriate instructional approaches. Accepted definitions are as follows:

1 *Method.* A way of doing something, a systematic mode or approach used to reach people (group, individual, or mass media contacts)
2 *Technique.* The form used to present material to be learned (lecture, panel, group discussion, or tour)
3 *Device.* The mechanical items and conditions used to facilitate learning (film, radio, special physical arrangements, slides)

Designing instruction is difficult because there is no best or most appropriate approach. Individual aptitudes and abilities vary so much that the programmer is usually faced with decisions for each programming situation. Criteria that are useful in the decision process include (1) objectives of the learning opportunity, (2) interests and other characteristics of the clientele, (3) previous experiences of the clientele, (4) availability of necessary equipment and resources, and (5) interests and capabilities of the programmer. In many cases, information about these criteria will not be available. The programmer will simply have to make the decisions. In making these decisions, the programmer should attempt to identify the combination of methods, techniques, and devices that will most effectively facilitate the involvement of the learner in such experiences as thinking, analyzing, practicing, clarifying, and critiquing. Again, the most important consideration is what the learner is experiencing.

12 Utilizing Effective Promotional Priorities

A continuing education program competes with a myriad of other programs, events, and needs for the public's attention, money, and support. However, you will be able to spread the word and generate interest about your program to the intended audience through carefully planned and implemented promotional activities.

Promotion is a communication effort involving elements of advertising, public relations, marketing, and news. It can range from informal discussions with community leaders to a sophisticated mass media blitz.

All successful promotional efforts start with an organized and inclusive plan that takes into account promotional objectives, audience and media characteristics, requirements, and deadlines. It is also important to use many communication channels and techniques to ensure reaching target audiences and to provide enough redundancy to your message to increase believability and acceptability.

13 Obtaining Resources Necessary to Support the Program

Citizens are entitled to continuing education as one important alternative to solving their problems and meeting their needs. The number of people who will seek education in the next decade is projected to increase. Obtaining adequate financial resources for continuing education is always difficult. The programmer must be extremely cognizant of the necessary resources in order to provide a quality program.

The program development process must provide for the legitimation and other supportive actions that will facilitate the organization's efforts to obtain continuity and adequate financial resources. Involvement of influential decision makers at opportune times in the programming process will provide for greater understanding and acceptance.

14 Determining the Effectiveness, Results, and/or Impact

A continuing education programmer should develop a concept of evaluation and then make the proper applications to meet the needs of the organization. Systematic evaluation is difficult and costly. Informal evaluation may be questioned. Thus, decisions about the application of evaluation are difficult, yet extremely important.

Recent literature on educational evaluation presents the main purpose as improving decision making; that is, the main use of evaluative data is input into the decision-making process. Program evaluation might be viewed as a process of judging the worth or value of a program. This judgment is formed by comparing evidence about what the program is with criteria about what the program should be. Thus, evaluation is a process of deciding that involves (1) establishing standards or criteria, (2) gathering evidence about the criteria, and (3) making judgments about what this comparison revealed.

An important approach to evaluation is that the continuing educator should judge programs on the basis of several separate but related characteristics. Some of the most common are:

Effectiveness. Did we get enough results? Did we attain our objectives? Did we avoid negative side effects?

Quality and suitability. How "good" were the experiences provided? How suitable were they for the particular clientele?

Contact. How many did we reach? What proportion of the potentials? Was there adequate balance; i.e., was it varied in serving all ages and income levels?

Importance. To the clientele, to society, to the mission of extension.

These are distinctly separate judgments. One should not be substituted for another. For example, the participants rating the program highly in terms of quality and suitability do not necessarily mean that it produced any results. Nor does the fact that we had extensive contact mean that the program was very efficient. But we may need to know how participants react to the program as well as what results are produced, and whether or not the range of contact was sufficient and the use of resources productive.

15 Communicating the Value of the Program to Appropriate Decision Makers

Many continuing education programs are supported by public funds. It is essential that the individuals involved in making decisions about funding programs obtain a clear understanding of the value and limitations of the program. Funders and influentials need to get a sense that the program is actually accomplishing important things. The different methods available for use in communicating with decision makers vary from the informal, face-to-face contact to the more formal research report. The continuing education programmer will need to develop a plan using the most appropriate content and medium for the various individuals and groups that need to be communicated with.

Program development is really designing a course of action to achieve a quality program. The fifteen concepts previously discussed are the essence of ideal planning. The programmer should use them as guidelines in implementing a process in a given programming situation.

In Chapter 1, we introduced three different types of programs. The following materials outline a framework for the development of each type of program. The concepts discussed in this chapter are made operational in these frameworks to the extent that is necessary and desirable.

DEVELOPMENTAL FRAMEWORK FOR PROGRAM DEVELOPMENT

The description of a developmental framework for programming is complicated because the process is dynamic and constantly being adapted to the actual situation. We will identify the phases in sequential order; however, the actions involved in the process overlap the various levels of the framework. Also, it is important to recognize that actions within the various phases may be happening simultaneously or may take place in a completely different sequence.

Phase 1 Identification of the Basis for Programming

- The philosophical basis for program development in the agency or organization should be clearly identified.
- The continuing educator should develop a working philosophy as the basis for program development. The beliefs that the continuing educa-

tion programmer has about education, the learner, the teacher, and programming should be clearly identified.

• Broad policies and procedures for program development should be defined, understood by, and communicated to all concerned.

Phase 2   Situational Analysis of Community and Clientele

• Collect and analyze present and past situational data, facts, and trends to effectively understand the situation. Consider data from and about people and communities or other geographical areas, data from the discipline fields, relevant data about society as a whole, and the basic institutional documents and philosophy that establish programming responsibilities and limits.

• Involve potential target clientele and influentials directly or through groups to study, interpret, and make decisions about programming needs and programming feasibilities.

• Study the present program and responsibilities of other agencies and institutions to avoid duplication.

• Analyze the available resources to determine if an adequate program to meet the problem or need can, in fact, be implemented at this time or if additional resources are needed.

Phase 3   Identification of Desired Outcomes

• Work with potential clientele to define and refine needs and set priorities so that the clients are committed to the program.

• List the general outcomes to be attained through the program, based upon the analysis of the situation. If possible, these outcomes should reflect the social, economic, and/or environmental changes to result from the planned program. In many instances this will be done in advance by the professional in consultation with clientele. In other cases, the professional and the clientele will define the expected outcomes while they work together in the actual program.

• For each general outcome, identify the specific growth and development that must occur in participants for the overall outcome to be attained. These are called specific objectives. In programs where it is important that most participants attain a minimum level of knowledge or skill, clearly indicate who is to be taught, what level of change is to take place in the individuals' understanding, belief, or action, and what is to be taught (specific unit of content). Consider the participants' entry level of knowledge.

• Order the list of expected outcomes into a meaningful sequence. A logical order from the sense of the discipline may not be logical from the standpoint of the learner.

• Check the list of general and specific outcomes to be sure that:
  a They are directly on target with the analysis of the situation and promise to be of value to the participant and the larger society.

    b They are actually attainable within the specific programming situation—these clientele, this amount of time and energy, etc.

    c The outcomes are seen as general targets for the majority with some flexibility for individual learners to achieve their own individual needs.

• Make decisions about program priorities based on a set of criteria for determining what is most urgent and important. Use information from the analysis of the community and clientele.

Phase 4   Identification of Resources and Support

• Determine whether adequate resources, including people, time, money, and materials, are available to meet the needs of the program. Also, determine whether the resources will be available when needed.

• Identify the people with the appropriate expertise representing various disciplines or fields of knowledge that are necessary for the program to be effective.

• Determine whether the individuals involved in providing leadership for the program have adequate time to devote to all phases of the program.

• Determine whether adequate financial resources are available to carry out the program.

Phase 5   Design of an Instructional Plan

• Identify the kinds of learning experiences that participants or others will need in order to achieve the desired outcomes. (What must they see or hear, practice, discuss, etc.?) In what sequence? Consider variations suitable to the background of the clientele (educational level, social experience, etc.).

• Decide what responsibility you will share with the participants for attaining the objectives. This probably should agree with the amount of responsibility participants have for determining what they will learn.

• Identify the instructional approach and specific activities necessary to provide the participants with the experiences they need to bring about the expected outcomes (a course, an intensive saturation by mass media, a conference or institute, a workshop, individual consultation, or a combination of these are examples). Analyze theories and practices that facilitate learning and select methods, techniques, and devices accordingly. Use innovative approaches wherever appropriate.

• Identify the roles staff members are to perform and other instructional resources.

• Decide what materials will need to be developed or prepared and how much lead time is needed.

Phase 6   Program of Action

• Select the content, activities, and events that should be provided to *(a)* create awareness and interest in the program, *(b)* provide the learning experiences necessary to help learners attain the expected outcomes, and *(c)* provide for adequate follow-through.

• Organize what is to be taught or done in the program in order to achieve some continuity in the opportunities provided. Organize the action so learners can participate efficiently.

• Develop a working calendar that includes timing of promotional activities, preparation time for support materials, interaction with resource people, and the sequence of activities involved in program implementation and evaluation. The calendar of activities should provide for *(a)* logical sequence and continuity and *(b)* specific responsibilities and preparation time.

• Carry out the plan, making adjustments as necessary. Use resources as effectively as possible.

Phase 7   Accountability of Resources

• Plan evaluation into each of the programming phases; evaluate the design before implementing, evaluate progress and quality during implementation, and plan for final evaluation.

• For any evaluative activity, define precisely why you will be evaluating. How will you use the results? Evaluation is often most valuable if it can be used to make decisions about this or similar programs.

• Determine what kind of judgments are necessary for your particular purpose. Do you need to determine how well the program attained its planned outcomes? its efficiency in attaining results? or its overall importance and value?

• Specify the criteria you will use to make your judgments. Identify the kinds of evidence you will need to determine whether the criteria are met. If you are judging how well the program has met its commitment to certain outcomes, be sure each specific outcome includes a criterion for observable performance.

• Identify what evidence will be needed and how it will be collected, processed, and interpreted.

• Develop your judgments about the program and use the results. Who else needs to know about them? In what form?

Phase 8   Communication of the Value of the Program

• Provide reports on the value of the program to key resource people, participants, advisory groups, and influential decision makers. Such reports should take different forms for different audiences. They may vary from informal, face-to-face comments to formal, evaluative documents. No matter what form they take, each report should consider the following: need for a program, what the program was, educator's role, major results, benefits, action, and the reactions of the participants and others involved.

• Follow up with appropriate individuals and groups to clarify any concerns or questions about the role of the program.

INSTITUTIONAL FRAMEWORK
FOR PROGRAM DEVELOPMENT

An institutional framework for programming follows a more structured approach than did the developmental framework. The word institutional implies that the program is derived from the knowledge base of the institution or organization. Growth and improvement in individuals' basic abilities is the primary emphasis. This assumes that the programmer will know or quickly identify the cognitive knowledge, affective processes, or psychomotor skills to be taught.

This approach is most applicable to programming efforts aimed at individual learners. As a result, this framework does not emphasize situational analysis and establishment of programming relationships. Time and effort is given to analysis of the learners and their situation; however, this analysis is focused on determining the level and methods for teaching the subject matter. This framework puts more emphasis on the discipline as a basis for identification of objectives than on the problems of communities or people.

Since the emphasis is on helping learners, the continuity, sequence, and integration of the learning opportunities is important. The effectiveness of institutional programs is generally evaluated by the extent to which learners have mastered the content of the program. This framework is useful in developing certification programs, mandated in-service activities, and other such efforts aimed at individuals.

Phase 1   Defining Target Clientele

- Identify the clientele to be involved in the program. If the target clientele are affiliated with institutions, professional associations, or community groups, then linkages or relationships should be established. This relationship involves understanding the purpose and procedures for the program development effort.
- Identify background information about the target clientele. This would include the learners' needs, desires, characteristics, capabilities, practices, and problems.
- Explore the programs that are available from other agencies and institutions, to avoid duplication.

Phase 2   Specific Content Areas

- Study the needs. Consider the nature of the specific learners, the content to be taught, the design for instruction, and the aspirations and motives of the learners.
- Compare as precisely as possible the achievement or level of the learners with the proposed content to be taught. This may be done through pretesting procedures.

- Study the potential clientele. The programmer should study the previous educational experiences, social-economic status, participation patterns, and special interests of the potential clientele. In many cases, this information can be obtained through preregistration.

Phase 3   Identifying Instructional Approach

- What experiences (seeing, hearing, doing) will the learners have in each class, activity, or event.
- Promote the program through appropriate means, such as association newsletters, printed announcements, news media.
- Help the clientele who are going to participate to know about the purposes, format, and procedures of the program.
- Determine the relationship of the planned learning opportunities to continuing education units (CEUs), certification, or other standards.
- Identify the instructional resources necessary to effectively implement the learning opportunities.
- Identify the most logical sequence for the learning experiences that will be provided.
- Clarify the responsibilities for everyone involved.

Phase 4   Providing Instruction

- Provide quality instruction so as to bring out the abilities that are latent in the clientele.
- Be flexible so that the most appropriate methods, techniques, and devices are used to build motivation and interest.
- Provide effective communications so that everyone with a role or responsibility clearly understands what is happening and when.

Phase 5   Evaluation of the Program

- Determine to the extent possible what the learners have achieved through participation in the program. If pretest measurements were used, then the posttest should use measurements that are comparable.
- Make judgments about the results or achievements of the program. Should the learners have done better? Were the educational objectives achieved? Should the objectives have changed during the instructional part of the program?
- Make judgments about the instructional design or approach. Was it effective? How could it have been more effective? Were the learners satisfied?
- Determine how the results will be used in future programming. Will the results be shared with the learners? Will they be shared with other programmers? How will they be shared with administrators or financial decision makers?

INFORMATIONAL FRAMEWORK
FOR PROGRAM DEVELOPMENT

Informational programs focus on an immediate exchange of content. The programmer's major responsibility is to determine what new content should be provided and to utilize the most efficient medium for providing it.

Phase 1   Determine What Content
Is Available, Needed, or Desired

• Identify the content or knowledge that is available or requested. The programmer may decide that the available new knowledge should be disseminated to people. Or the learner might request knowledge to resolve curiosity, a need, or a problem.

• Utilize appropriate promotional techniques to help people become aware of the availability of new content or knowledge.

Phase 2   Provide Information or Knowledge

• The content or knowledge is provided through group, individual, or mass media approaches. The methods utilized will be based on resources, interests of the learner, and the type of content to be distributed.

Phase 3   Determine the Extent of
the Distribution of Content

• Record the number of people contacted or who requested content.

• Specific studies in some situations might be conducted to determine whether and how the client used the content.

• Influential decision makers should receive reports of the extensiveness and value of the program.

SUMMARY

Fifteen concepts that are considered important for the development of effective educational programs were introduced in this chapter: (1) establishing a philosophical basis for programming; (2) situational analysis of problems and needs or concerns of people and communities; (3) involvement of potential clientele; (4) levels of intellectual and social development of potential clientele; (5) sources to investigate and analyze in determining program objectives; (6) recognition of institutional and individual constraints; (7) criteria for establishing program priorities; (8) degree of rigidity or flexibility of planned programs; (9) legitimation and support with formal and informal power situation; (10) selecting and organizing learning experiences; (11) identifying instructional design with appropriate methods, techniques, and devices; (12) utilizing effective promotional priorities; (13) obtaining resources necessary to support the program; (14) determining the effectiveness, results, and/or impact; and (15) communicate the value of program to appropriate decision makers.

Understanding these concepts establishes the basis for selecting effective procedures through which the concepts can be implemented. As a follow-up to Chapter 1, three different program development frameworks were presented. Each framework includes several phases. Necessary actions or conditions to be achieved were included in each phase.

DISCUSSION QUESTIONS

1 Describe the relationship between program development concepts and procedures.
2 Select one of the fifteen concepts discussed and illustrate how its implementation might vary depending on the type of program development framework.
3 How would you generally describe the differences in the three program development frameworks presented?
4 Select a concept such as legitimation and illustrate how many different times it is utilized in a program development process.
5 Conceptualize and illustrate your ideal framework for program development.

SUGGESTED READINGS FOR SECTION I

Alinsky, Saul, *Rules for Radicals,* Vintage Books, New York, 1972.

Apps, Jerold W., *Problems in Continuing Education,* McGraw-Hill Book Company, New York, 1979.

Beal, George M., R. C. Blount, R. C. Powers, and W. J. Johnson, *Social Action and Interaction in Program Planning,* Iowa State University Press, Ames, 1966.

Bennis, Warren, *Changing Organizations,* McGraw-Hill Book Company, New York, 1966.

———, Kenneth Benne, Robert Chin, and Kenneth Corey (eds.), *The Planning of Change,* 3d ed., Holt, Rinehart and Winston, Inc., New York, 1976.

Berger, Peter L., and Thomas Luckman, *The Social Construction of Reality,* Anchor Books, New York, 1967.

Bergevin, Paul, *Philosophy of Adult Education,* The Seabury Press, Inc., New York, 1967.

Bernstein, Basil, *Class, Codes and Control,* Schocken Books, Inc., New York, 1975.

Campbell, Angus, and Phillip Converse, *The Human Meaning of Social Change,* Russell Sage Foundation, New York, 1972.

Eisner, Elliot W. (ed.), *Confronting Curricular Reform,* Little, Brown and Company, Boston, 1971.

Freire, Paolo, *Pedagogy of the Oppressed,* Herder and Herder, New York, 1972.

Goodenough, Ward Hunt, *Cooperation in Change,* Russell Sage Foundation, New York, 1963.

Hall, Edward T., *Beyond Culture,* Anchor Books, Garden City, N.Y., 1977.

Harrington, Fred Harvey, *The Future of Adult Education,* Jossey-Bass, Inc., Publishers, San Francisco, 1977.

Hass, G., K. Wiles, and J. Bondi (eds.), *Readings in Curriculum,* 2d ed., Allyn & Bacon, Inc., Boston, 1970.

Houle, Cyril O., *The Design of Education,* Jossey-Bass, Inc., Publishers, San Francisco, 1972.

Knowles, Malcolm, *Self-Directed Learning,* Association Press, New York, 1975.

Knox, Alan B., *Adult Development and Learning,* Jossey-Bass, Inc., Publishers, San Francisco, 1977.

Langer, Suzanne K., *Philosophy in a New Key,* 3d ed., Harvard University Press, Cambridge, Mass., 1976.

Lindeman, Eduard C., *The Meaning of Adult Education,* Harvest House, Ltd., Publishers, Montreal, P.Q., Canada, 1975.

Lippitt, Ronald, Jeanne Watson, and Bruce Westly, *The Dynamics of Planned Change,* Harcourt, Brace and World, Inc., New York, 1958.

Mead, Margaret, *Culture and Commitment,* Columbia University Press, New York, 1978.

Nisbet, Robert, *Social Change,* Blackwell, Oxford, England, 1972.

Pinar, William (ed.), *Curriculum Theorizing, The Reconceptualist,* McCutchan Publishing Corporation, Berkeley, Calif., 1975.

Reilly, Mary, *Play as Exploratory Learning,* Sage Publications, Inc., Beverly Hills, Calif., 1974.

Rothman, Jack, *Planning and Organizing for Social Change,* Columbia University Press, New York, 1974.

Smith, Robert M., George F. Aker, and J. R. Kidd (eds.), *Handbook of Adult Education,* The Macmillan Company, New York, 1970.

Zaltman, Gerald, *Processes and Phenomena of Social Change,* John Wiley & Sons, Inc., New York, 1973.

———, Philip Kottler, and Ira Kaufman (eds.), *Creating Social Change,* Holt, Rinehart and Winston, Inc., New York, 1972.

Section II

The Organization and Program Development

To extend knowledge and its application to people and communities is a major goal for institutions doing continuing education programming. The challenge is for institutions to effectively organize their resources and staff so that programs can have a major impact. Continuing education programming is uniquely different from residence teaching and research; therefore, each institution must organize so that the structure follows the intent and focus of the programs.

In Chapter 5, several guidelines for an organization doing continuing education are presented. Emphasis is given to the need for each institution to develop an effective structure. Also, a set of institutional assumptions for program development is given as an example. It is suggested that these assumptions provide a basis for program direction and programmer roles.

In Chapter 6, the roles of a continuing education programmer are presented. A review of the literature revealed a variety of potential roles. The suggestion is made that the roles will be affected by the program development process used, the type of program, and the philosophy of the programmer.

Chapter 5

Institutional Concerns in Program Development

A philosophy has developed among legislators, citizens, and educators that continuing education institutions and agencies have a responsibility to be actively concerned with the issues and problems of people and of society. Our society depends on educators who are willing to accept increasing responsibility for moving ideas toward action, to accept the responsibility for developing the necessary knowledge, and to apply useful knowledge toward the solution of society's major ills.

The fate of our democratic society depends upon the consent of the governed. The larger, adult segment of our population has the need for and the right to the resources of educational institutions throughout their entire life-spans. Now, more than ever, there is the urgent need for adults to learn and interact in continuing education activities. It is now that the educational programs and services of institutions and agencies must be directed toward helping adults at all income levels meet the challenges of tomorrow. Situations such as the energy crisis, unemployment, urban neighborhoods are all going to create drastic changes in the future. The people must be involved in understanding and working for cooperative solutions to these situations. This is the challenge.

STRUCTURAL GUIDELINES FOR
PROGRAM DEVELOPMENT

Educational institutions need to organize their resources to most effectively and efficiently serve the needs of all people. The appropriateness of any approach for any specific institution depends on many different factors. Regardless of the approach, historical experiences have shown that certain structural guidelines are important. Following are brief explanations of these guidelines that the institution and the continuing education programmer may want to consider:

1   An institutional philosophy and commitment to utilize knowledge to contribute to the solution of needs and problems of people and society are essential. They are necessary in order to motivate and reward staff for relating their disciplines and expertise to current social issues and problems.

2   Linkages must be established by the institutions doing continuing education with a research/knowledge base for the expertise necessary to solve community and social problems. Unless there is continuous interaction with new research/knowledge, the capacity of the continuing educator to solve needs and problems diminishes.

3   Cooperative and direct arrangements and linkages for relating to people and groups in communities, professionals, professional associations, and target clientele in various organizations or agencies need to be established and maintained. This will help the continuing educator understand people and their problems, and cause them to adapt their knowledge or expertise to those needs and problems. Such direct relationships also provide feedback to researchers so they can adapt their research to the current problems of society.

4   A continuing education institution or agency must be free from direct political control and the influence of governmental agencies. It is recognized that state agencies and elected officials have the right and responsibility to identify and state priorities. But the continuing educator, along with the affected people, must have the freedom to pick and choose the most important programming needs.

5   The administrative leadership of the continuing education institution must derive the means for the adequate financial support of programs. Financing continuing education may come from a variety of sources—federal and state government, communities and cities, grants, and client fees. A continuing education program supported solely by client fees will not always be able to focus on priority needs. A marketing philosophy develops so that the programmer must be more concerned with meeting targeted fees than priority problems. A philosophy of establishing fees on the basis of intent of program and responsibility to pay is very desirable.

6 An institutional structure for program development should provide for the involvement of people in identifying problems or needs and deciding on a course of action to resolve them. This can be achieved if the continuing education programmer is willing to accept this philosophy and to provide for local citizen input through continuing relationships with local communities, professional associations, and other groups.

7 An organizational programming structure for continuing education must never be considered permanent. Problems change; they are altered, reassessed, redirected, and sometimes they disappear. The continuing education resources must be able to shift the direction of staff and materials within short periods of time.

8 An institution must be willing to provide professional recognition and appropriate rewards to staff who make significant contributions to continuing education programs.

ASSUMPTIONS FOR PROGRAM DEVELOPMENT

A continuing education program should grow out of the mission and goals of the institution or agency. The activities of the various disciplinary units of an institution should be clearly related to the overall purposes of the institution. The statements of purpose and goals should be expressed so as to provide a positive guide for the development of programs.

A statement of mission for continuing education might be as follows:

> The primary concern of this institution is to continue to focus its resources on the present and future cultural, social, educational, intellectual, and economic needs of the adult population of the state.

Broad statements of mission and goals need to be further interpreted in order to provide specific guidance in the development of programs. One approach to achieving this interpretation is through the identification of a set of assumptions. Here, we define an *assumption* as something that we accept or take for granted. Assumptions can provide the basis or specific guidance for the programmer in the development of programs.

Following are several trends and assumptions about the future that might provide a basis for programming. This is an illustration. Each institution should develop their own assumptions.

Citizens Entitled to Public Education

The right to education is basic to a free society, since its fate depends upon the informed consent of the governed. That right should extend not only to children and college students but to all citizens, regardless of age. The adult segment of the population has the need for educational resources throughout their lives. There is a greater need now than ever before for educated, informed adults to solve community and statewide problems, to become involved in the structures, institutions, and laws by which they live. Educational programs, services, and resources must be directed toward helping adults fulfill social, economic, political, and personal responsibilities today and to prepare creatively for the future.

Level of Education and Participation

Many recent studies have shown the effect of education on people's interest in continuing education. The higher the number of years of formal schooling, the greater the interest and willingness to participate in educational activities. One survey revealed that only 10 percent of those who had not finished high school were interested in further education but that over 80 percent of college graduates wanted more education. As the trend toward more formal education for citizens increases, therefore, so will the demand for continuing and informal educational opportunities.

Population

By 1985, the number of adults aged 25 to 34 will increase by 10.2 percent. The number in the 35 to 44 age range will increase by 22 percent. The 25-and-over age group will increase in number from 36,172,000 in 1980 to 41,086,000 in 1990. Between now and 1990, the 25-to-34 age group will be the largest. Clearly, the potential candidates for continuing education are growing at a much more rapid pace than ever before.[1]

Education via the Communications Media

There is an increasing trend for people to learn via the communications media rather than through courses and institutions. A communication system—radio, television, telephone, newsletter, and dial-access program—provides an extensive educational delivery system that can reach almost every citizen to provide education and information.

Education's Contributions to Specialized Groups

Publicly supported agencies have an obligation and a responsibility to contribute educational programs for the benefit of people who may be ignored by traditional educational approaches. Minority groups, the disadvantaged, women, the elderly, and the handicapped need education to help them gain full participation in the responsibilities and benefits of the society, and to help them live fully satisfying lives. Nontraditional methods, approaches, and programs must be provided to meet the needs and interests of these groups.

[1]"Projections of the Population of the U.S.: 1977 to 2050," U.S. Bureau of the Census, Current Population Reports, Series P-25, 1977.

Certification and Recertification of Professionals

A significant trend among the professions today is for established professionals and paraprofessionals to periodically meet standards for certification and/or recertification. These professional requirements are developing because of state and federal legislation, self-imposed standards of professional associations, and consumer demand. In many cases, such continuing education is mandatory. Examples of the fields involved include teachers, soil testers, nurses, physicians, dentists, dental hygienists, chiropractors, nursing home administrators, psychologists, veterinarians, judges, police and fire personnel, dietitians, physical therapists, optometrists, lawyers, pharmacists, engineers, and many municipal, state, and federal civil servants. Certification and recertification requirements are based on the professionals' need to keep abreast of new developments and to use the most recent research findings in their fields of specialty. Educational institutions should be responsible for facilitating the use of new knowledge to serve the public.

Professional Degree Requirements

In many fields today, the continuing education unit (CEU) is used as the basis for continuing or advancing in the profession. Often, a specific curriculum is required to achieve the necessary CEUs. This alternative to advanced degrees is being pursued by many professionals. Educational institutions must continue to expand their response to this significant change in advanced degree requirements.

Education of Elected Government Officials

Municipalities, school districts, townships, counties, and other government units have elected officials who are responsible for making decisions about efficiency in government operation and for services that address the needs of people. Changing state and federal laws require local interpretation and application. The local government units are essential in solving community and regional problems. Changing population distribution, along with public demand and newly enacted legislation, requires that elected officials be as up to date as possible in order to plan, organize, and provide services for community needs.

Education for Personnel in Governmental Agencies

State and local government agency employees need new knowledge and methods to serve people effectively and provide efficient services for the tax dollars that support them. If the states are to continue to provide services to their citizens, these employees need continuing education and training to do their jobs most effectively. The multiplier effect is evidenced by the countless number of people these agencies serve daily.

SUMMARY

The major objective of continuing education programming is to extend knowledge for use by people and communities. Thus, the problems or concerns of people become the critical rather than special interests of staff. The previous statements are an example of a philosophical position that institutions interested in continuing education must clarify. This clarification of mission and commitment to continuing education provide necessary guidance for program development and for roles to be assumed by the programmer.

DISCUSSION QUESTIONS

1 Review and critique mission statements of institutions doing continuing education.
2 What is your belief about the role of an educational institution?
3 Should adults be expected to pay for continuing education programs?
4 Should professionals be required to participate in continuing education programs?
5 Of what value are the programming assumptions of an institution?

Chapter 6

The Role of
the Programmer in
Program Development

Change is a common and challenging experience all of us share. We share this experience as initiators of change or as passive recipients or perhaps, more often, as active resistors of change. Regardless of our role, we are a part of change and change affects our lives.

Because people want to maintain some control over their lives, change can present a threat to this control. Moving from the tried and proved to the relatively unknown introduces an element of risk. The less a person understands about change, the more ambiguous and threatening change may seem. However, one thing remains certain about change: It is enduring and always occurring.

Given that change of some type is constantly affecting people suggests that people are constantly acting as either a target of change or as an agent of change, and often both at the same time. The degree to which a person acts as agent or target, and indeed the level of change involved, depends primarily on the person's position in a given social system. The continuing educator, for example, often defines her or his professional role as that of a change agent. The organizations that the continuing educator serves and the nature of the problems being focused upon help to define the parameters and participants involved in the change process.

The development of programs that focus on change is perhaps a more challenging and awesome responsibility than adjusting to change. Not only must programmers provide initiative in deciding what changes are needed, but they must also provide leadership concerning how these changes can be realized. Unless the programmer has an understanding of the concepts in program development, all efforts will often be based on trial and error. This will likely be inefficient and ineffective. One can learn from experience; however, should a continuing education programmer learn only by trial and error in a dynamic and rapidly changing society?

There are many programming roles that a programmer should know about and be skilled in utilizing. Several roles are explored in this chapter and a few practical questions that seem important for the programmer to think through are raised.

FACTORS AFFECTING THE ROLE OF THE PROGRAMMER

Rothman[1] outlines four major variables that affect the role of the programmer: (1) the dynamics of the change process, (2) community factors, (3) organizational factors, and (4) personal attributes of the programmer.

The Dynamics of the Change Process

The change process itself affects the role the programmer performs. The objectives of the program directly affect the programmer's role. For example, if the goal of the program is to promote predetermined goals, an advocate or demonstrator role might be used. If the objective of a certain programming segment is to generate ideas for solutions to a problem, an encourager or facilitator role might be more appropriate. Likewise, different roles are appropriate for the various phases of the programming process. Situation analysis, goal setting, implementing, and evaluating will have unique requirements that affect role. Finally, the environment in which the programming is taking place affects the programmer's role. For example, a developmental program as described in Chapter 4 is generally a changing, flexible situation as compared with more institutional, predictable programs. The developmental programming situation will require multiple roles, whereas the informational-type program might require one or two major roles.

Community Factors

Many community structural variables may affect the range of roles performed by a programmer. Size, governmental structure, racial mix of the

[1]Jack Rothman, *Planning and Organizing for Social Change*, Columbia University Press, New York, 1974.

population, and other demographical factors have an effect on the appropriate roles for a programmer. Similarly, the cultural norms in the community impose certain restrictions on the role of the programmer. The needs and responses of the client are also a major factor in shaping the programmer's role. Rothman presents data that suggest that low-income clients respond better to "socializing" roles.

Organizational Factors

The organization for which the programmer works obviously has an effect on the role(s) she or he performs. The structure of the organization may limit the use of certain roles. A person working in a given organization may not be able to utilize conflict strategies or roles that coerce opposing community groups. Rather, they will need to use roles and strategies that neutralize the opposition and maintain community stability.

Agencies tend to develop traditional modes of practice that influence the roles of professionals working within that agency. Thus, a programmer must be aware that certain roles may not be accepted simply because they are different. Closely tied to this aspect is the role expectation and responsibilities of the position occupied by the programmer and the extent of the programmer's identification with that position. Rothman suggests three types of positions that call for differing roles: The politician who defends the agency before the outside world; the administrator who supervises the execution of agency programs; and the professional who uses professional, technical, or scientific tools.

Two final organizational factors influencing the role of the programmer are the relative power and resources of the employing agency. The degree of power available to the programmer, especially through the resources or prestige of the organization, has considerable effect on the roles one can perform.

The Programmer's Personal Attributes

There is a great deal of support for the idea that the programmer's personality gives certain emphasis to prescribed roles as discussed above. Personality factors may create new roles within the organization's normative boundaries. In addition to personality, the programmer's perceptions of clients and problem situations contribute to role performance. If the programmer believes that people are capable of making decisions and taking control of situations in their lives, she or he is likely to utilize roles that encourage participation. If the programmer sees them as basically dependent and incapable, more authoritarian roles may be used. Similarly, the programmer's value orientation affects role. If the programmer values participation over fast answers or solutions, the role will reflect this value.

Another factor influencing the role of the programmer is the homogeneity of the programmer and the clients. Such things as race, sex, religion, and other cultural differences could affect the roles a programmer is able to perform in educational programs. A person with a background from a high socioeconomic class may have difficulty communicating with people from low socioeconomic classes.

Each of the factors discussed above not only influences the role of the programmer but also has a reciprocal influence on the others. As Figure 6.1 illustrates, the four variables function within a governmental structure and a society. The arrows between each of the variables and the society and government structure illustrate the wide range of interrelationships.

TYPES OF ROLES

As was pointed out in Chapter 1, program includes two major aspects. One of these aspects relates directly to achieving educational ends; the other focuses on maintaining the organization as a viable social unit so that it can continue to fulfill its educational function. Organizational factors influencing role, as discussed above, relate to both of these functions to some extent. Material in the following sections examines the types of roles a programmer might assume in striving for educational or maintenance ends. Several specific roles as described by a number of different authors are explored. Roles designed to achieve program goals are discussed, and these are followed by an examination of maintenance roles.

Figure 6.1   The Programmer's Role

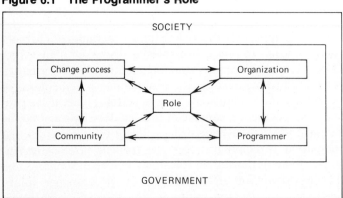

Roles Aimed at Program Goals: Robinson and Clifford

Robinson and Clifford[2] discussed five leadership roles that we can portray in different scenes within a community organization. Each role is described in terms of role expectation and behavior.

The Activator   The Activator initiates activity by introducing subject matter. In this role, the Activator involves people through questioning, active listening, and providing support and approval. Assimilation takes place by structuring and organizing ideas and clarifying and formulating objectives. Reinforcement is provided through personal and research support, and personalizing (e.g., "I think your plan is a good one"). The Activator solidifies by reviewing and summarizing discussions and decisions, specifying and confirming agreements.

The Controller   A Controller's behavior is perceived as a power-application role. In this role, the Controller is very active, but rigid, acting out behavior consistent with the belief that people need strong direction. The Controller often works within a directive organization and uses power over others to regiment, judge, reward, or punish.

The Martyr   The Martyr's behavior is a guilt-producing role. The Martyr tries to impose her or his values and policy on everyone. Rules may become ends in themselves rather than means to an end. This role seeks to win support from group members by making them feel guilty if they violate organizational norms or are disloyal.

The Cavalier   This is a pleasure-providing role in which the programmer wins the group over through fun and games. The Cavalier wants to be liked by everyone and provides an unstructured and permissive work environment. The Cavalier is extremely flexible and permissive to the extent that tasks are often not accomplished.

The Abdicator   The Abdicator is really not a leader at all but withdraws from a situation of responsibility. Action is postponed and responsibility avoided so that others are required to make decisions and promote activity. This role is often seen in organizations burdened with conflict and crises.

Robinson's descriptions of roles are based primarily on the organization and programmer variables as described earlier. The Controller and

[2]Jerry Robinson and Roy Clifford, *Leadership Roles in Community Groups,* North-Central Regional Extension Publications, no. 36-3, University of Illinois at Urbana-Champaign, 1974.

Activator roles are similar to descriptions of autocratic and democratic leaders, respectively, while the Cavalier and Abdicator roles resemble the laissez-faire leadership style.

Roles Aimed at Program Goals: Gallaher and Santopolo

Gallaher and Santopolo[3] described the role of the programmer in terms of a change agent. They discussed four different roles: Analyst, Advisor, Advocate and Innovator.

Analyst   The programmer's main commitment is to interpret a situation for a client or group. The client or group feels the need to understand a particular problem area and is not yet concerned with obtaining advice or solutions. The Analyst must carefully examine all available data and help the client or group appreciate the need for an objective analysis of the situation. It is important for the programmer to know when only analysis is expected. Otherwise, the programmer-client relationship can be damaged by giving advice, advocating an alternative, or attempting an innovation when the client desires to postpone. This role, more than any other, is basic to the success of a continuing education programmer.

Advisor   The programmer's main commitment is to present the client with alternatives applicable to a given situation. It should be stressed, however, that success in this role is tied closely to the programmer's ability to analyze. To advise is to present alternatives to the client but leave the decision-making process mainly to the client.

Advocate   When the programmer's main commitment to a client is to recommend a specific alternative, the programmer is performing the role of Advocate. As in the Advisor's role, success in this role relates directly to the analysis that precedes advocacy. A continuing education programmer must understand the range of alternatives possible in a given situation. The programmer is then in a better position to advocate and support the alternative that appears to best suit the client's problem.

Innovator   When the programmer's main commitment to a client is to create an innovation to satisfy a specific need, the programmer is performing the role of Innovator. One area of innovative activity commonly engaged in by the programmer is the role of linking or relating knowledge systems to the client's needs.

[3]Art Gallaher and Frank Santopolo, ''Agent Roles,'' *Journal of Cooperative Extension*, vol. 5, no. 4, Winter 1967, pp. 223–230.

Roles Aimed at Program Goals: Franklin

Franklin[4] described role in terms of certain educative styles. He indicated that programmer style or role depends on three factors: (1) methods of interacting with client system (individuals, group, or multigroups), (2) underlying purpose, and (3) philosophy of what constitutes help. Through extensive personal observation of extension in West Virginia, Franklin has compiled five basic programmer styles as follows.

Instructor "The strategy in this style is to induce change through promulgating information, or through transmitting conclusions arising from (the agent's) own investigation."[5] The Instructor style is perhaps best illustrated by the role of the expert in our society. Certain individuals, by virtue of their education, experience, or social standing, have privileged access to certain knowledge that they then bestow on those in need. An example of this style is the university professor who lays special claim to knowledge in his or her field by virtue of a degree and in-depth study. Students are then instructed. Many continuing education programmers assume this role from time to time in their programming efforts, though rarely in as pure a form. The programmer who is prepared to specially answer the client's questions assumes the Instructor role. This role is usually most appropriate in institutional and informational types of programs as described in Chapter 4.

Paterfamilias Franklin writes that "this type of change agent relates consciously or unconsciously as a 'father' to the client group . . . he believes he knows better than the group what is best for it."[6] The clientele always have someone to depend on; consequently they are not being prepared to assume self-directed learning responsibilities.

Advocate In the Advocate role, the programmer takes a position on what direction she or he would like to see the clientele pursue. Part of the Advocate role is to convince the clientele that the Advocate's position is most desirable. This role is often assumed by a politically oriented programmer. For example, a programmer may want to help prison guards become more sensitive and responsive to the feelings and needs of the prisoners. The programmer enters the prison to convince the guards that this is a good idea, and programs are designed to achieve that objective.

---

[4]Richard Franklin, *Toward the Style of the Community Change Educator,* National Training Laboratories, Institute for Applied Behavioral Science, Washington, D.C., 1969.

[5]Ibid., p. 5.

[6]Ibid., p. 6.

Many programmers are excited by the Advocacy role because it allows them to become a more visible, active part of the change process.

Servitor   In this role, the programmer "is the implementor of decisions, the executive secretary. He may be able to influence those decisions, but only within circumscribed boundaries."[7] Most often the programmer will assume this role for one of two reasons. First, the programmer might be reacting against the role of Paterfamilias or Advocate. For fear of dominating the clientele, the programmer goes to the opposite extreme and allows the clientele to dominate. Second, the programmer's power position relative to the clientele may force the role upon her or him. New and inexperienced programmers often assume the Servitor role as a safe, realistic way to "learn the ropes."

Community Change Educator   The Community Change Educator is more concerned with the process of change than with its contents. As Franklin puts it:

> He takes initiative in generating a learning environment for change. Aims and means merge in this focus. . . . The CCE (Community Change Educator) comprehends both cognitive and emotional data in the situation as integral to the change process, relates collaboratively with the client, helps enlarge the number of available options, and perceives the decision for change as the responsibility of the client group.[8]

Franklin sees the Community Change Educator's goal to be a situation of "interdependence" for the clientele. That is, the clientele are responsible for change and its diffusions in the community.

Although it is obvious that Franklin prefers the Community Change Educator role to the other four, he does not obviate the others completely from the program development process. In fact, all five roles can be present in a client-programmer relationship. The assertion of a particular role over the others depends largely on how the programmer perceives the clientele. The types of program described in Chapters 1 and 4 also have an important influence. The Community Change Educator style appears most ideal for developmental-type programs and may be less ideal for institutional or informational programming.

Roles Aimed at Program Goals: Biddle and Biddle

Biddle and Biddle[9] hold a view of the continuing educator's role that is

[7]Ibid., p. 7.

[8]Ibid., p. 9.

[9]William W. Biddle and Loureide J. Biddle, *The Community Development Process,* Holt, Rinehart and Winston, Inc., New York, 1965. Reprinted by permission of Holt, Rinehart and Winston, Inc.

similar to Franklin's. They summarize the continuing educator in community development as:

> . . . "the encourager" of indigenous participant growth. Great skill is required of the community developer to strike a proper balance . . . that gives the maximum encouragement for participants in the process to achieve a momentum of their own. The balance of initiative shifts from time to time throughout the process. The encourager's initiative is usually greatest in the early stages, and then tapers off as the local citizens gain in confidence and competence. But his initiative may increase, then decrease again, and may take a variety of forms, if the process bogs down. His decision to speak up or to remain silent, to offer guidance or to let people find their own way, depends upon his sensitivity to their need, but even more upon an awareness of the process and of the encouragement needed to maintain its vigor.[10]

This perspective, like Franklin's, suggests that the programmer's ultimate role is dynamic in nature. Roles may change throughout the program development process. The programmer's knowledge of the clientele is crucial in making correct decisions about potential roles.

Franklin's concept of the Community Change Educator derives somewhat from Lippitt's[11] construct of the change agent. Instead of the more general term "role" to describe the continuing education programmer's repertoire of behaviors and functions, Lippitt speaks of functions very specifically. They can be thought of as a role only when considered as a whole.

Lippitt writes:

> The change agent must assess the client's readiness to enter into a helping relationship, and he must determine whether or not the client possesses sufficient motivation and capacity to hold up its end of the partnership. This involves, as we have seen, an appraisal of the change and resistance forces which are present in the client system at the beginning of the change process as well as others which may be revealed as the process advances. Being continually sensitive to the constellation of change forces and resistance forces is one of the most creative parts of the change agent's job.[12]

More specifically, Lippitt outlines these functions in the following ways.

Mediating and stimulating new connections with the client system   He describes this role as follows:

> In any established system the pattern of internal relationships is well stabilized. Usually it is also accepted without question by the members of the

---

[10]Ibid., pp. 81–82.
[11]Ronald Lippitt, *The Dynamics of Planned Change,* Harcourt, Brace & World, Inc., New York, 1958.
[12]Ibid., p. 104.

organization: no alternative pattern of relationships occurs to them as possible or even desirable. Hence, the position of change agent as an outsider gives him a unique view of these relationships which is often quite different from that of insiders.[13]

The change agent or programmer, through an analysis of the client system, begins to communicate an understanding of how it works or does not work with the clientele. For this strategy to be effective, a high level of trust must be built up between the programmer and the clientele. In a sense, "the change agent holds up a mirror in which the client system sees itself more clearly than it did before. . . ."[14] If the trust level is not high, holding up this mirror will only cause defensiveness.

Presenting expert knowledge on procedures   In this role, the programmer does not directly try to influence the client system or its goals. Instead, the programmer offers services in organizing more effective procedures—better means to achieve existing goals. A programmer is consulted by an organization whose members feel frustrated over getting too little accomplished. When an analysis of that organization reveals that its leadership is not delegating authority, programs are then designed to help the organization confront this problem.

Providing strength from within   In this strategy the programmer actually becomes part of the system to help change it. This function is very similar to Franklin's category of Advocate. Lippitt writes that "the change agent uses whatever power he possesses to strengthen one view relative to the other."[15] This category includes the union organizer who joins with workers to increase their strength vis-á-vis management and "the community worker who tries to mobilize the residents of a city block group in their fight for better living conditions."[16]

Creating special environments   The programmer perceives that a certain change is necessary for the clientele, and attempts to establish "environments or situations in which the client system will find it easy to learn something new or strange."[17] The social worker who attempts to bring people off the streets and into a settlement house is operating on the basis of this assumption. Another example is the group dynamics facilitator. This facilitator brings people away from their everyday activities and

[13]Ibid., p. 105.
[14]Ibid., p. 108.
[15]Ibid., p. 108.
[16]Ibid., p. 108.
[17]Ibid., p. 112.

into a group setting where they will be more open to exploring the meaning behind their behavior. The instructor of a class on aging who takes the students into a nursing home knows that the new environment will provide practical learning about the relationships of the elderly and society.

Giving support during the process of change   Change is often feared because it involves the unknown and certain levels of risk. In this function, the programmer works to reduce clients' fears. Lippitt writes that "one way of helping is to encourage and support the client system's belief that change is actually possible."[18] Another is to encourage clientele to try something new. A third is to make sure that clients are aware of their positive and negative feelings about change. Finally, once changes have been made, "the client system may be doubtful about its ability . . . to progress further."[19] The programmer then works to give clientele a feeling of self-confidence in their ability to sustain change.

Throughout Lippitt's description of the change agent's function, the one factor of vital importance is a climate of mutual trust between the programmer and the clientele. Thus, another function of the programmer is to establish a climate of mutual trust.

Establishing a climate of mutual trust   Essentially, mutual trust is effective communication between the programmer and the clientele. Several qualities make for trust or effective communication. The concept of trust must be viewed as a process, a development, not a series of isolated parts. Five qualities make for trust in the change relationship. First, the programmer demonstrates an ability to empathize with the client's situation:

> We listen with understanding. . . . It means to see the expressed idea and attitude from the other's point of view, to sense how it feels to him, to achieve his frame of reference in regard to the thing he is talking about.[20]

Second, the programmer has an attitude of respect in that the clients are valued for just being as well as for their contribution to the relationship. Third, the programmer demonstrates a genuineness of self. The programmer is open, without the need to behave or act in a way false to what she or he is. Fourth, the programmer is willing to self-disclose. The programmer not only "listens" as stated in the first quality, but also is willing to share experiences, thoughts, and concerns with the client. Fifth, the pro-

[18]Ibid., p. 114.
[19]Ibid.
[20]Carl Rogers, *On Becoming a Person,* Houghton Mifflin Company, Boston, 1961, pp. 331–332. Reprinted by permission of Houghton Mifflin Company.

grammer demonstrates the ability to verbalize spontaneous feelings with the client. In reviewing these five qualities, the attitudes of sensitivity, awareness, and respect of client and self are represented as is the ability to respond and act upon those qualities.

Although establishing mutual trust is a very complex function for the programmer, it is vital to one's success as a programmer. It is the foundation upon which all the other functions that Lippitt speaks of are built. Consequently, it must be the programmer's first priority, the stepping stone from which other changes are reached. As suggested in Chapter 4, Lippitt's ideas relate more directly to developmental programs.

Roles Aimed at Program Goals: Knowles and Verner

Knowles[21] reviews the functions of the continuing educator from a holistic view of program development. These functions are: diagnostic, planning, motivational, methodological, resource, and evaluative. Knowles describes the continuing educator's role as it relates to the continuing development of the program and asks the basic question: What part does the educator perform in the program development process? The various functions outlined by Knowles are described and illustrated through the experiences of an Extension Community Development Programmer.

The diagnostic function   In this role, the programmer helps the learners diagnose their needs for particular learnings within the scope of the given situation. For example, an Extension Community Development Programmer working in a rural and unzoned county begins to hear complaints about a man who has bought farmland and converted it into a junkyard. Realizing this as a potential problem, the programmer talks with local officials and certain individuals in the various towns and townships. From these conversations, it is learned that the junkyard is not the only perceived problem. Other land-use conflicts are also seen as problems. The citizens favor preservation of the rural and scenic character of the land. The programmer discovers concerns about the uncontrolled spread of mobile homes, improper sewage facilities at new homesites built by city people, unplanned construction of industrial parks, the conversion of farmlands into apartment complexes, and so on. On the other hand, the programmer finds that many people fear zoning ordinances because they might have to surrender some of their cherished local autonomy to countywide authority. The clients are torn between an obvious problem that needs solution, and a solution that is a potential problem. The agent diagnoses a need on the part of the people to learn more about the problem and the implications of various solutions.

---

[21]Malcolm Knowles, *The Modern Practice of Adult Education,* Association Press, New York, 1970, p. 22. Used by permission of Follett Publishing Co.

The planning function Here, the programmer helps the learners plan a sequence of experiences that will produce the desired learnings. In response to the problem, the programmer helps organize a citizens' group to review land use in the county and to produce a coordinated land-use plan. The group lists objectives they hope to accomplish: First, they will survey the full extent of the problem in all parts of the county; second, they will put together a comprehensive land-use plan; third, they will offer various recommendations to make this plan a reality.

The motivational function Here, the programmer creates conditions that will cause the learners to want to learn. While the citizens' group is active, the programmer works to keep people involved and interested. She or he meets with individuals on the committee, over coffee at their work places, for instance, to discuss various aspects of the project. In this way, the programmer helps to assure their continued commitment.

The methodological function In this aspect, the programmer selects the most effective methods and techniques to produce the desired learnings. Basically, we will be concerned with four methods or formats of education, as outlined by Verner.[22] These four methods are individual learning, group learning, large meetings, and learning via the communications media. The citizens' group will likely use all methods, and the programmer will have a role in each. First, the programmer contacts all the members of the group on a one-to-one basis. On these occasions much individualized education can take place because the specific problems of each member can be considered. Second, learning takes place when the group meets to discuss the development of the project. The programmer organizes and facilitates these group meetings. Third, the group can get greater involvement by holding town meetings on the land-use problem. Again, the programmer performs an organizing role for this function. Fourth, articles in the local papers, radio broadcasts, and so on, can do much to disseminate the citizen group's land-use plan. The programmer has a central role in evolving and conducting these kinds of programs.

The resource function Here, the programmer provides resources necessary to produce the desired learning. In this role, the programmer might bring in various experts and interest groups to present their points of view to the group. Also, the programmer can supply audio-visual equipment, arrange a meeting place, help publicize the meetings, and prepare handouts.

---

[22]C. Verner, "Definition of Terms," in G. Jensen, A. A. Liverright, and W. Hallenbeck (eds.), *Adult Education Outlines of an Emerging Field of University Study,* Adult Education Association, Washington, D.C., 1964.

The evaluative function   This role focuses on helping the learners measure the outcomes of the learning experiences. After the land-use report is completed, the programmer can help the group evaluate its impact. Together, they can determine the county's progress in accomplishing the recommendations of the report. If progress has been slow, the programmer's role and the six functions described might be repeated.

Roles Aimed at Organization Maintenance

Various roles for the continuing educator in program development will be described in this section. Again, it is important to understand these roles so they can be performed when necessary in the various responsibilities of program development. The second category of behaviors focuses on the programmer's role in maintaining the viability of the organization and the program.

Knowles[23] stresses the importance of a maintenance role for the continuing education programmer that involves management at the organizational level and must be in operation for effective development of adult programs. In the maintenance role the programmer is less concerned with educational ends than with maintaining the organization as a viable social unit so as to continue its educational functions. Such activities may be referred to as administrative management and administrative leadership.[24]

A programmer might coordinate a community health education program begun by a group of citizens and supported by the local pharmacists, doctors, nurses, and dentists. Part of the role is to maintain the health education program as a viable entity. In a sense, the programmer performs a variety of service functions; for instance, obtaining space for the group's counseling program or providing leadership in resolving personal differences among people actively involved. Finally, the programmer makes sure that the bills are paid, that funding is forthcoming, and that money is allocated in accordance with group wishes. In brief, the continuing educator is responsible for the internal well-being of the organization.

Knowles speaks of the changing nature of the role of the continuing educator. He says that "his [adult educator's] function has moved increasingly away from being remedial toward being developmental— toward helping his clients achieve their full potential."[25] This view of the continuing educator's role is similar to Franklin's concept of the Community Change Educator, Biddle and Biddle's concept of the Encourager, Lippitt's concept of the Change Agent, and Robinson and Clifford's concept of the Activator. These concepts imply that adults have the potential for unlimited growth and development in achieving a better life.

---

[23]Knowles, op. cit.
[24]Rothman, *Planning and Organizing*.
[25]Knowles, op. cit., p. 34.

PROGRAMMER ROLES IN PROGRAM DEVELOPMENT

On the basis of this review and discussion of roles, it is suggested that there are four major roles essential for the continuing education programmer.

The Analyst

Gallaher and Santopolo suggest that this role is basic to the success of any change agent or continuing education programmer. The role is one of taking stock of the programming situation and helping the clients diagnose the need. It is essential for defining the problem or need in all types of programs. This role should be performed through a variety of different actions in programming, such as deciding on learning experiences, considering the resources, developing the plan for evaluation, or communicating the results. It also combines some aspects described as Advisor by Gallaher and Santopolo and the resource function described by Knowles.

The Stimulator

A stimulator role might also be called an "activator" or "motivator." It is essential for clients to gain enthusiasm for the program. This enthusiasm may be lacking for a number of reasons, including feeling inadequate to solve the problem or meet the need, lack of knowledge of process and resources, and conflict between individuals and groups. This role would be closely related to Robinson and Clifford's Activator, Gallaher and Santopolo's and Franklin's Advocate, and Knowles's motivational function. The programmer would act as a stimulus to keep the process moving, to see the clients involved, and to make contacts with the necessary individuals with influence and resources.

The Facilitator

This role suggests that there is a need for the programmer to link the needs of the clients with the appropriate knowledge or resources in an efficient and effective manner. A facilitator is related to Gallaher and Santopolo's description of an Innovator: "one who can create an innovation to satisfy a specific need" and Lippitt's suggestion of a need for a change agent to create special environments. The role of facilitator suggests the need for someone to establish environments conducive for learning by clients. These environments may be formalized learning opportunities or opportunities for an expert to relate to the clients in their own situations. This role suggests that an essential ingredient is knowing the client group well and having the process and expertise to create situations conducive to promoting and teaching through a variety of opportunities.

The Encourager

Most adult clients or students feel a certain amount of uneasiness in a programming situation, especially if such activity is new to them. They are unsure of their personal abilities and of the group's potential. An essential ingredient necessary in order to help each individual develop his or her full potential is the establishment of a climate of trust. This climate can be promoted through the use of an encourager role—helping people and groups realize their potential. Such a role includes aspects of Franklin's Paterfamilias role, and Lippitt's reference to programmer support of clientele during the change process.

DYNAMICS OF ROLE PERFORMANCE

In this chapter four factors were identified as affecting role. Also illustrated was the potential for a wide range of roles for the continuing education programmer. The last part of the chapter explores more specifically some of the dynamics and problems involved in actually performing roles. Rothman et al.[26] outlines several considerations in making effective use of role.

Role Set

The literature emphasizes the need for flexibility in assuming roles so that a particular role is suitable for the situation. Some situations require only a very limited number of roles for the programmer to be effective, others require a large number of roles. Rothman et al. refer to this as limited versus multiple role sets. They suggest that many programmers accept a limited role and consequently do not perform effectively in situations where assuming multiple roles is required. They state:

> Diagnosis of one's role set should hypothetically contribute to effectiveness in community practice. Not only might the practitioner be better able to determine the particular roles to employ under given conditions, but this framework might also help him to move from a limited to an extended role set and back again flexibly as circumstances require. As a rule of thumb, a broader role set is suggested when a practitioner is in a decentralized structure or when he is using a high-intensity approach with distrustful groups. Employing this general framework, experienced practitioners can discern many additional criteria for determining the appropriate scope of role set.[27]

[26]Jack Rothman, John Erlich, and Joseph Teresa, *Promoting Innovation and Change in Organizations and Communities,* John Wiley & Sons, Inc., New York, 1976, pp. 134–167. Reprinted by permission of John Wiley & Sons, Inc.
[27]Ibid., p. 64.

In a similar manner, Robinson and Clifford[28] stress the need for a good leader to remain flexible. A good leader is concerned with making the group a more productive team. This is achieved by making maximum use of the combined skills and knowledge of all the people involved. This function was described earlier as the Activator role.

Flexibility in assuming roles is especially important in developmental programming. In need analysis the Analyst role is extremely important, while the Advocate role may be necessary when research strongly supports a given course of action.

Role Conflict

In situations where there are multiple influences on roles, the programmer may have conflicting expectations regarding role. Rothman et al. state:

> Human service workers often find themselves caught up in a "cross-fire" of differing expectations regarding their work roles. Their own assessment of desirable goals may vary from those of supervisors, board members, community leaders, public officials, and others. Within the agency system different constituencies may have different views of a particular practitioner's roles. For example, clients and administrators may differ on how agency services of various kinds should be delivered.[29]

Role conflict situations are often extremely difficult for the programmer working in a community with a variety of interest and support groups. Several approaches have been suggested for dealing with role conflict:[30]

1　Selecting one role for emphasis
2　Meeting or balancing competing expectations
3　Withdrawal from expected role behavior
4　Realistic action to change the role definition
5　Aggressive and symbolic adjustment patterns

Rothman et al. suggest that realistic action may be used in redefining the role. This should be done by "achieving role consensus among competing reference groups, by eliminating the position, or by removing the actor from the situation."[31] Other alternatives may be less productive.

The best solution to role conflict according to Rothman et al. is to blend and balance expectancy within the existing role. This can be accom-

---

[28]Robinson and Clifford, *Leadership Roles*.
[29]Rothman et al., op. cit., p. 134.
[30]Ibid., p. 137.
[31]Ibid., p. 67.

plished by clearly identifying and specifying the role and then obtaining mutual agreement from those related to or concerned with the role. Time taken from ongoing operations to clarify roles and tasks is usually well worthwhile. However, note that role ambiguity and lack of role consensus may at times promote creativity and pursuance of "multiple valued objectives." For example, when a third party asks a programmer to meet with a group of interested adults for the purpose of establishing an educational program, the programmer may not have a clear idea of what the group's intent is or how the third party saw the planning role. The adult participants or third party may have established objectives prior to asking the programmer's assistance or they may expect the programmer to direct the formation of these. In this situation, the programmer must pursue the clarification of types of leadership with the group and the educational objectives. The group members, third party, and programmer will all be involved in offering various alternatives, discussions of the alternatives, and selection of relevant roles and purposes. Within the process, new combinations of elements will give rise to action not conceived or previously taken.

Role Orientation

Closely tied to the idea of role conflict is what Rothman et al. term role orientation. They suggest that professionals hold one of three basic role orientations that determine the degree to which the various factors affect role. A professional orientation implies a high concern with professional values and standards. A bureaucratic orientation refers to a preoccupation with the policies and norms of the employing agency. And finally, a client orientation connotes primary attention to the needs of those served by the agency.

Role orientation has definite implications for the continuing education programmer. If a programmer has a strong professional orientation, the important problems and needs of the clientele may never be considered in programming. Specific efforts should be made to help programmers become aware of their orientation and strive for a balance of the three orientations. Again, this points out the importance of programmers developing their own working philosophies as guides in developing and utilizing roles in programming.

SUMMARY

There are several factors that affect the role of the programmer in continuing education programming. These are (1) the dynamics of the change process, (2) community factors, (3) organizational factors, and (4) personal attributes of the programmer. In the second section of this chapter, various possible roles for the continuing education programmer were reviewed. Several role perspectives were explored, including roles viewed from the perspective of leadership, change, and function. Four roles were suggested for the continuing education programmer. In the final section of the chapter we explored certain considerations in applying roles in programming. We emphasized that the programmer must be involved in performing a variety of roles if program development is to be effective.

DISCUSSION QUESTIONS

1 In continuing education programs, identify and describe the roles and responsibilities of the programmer in dealing with situations characterized by *(a)* apathy among people, *(b)* conflict of basic philosophies within the society, and *(c)* conflict within the organization of program priorities.
2 Illustrate how roles performed by the programmer will change when the tasks of need analysis and program design are being completed.
3 Discuss how roles might change in developmental-, institutional-, and informational-type programs.
4 What are your beliefs about the role of the continuing education programmer in advocating change?
5 Discuss situations in which a continuing education programmer may get involved in role conflict.

Section III

Involvement of People in Program Development

"A man becomes more and more a free and responsible agent the more he, at all times, knows what he is doing in every sense of the phrase, and the more he acts with a definite and clearly formed intention."[1] Few continuing educators would quarrel with Hampshire's philosophy. In fact, we really say the same thing when we argue that "it is right" to involve our clientele in program development. The concept of involvement is generally viewed as necessary and something we should do in programming. In this section, several critical issues and concerns relating to the purpose, role, and methods of the involvement process will be focused upon.

In Chapter 7, a rationale for the involvement of people will be developed. It is suggested that the factors affecting clientele involvement include the nature of the planning task, functional roles, and planning ideologies.

Ideas on the methods and procedures for involving people are presented in Chapter 8. The advantages and disadvantages of the different methods are discussed.

In Chapter 9, advisory committees are discussed. The emphasis is on concerns relating to the committees becoming an effective study group.

[1]Stuart Hampshire, *Thought and Action,* Chatto and Windus, Ltd., London, 1959, p. 177.

Chapter 7

A Rationale for Involvement of People

"All changes should be introduced with the fullest consent and participation of those whose daily lives will be affected by the change."[1] This statement of well-known sociologist Margaret Mead symbolizes our concept of the involvement of people in program development. The emphasis on involvement in decisions about the program represents a departure from planning for to planning with people.

The literature reveals a wide range of disagreement on the notion of involvement in the decisions when developing programs. This variance is true when we consider social action, education, or community development programs. Two opposite views can be clearly identified.

A CONCEPT OF INVOLVEMENT

The first view of involvement is embodied in the concept of power or control. Arnstein, for instance, defines participation as "the redistribu-

---

[1]Margaret Mead (ed.), *Cultural Patterns and Technical Change,* The New American Library, Inc., New York, 1955, p. 289. Reprinted by permission of UNESCO.

tion of power that enables the have-not citizens, presently excluded from the political and economic process, to be deliberately included in the future."[2] This concept depicts a ladder of citizen participation that begins with manipulation at the bottom and moves up to citizen control at the top. The underlying theme is one of conflict: The have-not citizens against the powerholders. It is suggested that change results from confronting existing power centers with a new power center based on the size and dedication of its groups rather than on the control of wealth or institutions. The conflict pushes the existing power center to negotiate. Saul Alinsky, addressing his organizers, stated: "That organizer dedicated to changing the character of life of a particular community has an initial function of an abrasive agent . . . to a point of overt expression, to search out controversial issues, rather than to avoid them. . . ."[3]

The basic purpose of this type of participation is to drastically alter the power structure. The definition of the problem is seen in terms of the whole system as it relates to both internal and external environments. One approach to social change theory sees society exactly in these terms. The basic assumption of conflict theories is that all social organisms are inherently unstable, and change, therefore, is the working out of conflicts.

Conflict strategy is based on the premise that "prevailing arrangements of power can only be altered by power." Alinsky goes on to suggest that "to make even good will effective it must be mobilized into a power unit."[4]

The danger of conflict strategy is that it may merely amount to manipulation of the many by the few. One of the major objectives of participation is to effect psychological changes in the participants themselves that will better prepare them to participate in all changes that affect them and their environment. When this objective is not achieved, the whole process may become one in which a few leaders emerge as representatives of the group. The process may also attempt to rigidly control the participants, a condition that gave rise to the cry for participation in the first place, that human beings are reduced to mere objects. And, as Paolo Freire aptly observes, "[People] cannot enter the struggle as objects in order *later* to become men."[5] In the words of Irvin Kristol:

[2]Sherry P. Arnstein, "Eight Rungs on the Ladder of Citizen Participation," in E. Cahn and B. Passett (eds.), *Citizen Participation: Effecting Community Change,* Praeger Publishers, Inc., New York, 1971, pp. 71–72.

[3]Saul Alinsky, "From Citizen Apathy to Participation," paper presented at the Sixth Annual Conference, Association of Community Councils of Chicago, October 19, 1957, Industrial Areas Foundation, Chicago. Quoted in John Hall Fish, *Black Power/White Control: The Struggle of the Woodlawn Organization in Chicago,* Princeton University Press, Princeton, N.J., 1973, pp. 28–29. Reprinted by permission of Princeton University Press.

[4]Ibid., p. 25.

[5]Paolo Freire, *Pedagogy of the Oppressed,* Myra B. Rames (trans.), Herder and Herder, New York, 1972, p. 55.

> . . . participatory democracy requires that all people be fit to govern: and this in turn requires that all people be made fit to govern, by rigid and uniform educational training, constant public indoctrination, close supervision of private morals and beliefs, and so forth.[6]

It should be emphasized that the conflict approach is not the only approach to social change. It is misleading to imply that participation always entails conflicts of interest.

The functional approach to social change maintains that the major function is to provide the means for increased collective effectiveness. Societal needs become organized in and represented by specific institutions. But the social system is an interdependent unit and, as specific institutions multiply, the problem of interdependency and integration becomes central to planning for change. Collective effectiveness is realized only if all societal needs are met in a balanced fashion. When the needs of one subsystem are not recognized, that subsystem must push its weight to offset the imbalance and move toward integration.

Our approach to social change parallels that of the Institutional Building Model. The basic premise of this model is that change is introduced primarily in and through formal organizations. The model applies to situations where change agents enjoy some official sponsorship and attempt to impress their goals on the social system; the components of the system related to the proposed innovations must be influenced, and not coerced, to accept the innovations; formal organizations are the vehicles through which change agents develop the technical capacities and commitment to change. It should be clear how this model differs from conflict strategy. These underlying assumptions are not always explicitly stated with respect to the concept of participation.

In the Institutional Building Model the change agents are identified as the leadership, with professional and political attributes, that facilitates the change process. Their basic tasks are to define problems, values, objectives, and operating styles of the organization; translate problems and needs into programs through policies and action measures; mobilize and develop human and physical resources; combine these resources into structures of authority, communication, and effective actions that enable the organization to carry out its programs.

Mobilizing and developing human resources into structures that enable the organization to implement its programs is most effective through the direct participation of those the organization serves. Thus, participation is defined in institutional terms.

---

[6]Irvin Kristol, "What's Bugging the Students?" *The Atlantic Monthly*, vol. 216, November 1965, p. 111.

It is a structured form of participation. As Lewis Feuer[7] convincingly argues in discussing "participatory democracy," an unstructured form of participation is just another way of legitimizing an undemocratic reality. Participation may be defined as a function of differentiation. The two broad features of this definition are: Decentralization or dispersion of authoritative decision making from the top of institutional hierarchies downward and from within the organization outward to the people affected by the decision; and direct involvement of citizens in the decision-making process. This kind of involvement is further distinguished from that kind of "contact involvement" that Riesman[8] made famous by his term "the lonely crowd." Thus, our concept of participation includes cases that might be appropriately called "contact participation," such as a public hearing that allows participation on a consultant or advisory basis. This is viewed as a part of the total participation process. Authority is an important ingredient in the concept but not in the same sense that it was in the conflict approach. Authority is an integral part of the decision-making mechanism. This is not by way of advocating participation as an absolute value that must be maintained at all times, but as a process that must be adapted to ever-changing situations. The limits of participation are determined by conditions prevailing in the situation at any given time.

Thus, the conflict approach to citizen participation has emerged as a major idea in recent years. Again, we do not advocate it as an effective approach in the development of continuing education programs. We do, however, advocate the second approach discussed, which is based on functional theory within the framework of the Institutional Building Model. Participation was defined as the process that helps integrate the ever-increasing differentiated functions and institutions in the social system. The lack of such integration is seen as a major characteristic of the change process.

REASONS FOR INVOLVEMENT OF PEOPLE

Just as John Dewey's[9] philosophy of progressive education and learner involvement was misinterpreted by many curriculum planners in formal education, the concept of clientele involvement in program development has been similarly misinterpreted by continuing educators. Involvement does not always mean involving groups in laborious analyses of "the situation" to identify "the relevant needs."

[7]Lewis Feuer, *The Conflict of Generations: The Character and Significance of Student Movements,* Basic Books, Inc., Publishers, New York, 1969, pp. 408–412.

[8]David Riesman, *The Lonely Crowd,* Yale University Press, New Haven, Conn., 1976.

[9]John Dewey, *Interest and Effort in Education,* Southern Illinois University Press, Carbondale, 1975.

The literature on participatory activities presents various reasons and justifications for involvement. Several reasons are advanced for the cause of participation:

- The first rationale is based on the idea of the town meeting, the educability of the citizen, and the belief in reason, with the end product being understanding, consensus, and wise decisions.
- A second rationale is based on the principle of securing the consent of the public but tends to deny the viability of the idea of the "public interest." Instead, it emphasizes the group basis of politics, group interaction, conflict, and accommodation as the way to formulate sound decisions.
- A third rationale is based on the idea that citizen involvement provides the programmer with better information about the wishes and needs of the people and also to avoid misunderstandings and misconceptions that may occur.
- Another rationale sees participation as a vehicle for social therapy; that is, an opportunity for the disadvantaged to participate in decisions that affect them with the ultimate end of counteracting their alienations.
- Another rationale argues for participation as a means to alter the power structure. It is strongly argued that "citizen participation is a categorical term for citizen power."[10]
- Participation is seen as a way to legitimize programs. This rationale argues that the involvement of people will speed up the process of change and reduce resistance to the program.
- Another rationale is to facilitate the teaching-learning process, especially in the case of planning educational programs. The argument maintains that participation promotes an active kind of learning that is not only more permanent but also more available.
- Participation is seen as a way to mobilize resources because "short of total war, a free government is incompetent to marshall the full resources of its people by compulsion."[11]
- A final rationale for citizen participation is that it is an end in itself. This argument maintains that participation is by nature an affirmative activity seeking to exercise the initiative, creativity, and self-reliance of the individual.

These nine reasons for involving citizens in decision making have important implications for program development. They provide three basic premises for support of the concept of citizen involvement in program development. These are:

[10] Arnstein, op. cit., p. 71.

[11] E. S. Cahn and J. C. Cahn, "Maximum Feasible Participation—A General Overview," in E. S. Cahn and B. A. Passett (eds.), *Citizen Participation,* Praeger Publishers, Inc., New York, 1969, pp. 16–17.

1 More accurate decisions about the relevant needs and opportunities for which continuing education programs will be reached when clientele are involved in making those decisions. It is believed that people, when provided with the real facts of the situation, will identify their most critical problems.

2 The involvement of clientele representatives will speed up the process of change. It is assumed that those who are involved will aid in diffusing and legitimizing subsequent educational programs.

3 Involvement in program development is a learning experience. Participants should be better informed and better prepared for active leadership in the process of change.

Of these three premises, many writers suggest that involvement for the purpose of identifying the most relevant needs and opportunities is most important. According to VandeBerg:

> The primary purpose of any planning is first and foremost that of developing a sound, defensible and progressive course of action—a plan. In the process followed, many other benefits might accrue—such as the education of participants—but we want a plan that can and will be used.[12]

No one would dispute the notion that the end result of any planning effort ought to be a sound, defensible, and progressive plan. However, not everyone agrees that involvement of clientele is the only way to realize this goal. Brower,[13] in his analysis of the philosophical dilemma of the adult educator, identifies four alternative approaches to program development: (1) the academic approach, in which professional authority is primary; (2) the grass-roots approach, in which the learner primarily makes the decisions; (3) the education-for-reality approach, in which the educator and the learner are mutually involved in developing the program; and (4) the propaganda approach, in which programs are developed by a third party excluding both the learner and educator. The programs of various agencies or organizations that promote or sell their particular ideas and vested interests are examples.

There is ample evidence to suggest that the answer to this dilemma does not lie entirely in one approach versus all others. Consider, for example, the number of "canned" programs, planned entirely by professionals, that have been received apathetically by clientele; or the studies that show that problems identified by citizen planning groups sometimes have no basis in the social and economic facts of the community. Whale

[12]G. L. VandeBerg, "Guidelines to Planning," *Journal of Cooperative Extension,* vol. 3, no. 2, Summer 1965, p. 79.

[13]S. L. Brower, "Dilemma of Adult Educators," *Journal of Cooperative Extension,* vol. 2, no. 2, Summer 1964, pp. 113–119.

and Boyle[14] suggest that limited rationality can be anticipated from group planning unless the educator expends much more effort in training and working with citizen planning groups than has been the case so far.

One error made by the proponents of citizen involvement and previous research efforts has been a tunnel vision attempt to identify the program development process, rather than processes. The approach to date has in many ways resembled the early efforts of social scientists to define leadership by using only personality theory, while failing to recognize that the context of leadership affects those who can and should perform a leadership role.

The assumption that the best plans are those in which local people are involved so they can identify needs and opportunities has channeled research efforts into a search for (1) criteria by which local people who will be effective planners can be selected, and (2) ways for citizen committees to function more effectively as problem-solving groups. The possibility that involvement of local people through group problem solving may not only be inefficient for a given situation but also an inaccurate process for determining program foci, has received little attention. This is not to argue against involvement but rather to question the purpose of involvement. This question has direct implications for those responsible for program development in terms of who should be involved and how.

FACTORS AFFECTING CLIENTELE INVOLVEMENT

There are several factors that seem important in making the practical decisions about who, how, why, and when to involve clientele in programming. Those factors that will be discussed are nature of planning task, functional roles, and planning ideologies.

Nature of Planning Task

Much of the present literature on the process of program development appears to have originated from research findings in group dynamics, particularly the work on group problem solving of Bales[15] and his associates. Continuing educators, particularly those in developmental programming, have prescribed group problem solving as standard operating procedure without regard to the nature of the problem confronting the group. This practice does not take other relevant findings from group dynamics research into consideration. For example, it has been clearly demonstrated

---

[14]W. B. Whale and P. G. Boyle, "Group Decision Making," *Journal of Cooperative Extension,* vol. 4, no. 2, Summer 1966, pp. 109–115.

[15]R. F. Bales and F. L. Strodtbeck, "Phases in Group Problem Solving," in D. Cartwright and A. Zander (eds.), *Group Dynamics Research and Theory,* 3d ed., Harper & Row, Publishers, Inc., New York, 1968, pp. 389–398.

that group problem solving is superior to individual problem solving only under certain task conditions: (1) those that are complex and can profit from a division of labor, and (2) those in which individual decisions are subject to random error so that collective decision making tends to reduce error through cancellation. Not all problem areas that confront program planners are constant in terms of these variables.

Several small group researchers have commented on this point. Hoffman[16] has suggested that, until a taxonomy of task problems is developed, further investigation into the nature of group problem solving is unlikely to be very fruitful. Some authors have made attempts in this direction. Fiedler[17] attempted to operationalize Shaw's[18] four criteria for classifying group tasks. These include (1) decision verifiability—how objectively and well the correctness of the solution can be demonstrated; (2) goal clarity—how clearly task requirements are stated to or known by the group; (3) goal path multiplicity—how many procedures are available for performing the task; (4) solution specificity—how many correct solutions exist. Fiedler used these criteria to develop an index for group task structure. The findings suggest that citizen involvement in program development is less important under conditions of high task structure because the opportunity for division of labor and error reduction is much lower than with low structure tasks.

There is evidence also that business management planning has recognized that the nature of the planning task has relevance for the process to be followed. Delbecq[19] suggests a categorization model involving three decision-making procedures: (1) routine decision making, in which the problem is clear and highly specialized inputs of information are needed to arrive at a solution; (2) creative decision making, whereby decisions evolve apart from the expertise of the specialist and an objective basis for making decisions is lacking—in this situation, the opinions and ideas of the group become all-important; (3) negotiated decision making involving opposing factions with conflicting opinions about ends or means or both. In the context of program development, clientele involvement for the purpose of need identification is less important in the first instance and much more important in the latter two situations.

[16]L. F. Hoffman, "Group Problem Solving," in L. Berkowitz (ed.), *Advances in Experimental Social Psychology,* vol. 2, Academic Press, Inc., New York, 1964, pp. 99–132.

[17]F. E. Fiedler, "The Contingency Model: A Theory of Leadership Effectiveness," in H. Proshansky and B. Seidenberg (eds.), *Basic Studies in Social Psychology,* Holt, Rinehart and Winston, Inc., New York, 1965, pp. 538–551.

[18]Nathan C. Shaw (ed.), *Administration of Continuing Education,* National Association for Public School Adult Education, Washington, D.C., 1969.

[19]A. G. Delbecq, "The Management of Decision Making within the Firm: Three Strategies for Three Types of Decision Making," *Academy of Management Journal,* vol. 10, no. 4, December 1967, pp. 329–339.

Last[20] classifies planning tasks or the program development situation somewhat differently. He imagines some situations involving decisions that are subjective and others that are objective. He defines subjective tasks as those in which emotion (feelings, values, and opinions) serve to guide a person's actions. Objective tasks, in contrast, are those in which people rely primarily on their intellectual faculties (knowledge and comprehension of facts) for guidance in decision making.

He suggests there are five planning steps or phases to decision making and relates them to an objective-subjective scale. When arranged along a continuum, as in Figure 7.1, the most subjective of these tasks appears to be the selection of alternatives for action. This is clearly a "value-oriented" task. A person carries it out in response to her or his feelings and opinions. Human judgment is the overriding input in the decision. The task represented as the most objective is the identification of alternatives. Alternatives are generally based on factual information. Hence, this kind of task is particularly "fact-oriented." The other three tasks are more intermediate in their degree of objectivity or subjectivity. They are not purely value-oriented or fact-oriented, but rather a combination of the two. Goal determination is a predominantly subjective task, but evaluation of alternatives is mostly objective. Problem identification

[20]Donald Last, "Principles and Practice of Citizen Involvement with Special Reference to Regional Planning in Dane County, Wisconsin," Master's thesis, University of Wisconsin-Madison, 1972.

Figure 7.1   Subjective-Objective Range of Key Planning Tasks or Steps

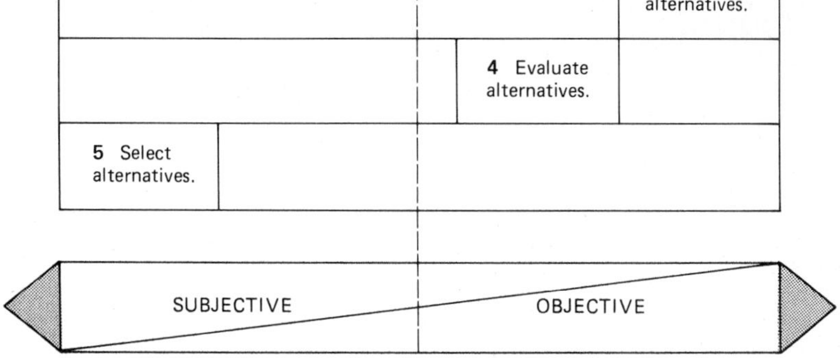

is positioned in the center of the continuum to indicate its equally subjective and objective nature.

Last goes on to suggest that the planning authority of the citizen and the professional planner are inversely related. A very active decision-making role for the citizen is supplemented by a rather passive decision-making role for the professional. As the citizen's influence decreases, the professional's increases until the professional has most of the decision-making authority. In extreme situations either the citizen or the professional may exercise exclusive decision-making power. In some instances, decision-making authority may be equally shared. In short, the planning authority of the professional supplements the citizen's and vice versa. The more actively a person participates in a planning activity, the greater the possibility of that person influencing the decisions.

Last noted further that the decision-making role of the professional, in relation to the citizen planning group, depended largely on its nature and the professional's perception of the objectivity or subjectivity of the task. Whether the citizen or the professional should perform the dominant planning role is a consequence of how subjective or objective the task may be. The professional should have most of the planning authority for those tasks that are objective. For the most objective of tasks, in fact, citizen involvement may not even be necessary. However, when planning tasks are subjective, the people to be affected by the planning should have the greatest share of the decision-making authority. In such cases, representatives of the planning organization should not attempt to impose their own views on the citizenry.

Last's concept then suggests that depending on the subjective-objective nature of the decisions, there can be a wide range in the degree of citizen involvement in a given planning activity. They may be either the sole decision makers, the predominant decision makers, decision-making partners, minority decision makers, or even roleless nonparticipants.

Following are two examples of programs that a continuing education programmer might be promoting:

- Programs to help families in need deal with family stress, violence, nutrition problems, divorce, and death
- Programs to help small businesses with new developments in insurance, accounting, data processing, mergers and acquisitions, leasing and tax management

In the development of the programs to help families, the potential clientele probably should have a major role in the program decisions. Many of the decisions about needs, objectives, and learning experiences would involve feelings, beliefs, and values. In the second example, the programs for small businesspeople would probably be based on a lot of objective facts and new knowledge. The programmer would be able to make objective decisions and probably have less need for clientele input.

Maier[21] suggests there are two aspects to any decision that have relevance for involvement: (1) its purely objective or impersonal attributes—the quality aspect—and (2) its attractiveness or desirability to those who must live with the decision—the acceptance aspect. The first depends upon objective data (facts in the situation) and the second upon subjective data (people's feelings).

According to Maier, problems can be examined according to which aspect—quality (Q) or acceptance (A)—is most important. Problems classified as Q/A (quality first) are those that can be solved on the basis of objective data. Acceptance, though important, is of secondary concern and may be gained either by imposing the decision, by using the legitimate and/or reference power bases of the person(s) making the decision, or by using a participative approach that encourages discussion of the decision(s) to develop understanding. A/Q (acceptance first) problems are those for which objective data are either not available or not helpful in making effective decisions. In such instances, the subjective input (feelings, values) of those to be affected is primary.

The above discussion suggests that the specific task confronting a decision-making group should be viewed as a random variable. In other words, tasks vary in terms of the inputs required to arrive at high-quality and acceptance decisions. The two major sources of variability are (1) the degree to which decisions can be based on objective data, and (2) the specificity of the problems that affect the number of potential alternative decisions.

In summary, the emphasis on the nature of the group task has not been emphasized in the literature in the area of program development. The result has been to focus on one approach to planning through the use of the clientele decision-making groups. This limited approach fails to recognize that the purpose of citizen involvement may vary a great deal depending on the planning task. The particular aspects of the task may also affect the type of background information to be considered and the nature of the orientation provided for the participants.

Some typology for classifying planning tasks is needed to make valid judgments about the purpose and process of citizen involvement in program development. Figure 7.2 provides an initial approach that might help clarify our thinking about citizen involvement in program development. The type of process to be followed, the roles of programmer and client, and the necessary resources will depend on the planning task. If the clientele involvement is necessary in order to discover the relevant needs, a

[21]N. R. F. Maier, *Problem Solving Discussions and Conferences,* McGraw-Hill Book Company, New York, 1963.

Figure 7.2 Typology of Involvement Tasks

Involvement task	Process	Roles	Resources
1 Q/A To identify relevant problems, needs, and opportunities on which the program should be based. Legitimation follows as a natural consequence.	Group problem solving. Add to data available.	Create an environment conducive to group problem solving. Select group. Select group members able to be creative. Thoroughly orient and train for group problem solving. Avoid influencing group.	Facts, trends, data that relate to problem area. Rational group members capable of analyzing data.
2 A/Q To gain understanding and acceptance of the program bases and legitimation of the subsequent educational program.	Diffusion process. Two-way flow of communication.	Utilize expertise and information related to problem area. Use all effective means of persuasion. Involve influentials of community.	Objective data that clearly indicate problems. Data that clearly indicate priority alternative. Strong legitimation from leadership.

group problem-solving model would be necessary. The relevant process for understanding and acceptance is simpler.

Some basis for making decisions about the purpose of citizen involvement is required. This basis lies in a thorough analysis of the nature of the planning task—the problem area within which the program is to be developed—rather than in a philosophical statement about the "goodness" of the idea of involvement. In adult education, an assumed position for one type of involvement or programming effort is often stated as being "better" or more highly valued than another. This assumption may be based upon an axiological value of how people think it *should* be done rather than on an analysis of the program's problem area. It should be stressed that several forms of involvement may be equally valued by the participants. Participants simply involved through implementing the programmer's decisions may feel their involvement is just as "good" as those participants who have joined the programmer in the planning nature of the problem and the programmer's and participants' orientation, which suggest the type of involvement to use.

Functional Roles

The term role may be used to describe an individual's level of influence in planning decisions, or it may refer to the functions performed. People perform a variety of functions in planning. A list of functional planning roles includes such things as recorder, coordinator, moderator, consultant, reviewer, designer, and originator.

The function of the recorder is to keep an account of the activities of the planning group for future reference. Such persons are information receivers. They have no means by which to contribute their knowledge or views during the planning process. Coordinators interact with the planning process only to the level of "housekeeping" responsibilities. They use their organizational skills to establish a comfortable or convenient time and place for meetings and help provide the appropriate tools and materials for orderly and efficient planning business. A person who functions as a moderator maintains a neutral position on all planning issues, entering into the planning process only on questions of procedure or to help the planning participants resolve their differences. The functions of recorder, coordinator, and moderator are "nonparticipatory roles" in decision-making authority. While such individuals may be present during the planning process, they have no voice in the actual deliberations.

Persons who perform the roles of consultant, reviewer, designer, or originator, however, do participate in the planning process. The consultant may be invited to prepare and present planning perspectives, if the planning groups want the advice of an outside expert during some phase of the planning effort. The reviewer is involved after the plan (or one of its component parts) has reached an advanced stage of development. Such a person evaluates the ideas set forth by the planning group. The functional roles of the consultant and the reviewer are weak ones because individuals performing them participate in the planning process, but only to a limited degree. The power rests with other members of the group who reserve the right to incorporate the advice of the consultant or not, or to change a plan based on the recommendation of the reviewer.

Examples of strong functional roles are the plan originator and designer. The originator is a planning group's chief discussion leader. The knowledge and viewpoints of such a person strongly affect the rate and direction of planning activity. More important, the originator is a key source of planning ideas generated from the group. The designer role is associated with such things as data collection, synthesis, and analysis (i.e., with systematically categorizing and assembling the component planning information into a more understandable and integrated unit). The designer may be responsible for writing or editing parts of an actual plan. Individuals performing the designer or originator roles exercise the most power in making decisions concerning the plans' content and scope.

Figure 7.3 Complementary Functional Roles of Citizens and Professionals

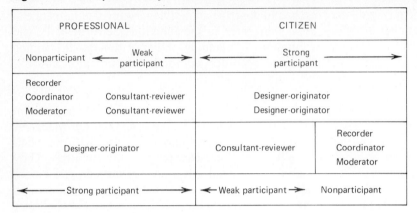

Just as the decision-making roles of the citizen and the professional planner are complementary, so also are the functional planning roles of these two types of people related. Figure 7.3 illustrates that when the citizen planner performs the function of designer or originator, the professional planner is limited to the functional role of consultant, reviewer, recorder, coordinator, or moderator. The reverse is also true. When the professional programmer performs the designer-originator function, the citizen is limited to weak or nonparticipatory types of functional roles.

This discussion of functional roles in the process of program development has real implications for the continuing education programmer. The question is whether the clientele perform as a weak or strong participant. If the purpose of involvement is to receive significant input to decisions on needs, objectives, and learning experiences, then the programmer should provide the opportunities for the client to assume designer and originator roles. If the client is to be a weak participant, the process should provide for those types of roles.

Planning Ideologies

As stated previously, citizen participation in planning should depend on the subjective-objective nature of the task to be performed. Ideally, the more subjective a task is, the more the citizen will be involved. Conversely, the more objective a task is, the less necessary it may be for citizens to participate. Unfortunately, society is not always ideal. Not everyone is governed by morals, ethics, or a democratic credo. In actual practice, the level or kind of citizen involvement in planning is not so much related to the character of the task as it is to the professional planner's philosophy regarding citizen participation.

It is probably true that while some institutions would like to recognize or respond to citizens' willingness to contribute to plans, they are unable to due to circumstances. However, other institutions deliberately refuse to acknowledge this kind of citizen interest. Thus, there is a wide variation in the amount of decision-making authority as well as in the roles of citizens in the development of educational programs.

Citizen participation, then, is often a function of how the professional perceives the decision-making and functional roles in relation to the roles of the citizens. The role perspective of the professional is strongly influenced by his or her philosophy. Several authors have recorded their views on this subject. Jakobson[22] states that all planners identify with one or more of six types of planning ideologies: utopian, scientist, humanist, bureaucrat, activist, or liberal. He examines the way planning goals are envisioned, and what planning techniques are employed by a planner in distinguishing between these ideologies. A person who uses a "scientist's" approach to planning, for instance, can be identified by a mechanical style and the use of systematically organized and rigorously analyzed (quantifiable) data to predict the consequences of possible actions.

Jakobson grouped several of these philosophies as to attitude concerning citizen participation and professional approach. He considers the utopian, scientist, and humanist ideologies to be "elitist" planning philosophies; whereas, the liberals, activists, and bureaucrats, assume a more popular attitude as planners. The latter represent deliberate, interpretative, or adaptive methods of planning pertaining to society.

Jakobson then considers patterns of concordance and conflict with respect to these ideologies. "In reality there is a conflict between these ideologies which represent the existing order—in other words, the establishment—and those which tend to question the validity of this order."[23] The scientist, bureaucrat, and liberal are those who use validating measures of facts, measured trend norms, and who work within existing institutions. However, the utopian, the humanist, and the activist advocate change and work outside establishments.

Brower writes of several different "approaches to educational program development" that span the full range of planning philosophies. Persons practicing an "academic approach," Brower says, exclude the client from any planning or programming decision making. "Those who hold rigidly to the academic approach are insulted by the notion that anyone other than the professional authority should or could determine . . . con-

[22]Leo Jakobson, "Toward a Pluralistic Ideology in Planning Education," in Ernest Erber (ed.), *Urban Planning in Transition,* Grossman Publishers, New York, 1970, pp. 266–275.

[23]Ibid., p. 270.

[24]Brower, "Dilemma of Adult Educators," p. 117.

tent."[24] In a "grass roots approach," the professional assumes a passive role. Such a philosophy "excludes the professional . . . from all but a bare minimum of the . . . process."[25] Midway between these extremes is the "education for reality approach." Persons subscribing to this philosophy insist that "both the people [students] . . . and the professional [be] involved in the total educative . . . experience."[26]

There are attitudinal differences among professionals concerning the involvement of citizens in program development. In fact, there may be an unlimited number of planning philosophies regarding citizen participation, ranging from a very favorable attitude to a very unfavorable attitude, with many intermediate attitudes between these extremes. Nonetheless, from a purely practical standpoint, a reasonable way to classify planning philosophies is to think of them in three categories: "elitist," "popular," and "compromise."

Planners classified as elitist feel that they should maintain all except a small part of the overall planning authority. Populist planners, in contrast, see for themselves a comparatively small decision-making role, and the planning authority of the citizen is predominant. Those planners who feel there should be an overall balance in the level of the planning influence of the citizen and the professional are considered to fit within a "compromise" philosophy.

SUMMARY

The literature on involvement in program development reveals a wide range of different ideas and suggestions. In this chapter we identified several reasons for involving people in decisions about programs. The focus of the ideas presented was that the purpose of the involvement task will determine the process to be followed, the roles of the programmer and the client, and the resources necessary for its completion. We suggested that the factors affecting clientele involvement include nature of planning task, functional roles, and planning ideologies. The implication for the continuing education programmer is that the design of the process of involvement should be based on the program situation rather than on the soundness of the idea of involvement.

DISCUSSION QUESTIONS

1 What is your philosophical basis for making decisions about involvement of people in program development?

[25]Ibid., p. 116.
[26]Ibid.

2 Please accept or reject and then justify the following statement: "The major reason for involving people in planning an educational program is to make them feel important. The often-stated reason of discovering the real needs of people is overrated."

3 Why would a continuing education programmer feel threatened by involvement of clientele in the decisions in program development?

4 How would the characteristics of a target clientele influence your decisions on roles and procedures for involvement?

5 Analyze the discussions on the nature of planning task, functional roles, and planning ideologies as factors of clientele involvement.

Chapter 8

Methods and Procedures for Involvement

In spite of increased interest, the idea of involving people in developing programs is very complex. The idea that we have not yet combined the reasons or purposes of involving citizens with the methods of involving them was developed in the previous chapter. In many situations, our methods lack a sense of purpose. We must establish congruence between our ends (purposes) and our means (methods).

Citizen involvement means including citizens in the program development process, connecting them to the process, or establishing situations that occupy their attention. It is a process that encourages the involvement of individuals in relation to groups and affects the persons involved to various degrees. Involvement thus includes a wide spectrum of activities. Simply gathering a group of people together in a room is a form of involvement, as is involving citizens who are actively pushing for adoption of certain plans.

Since the concept of involvement is broad, several assumptions should be made more explicit in order to understand the purposes and methods of citizen involvement in program development:

- People are involved already (if only indirectly); it is not a question of whether to involve them. Rather questions about involvement relate to purposes, methods, by whom, for whom, and at what stages of the program to involve them.
- Continuing educators have specific roles and responsibilities to perform which they should not abdicate to the clientele.
- As continuing education programmers we do not wish to be unethical or manipulative; all efforts at involvement are open and honest.
- It is not necessary for citizens to be involved all the time in all phases of program development process.
- Democratic participation does not necessarily mean total citizen control.
- We as professionals are in the best position to decide whether or not to involve citizens and how they should be involved.

Involving citizens in program development requires that we know our purpose for involving them before selecting the method to effectively involve them. We must "look before we leap." The method we select should depend on what we hope to accomplish.

Three major reasons for involving people in planning programs were suggested in Chapter 7:

- To gain acceptance of an already completed plan, to mobilize support, and to overcome resistance and feelings of alienation; acceptance of plans makes them easier to implement
- To make decisions on situations, needs, and problems and/or on the directions and solutions for those identified needs and problems
- To provide an educational experience for participants

Methods relevant to the first two will be discussed in the following sections.

INVOLVEMENT FOR
GAINING ACCEPTANCE FROM PEOPLE

A worthy purpose for involving people is to gain their acceptance for programs. Coch and French[1] long ago experimentally showed the benefits of involving people to reduce their resistance to change. One way to reduce resistance is to examine the reasons for it. Watson[2] classified reasons for resistance to change as follows: (1) personality reasons, such as

[1]L. Coch and J. R. French, "Overcoming Resistance to Change," in D. Cartwright and A. Zander (eds.), *Group Dynamics,* 3d ed., Harper & Row, Publishers, Inc., 1968, pp. 336–350.

[2]G. Watson, "What Do We Know About Learning?" in G. Hass, K. Wiles, and J. Bondi (eds.), *Readings in Curriculum,* 2d ed., Allyn & Bacon, Inc., Boston, 1970, pp. 286–290.

habit, dependence, selective perception based on past experiences, ego, insecurity, and self-distrust, and (2) social system reasons, such as conformity to community and group norms, interrelatedness of community and group subparts, vested interests, religious values, and rejection of outsiders.

Rogers,[3] a diffusion adoption researcher, provides five reasons why people do not accept change or new innovations: (1) a perceived disadvantage over present practice; (2) the new ideas lack compatibility or consistency with present values and ideas; (3) the new ideas are perceived as complex and difficult to understand and use; (4) people see little chance to try the new idea a little at a time; and (5) the new idea is too abstract and hard to communicate.

To reduce these identified resistances and enhance acceptance, the continuing educator can use the following methods:

1 Make new program development efforts less abstract and more observable and concrete to people's lives.
2 Reduce the complexity of ideas and make them more understandable and ready to use.
3 Show how the program will benefit specific client interests and its advantages over current practices.
4 Develop people's feelings of trust and credibility.
5 Divide programs into stages, phases, or subparts, which can be adopted separately if need be.
6 Create an understanding of new programs so they are not seen as threats to present values, norms, practices, or habits.
7 Create nonthreatening situations to help people see new opportunities or ways of doing things through illustrations and examples.
8 Provide encouragement to the dependent and the insecure so they can operate and personally benefit in different settings.
9 Allow the people involved to discover new ideas for themselves.

These suggested actions will help the programmer gain acceptance and legitimation. Methods imply certain general roles for continuing educators. For example, the roles of analyst, stimulator, facilitator, and encourager, as suggested in Chapter 6, are inherent in these suggested actions.

A new program will more likely be accepted if the idea or program originates with someone already accepted and trusted or if it relates to individuals' lives in an easily understandable way. Persons who are already accepted and trusted are also more likely to be the ones who can explain, interpret, and relate the program to others' lives.

We believe that two ideas are important to gaining acceptance of programs: (1) People's perceptions of the situational background of the prob-

---

[3]Evert M. Rogers, *Diffusion of Innovations,* Free Press, Glencoe, Ill., 1962.

lem must be analyzed, delineated, and communicated, and (2) the accepted and respected leadership of the community, the neighborhood, the association, or the group being worked with must be involved. Leadership in these systems must be developed and close relationships must be maintained. The idea of involving leaders is not new. Most continuing educators have discovered through experience that leaders are more apt to accept change. Forest[4] found both informal and formal community leaders to be more positive toward communitywide planning alternatives than the general citizenry.

The purpose of getting acceptance of programs from leaders of communities, associations, neighborhoods, and smaller groups is so the leaders will communicate proposed acceptance to others. Leaders are allowed to deviate from accepted norms because of past activities that have given them their leadership role.[5] Therefore, they can legitimize and facilitate change because they are credible and communicate well within the community, association, or group. By involving influential leaders, we can build a wider basis of support than by trying to involve all people or only isolated individuals. The necessary program support and acceptance has a greater chance of being expanded.

INVOLVEMENT FOR IDENTIFYING NEEDS AND MAKING DECISIONS ON PRIORITIES

Decision making is the process of choosing between two or more alternatives, actions, or solutions. We use the process of setting priorities among possible problem areas to focus our program on. This method involves a series of steps which, if followed objectively and logically, provide higher quality, more acceptable decisions.

Many models of the decision-making process have been proposed. Some have four steps; other models have as many as seven steps. One particularly useful model, presented by Stufflebeam et al.,[6] has the following four steps:

1 Creating awareness of decision situation, unsolved problems, and opportunities

2 Designing the decision, including putting the decision in question form, specifying responsibility, formulating alternatives, specifying decision criteria and rules

[4]L. B. Forest, "Commitments of Leaders as Predictors of Attitudes Toward New Social Issues in a Rural Community Social System," unpublished Ph.D. dissertation, University of Wisconsin-Madison, 1970.

[5]E. P. Hollander, *Principles and Methods of Social Psychology,* Oxford University Press, Inc., New York, 1967.

[6]D. L. Stufflebeam, W. J. Foley, W. J. Gephart, E. G. Guba, R. L. Hammond, H. O. Merriman, and M. M. Provus, *Educational Evaluation and Decision Making,* F. E. Peacock Publishers, Inc., Itasca, Ill., 1971.

3   Choosing alternatives based on information, rules, and specified criteria

4   Implementing alternatives, reflecting, and/or recycling if necessary

We can categorize types of decisions that emphasize certain steps more than others. For example, routine decisions need less time in steps 1 and 2 and are less complicated than nonroutine decisions. Decisions based on facts need less time in steps 2 and 3 and are easier than decisions tied to emotions, feelings, and values. Deciding on needs or problem priorities differs from deciding on solutions. Program development decisions involving citizens are probably best achieved by following some systematic steps in sequential order.

In making decisions on needs, problems, and opportunities, we should be very knowledgeable about the background situation. People need opportunities to see their situations more clearly and to discover the problems they can solve. Expanding people's knowledge of their own situations and needs can occur in three ways: (1) through people's insights and perceptions; (2) through systematic observation; and (3) through logical analysis of existing information and data. Involvement methods are designed to take advantage of all three sources to discover needs and problems.

The second step of the decision-making model—designing the decision making—depends on both the type of issue or concern under study and the previous involvement experiences of participants. For example, a recurring concern over which people have been extensively involved may need only a check of a few key persons to make a decision. A new issue, however, may need intensive involvement. A situation or problem that needs factual, scientific input needs less involvement to make a decision. Situations that are issue-oriented or attitudinal in nature may need far less factual, scientific data and much more value and feeling input from the people themselves in order to make the decision. When we design the decision-making process, our roles, actions, and resources will differ depending on whether the issue can be solved through factual data or whether it is a value-laden issue. We have less responsibility for choosing an alternative with an emotional issue, but our responsibility to design the proper decision questions is most important.

The third step of the decision-making process is choosing the alternative based on the already established criteria, design, and rules. One of our main roles in this phase of the decision-making process is to make sure all alternatives and options have been identified and analyzed before we make our choice. We also need to help citizens become more clear about what criteria they will use to make the decisions. There is nothing wrong with a value-oriented or emotional decision as long as people are aware of the emotions, values, and biases that dictate the decision.

Step 4 of decision making is implementation. In this step our role is to help citizens reevaluate their selection processes and selected alternatives, and to help them change direction if they need to. This reevaluation of alternatives will be easier if the citizens involved can understand how effective or appropriate the chosen alternatives will be.

INVOLVEMENT METHODS

People are involved in developing continuing education programs through a variety of different methods. A programmer will visit, consult, debate, and listen to clientele on a continuing basis. Much of this effort is casual, informal, or part of other tasks. This is a most important and beneficial type of programmer-client involvement. We should recognize, encourage, and integrate it with other involvement efforts.

In many program development situations it is necessary and desirable to use more formal approaches to involve people. Following are ten suggested methods for citizen involvement:

1 Task Force

A task force is different in its purposes from advisory or planning committees, as well as in its approach, operation, and eventual level of involvement. A task force is a small group of about fifteen persons assigned a specific task for a relatively short period of time. The task might be to search out all pertinent information about a specific problem; or to search out relevant data and come up with a list of alternative plans based on the data; or even to recommend an alternative plan, based on the data.

An example of involvement through task forces is a study group that analyzed the traffic situation in national parks. This panel of citizens was organized by the Conservation Foundation of Washington, D.C. After a year's study they flatly stated:

> . . . that private automobiles have no place in national parks; that homes on wheels are contrary to the park ethic; that the National Park Service should not provide vehicular campsite facilities and that private enterprise and all but rudimentary overnight accommodations should be phased out of the national park operations.[7]

Another example is a seven-person group in Milwaukee County, Wisconsin. This task force was asked to write an air pollution ordinance for

[7]Gladwyn Hill, "Study Group Asks Ban on Vehicles in National Parks," *The New York Times,* September 17, 1972.

the county based on federal standards and local needs. Extension environmental resource personnel were part of that task force and provided an example of technical experts and educators involved with interested citizens to work on decisions.

The task force method tends to be efficient because of its well-defined specific task, small group size, and short time for completion of the work. Second, it involves highly interested, knowledgeable citizens. Third, the chances are great for high psychological involvement and commitment to the final selected alternative because people can see the achievements in a relatively short time.

A disadvantage of the task force method is that it might exclude wide public involvement and may thus have low public accountability and acceptability.[8] Unless the task force is given real power, the decisions and alternatives may not actually be implemented and the effort could become a rubber stamp or an exercise in futility.

2 Ombudsman

An ombudsman is a professional paid by an organization or agency to represent the citizens. Sometimes, an ombudsman advocates positions in conflict with organizational policy and other principles. The ombudsman knows the inner workings of the agency and how to get things done for people. They are paid leaders and mediators. The advantage of this approach is a greater likelihood of involving the people who are generally not involved.

Disadvantages include the possibility of confrontation with long-term traditions, and which could be upsetting to many of the effective present policies. This approach must also answer questions about who to work with, what to advocate, what values should be encouraged, and the like. These questions must be thought through before an institution sets up an ombudsman.

3 Advocacy Planning

Advocacy planning is one form of the ombudsman concept. Several groups assumed to have an interest in a particular task are identified. For example, the Wisconsin State Highway Commission tentatively decided a new multilane highway was needed to let Chicago-Minneapolis traffic bypass the Madison metropolis. Many local citizens were up in arms. In advocacy planning the highway officials might designate one planner to work with the farming community around the proposed highway, another planner to work with environmentally concerned groups, and another to work with technicians and engineers to analyze and/or improve the exist-

---

[8]Thomas Appleby, "Citizen Participation in the '70's: The Need to Turn to Politics," *City*, May–June 1971, pp. 52–55.

ing highway system. Each group would advocate a plan that would integrate its own biases and ensure that each group's needs would be considered in the final decision.

Questions might be raised about this approach, such as how to use it with apathetic citizens. What if the "several interested groups" have different interests in what they advocate? These questions point out some disadvantages or problems with this approach to involvement. Nevertheless, it is a way to intensively involve a number of vested interest groups and to try and gain their acceptance and trust.

4 Formal Hearing

This approach (in many cases required) has been used by county boards, school boards, planning and zoning committees, highway commissions, and other public institutions to present a plan for goals and/or actions and then to hear testimony for and against the proposal.

It was used in the Brandywine project:[9]

> The key decision was that the project should be undertaken in two stages: first, planning, and second, implementation. Because we needed and wanted to develop the specifics of the plan together with the county and the townships, we were in no position to ask public officials for a commitment to implement whatever plan might take shape. No one, including us, knew what restrictions would be proposed for which properties or approximately what a particular landowner might be paid for his right to develop. We agreed that the townships should be asked to endorse the planning phase with the understanding that the commissioners would seek their reaction to the finished plan before deciding whether or not to proceed with the implementation stage.[10]

Extension community education agents have also used the process. In Columbia County, Wisconsin, agents used the method when an electric power company wished to put a huge power line across valuable farmland. A public hearing allowed both groups to air their views. Eventually, each better understood the other group's viewpoint and plans were made that satisfied both groups.

The advantage of this approach is that it offers a chance for all persons to express their feelings and ideas. One of the key outcomes of this sharing can be changes in understanding and attitudes. But past experience reveals that often only outspoken or strongly opinionated people will speak and arguments take the place of compromise. It is questionable whether the expressions are really representative when the silent people do not speak and many do not participate.

[9]Ann Louise Strong, *Private Property and the Public Interest: The Brandywine Experience,* The Johns Hopkins University Press, Baltimore, 1975.
[10]Ibid., pp. 48–49.

5 Unobtrusive Measures[11]

Unobtrusive measures are another way to gather information and discussion material. They are ways of taking a survey without asking respondents what they think. If we want to validate ideas and opinions gathered in more direct ways, we should look at the effects left behind by people's behavior.

The popularity of certain books in the library can be ascertained by the number of times they have been checked out or the amount of dust on them in the stacks. The amount of silt in a stream bed tells us the need for erosion control. The effects of an educational program on the use of fertilizers can be told by trends in local fertilizer sales. The variety of unobtrusive measures is unlimited and depends only on the imagination and creativity of those looking for such measurements.

One advantage of this involvement technique is that the data have been gathered as part of our ongoing activities and is a real-life measurement. Some disadvantages are that people have no feeling of involvement even though they are involved, and that past behavior is due to past social and individual pressures and may not reflect new directions. Nevertheless, it is a useful technique to gain better insights.

6 Brainstorming

Perhaps one of the most widely acclaimed methods for encouraging new insights, perceptions, and ideas is the brainstorming technique developed by Osborn.[12] This method is used in a group setting.

Several simple guidelines of brainstorming explain the technique: (1) a specific task is suggested; (2) a key person serves as a leader or facilitator in a free and open atmosphere established in part by a warm-up period on a nonsense task; (3) the leader encourages people to come up with as many ideas on the task as possible; (4) judgment on ideas is deferred; (5) quantity breeds quality—more ideas increase the chances for better ideas; (6) piggybacking on others' ideas is encouraged; (7) freewheeling is encouraged.

Groups and organizations that have used the technique have found several advantages: Many ideas are formulated and there is a high degree of involvement and interest if the environment is free and trusting. Disadvantages would include: the leaders need training; some adults hesitate to respond openly because of the risk of appearing stupid; judgments are postponed and discouraged; no decisions are possible; and the quality of ideas is not known until later.

[11]E. J. Webb, D. T. Campbell, R. D. Schwartz, and L. Sechrest, *Unobtrusive Measures,* Rand McNally & Company, Skokie, Ill., 1966.

[12]A. F. Osborn, *Applied Imagination,* 3d rev. ed., Charles Scribner's Sons, New York, 1963.

7 Content Analysis

Another way to get data to discuss with individuals at meetings is content analysis of news media and other materials that might reflect the current important problems and the attitudes people have toward them.[13] Content analysis uses a panel of judges to critically break apart the messages and substance of news articles so actual counts can be made of the favorable and unfavorable comments on various subjects. Forest[14] used this method to take into account the many letters and articles for and against certain U.S. Forest Service planning alternatives. The technique can systematize a great deal of unsolicited, unorganized, and unusable public opinion. It can unobtrusively involve many people while providing good information for decision making.

8 Nominal Groups

The nominal groups technique developed by Delbecq et al.[15] can be used within an already organized group setting. It is suggested as an alternative to brainstorming. The technique as outlined by its originators is as follows:

I   Problem exploration
   A   Divide group of people into smaller groups of six each.
   B   Have each individual write perceived needs and personal feelings on five-by-seven-inch cards.
   C   Have group consolidate personal feelings on large paper pads, avoiding any abbreviations and duplications.
   D   Review responses by total group.
   E   Vote on most crucial problems.
   F   Discuss problems and feelings.
   G   Explain the rest of the process and decide whether to continue with the next steps.
II   Knowledge exploration
   This phase involves scientific research persons.
III   Priority development
   This phase involves resource controllers.
IV   Program development
V   Program evaluation

The initial processes aim at getting individuals to express their concerns without pressure by the group. The individual ideas are then viewed by others and the group finally decides what needs are priority items. In

[13]Gordon W. Allport and Janet M. Faden, "The Psychology of Newspapers: Five Tentative Laws," *Public Opinion Quarterly,* vol. 4, December 1940, pp. 687–703.
[14]Forest, "Commitments of Leaders."
[15]Andre Delbecq, A. H. VandeVen, and D. H. Gustafson, *Group Techniques for Program Planning,* Scott, Foresman and Company, Glenview, Ill., 1975.

this way, both individual and group concerns are considered with little personal threat. This approach has been found to be a useful technique to involve a cross section of people. The specific advantages are: many unique individual ideas are generated; little training is necessary; individuals experience little social pressure; and a group consensus is possible. Some disadvantages are: it has no built-in way to obtain background data and other information that may need to be acquired through surveys or other approaches; even though the decision-making process is built through each of the phases, there is a tendency to close out various alternatives and to give the impression that answers and solutions are given from the top of the hierarchy; it could work against continuous involvement if citizens were to feel that their only role is to express their needs for someone else to solve them. In addition, superficial responses and acceptance may be interpreted as real commitment. Nevertheless, it is useful, in combination with other techniques, for making priority decisions on needs and solutions.

9 Surveys

The survey is a popular method for involving large numbers of people. It is often used when information or data need to be collected from widely dispersed clientele. It provides information from respondents that can be tabulated and discussed. Surveys can be carried out by personal interview, telephone interview, or mail questionnaire. Some advantages of this approach are a systematic involvement of large numbers of people, and the collection of a large variety of information. One of the disadvantages is that the client may not feel involved. Also, an opinion expressed on a survey is not a commitment to action. The information collected through surveys is often used in group situations.

10 Advisory Committees

An advisory or study committee is a very common approach for involving people in program development. There are two major types of committees, standing and special. Standing committees are those that handle a continuing and specific responsibility in program development, while the special committee is selected to do a particular job. The membership, the roles those members will be expected to perform, the procedures to be followed, and the resources needed will vary in accordance with the purpose of the committee. Advisory committees provide for the extensive and in some cases intensive involvement of the members. One disadvantage is that usually only small numbers of people can be involved.

SUMMARY

All continuing educators are faced with the question of how to best involve people in creating programs. It is a question of roles to be performed, methods to use, and the resources needed in the involvement process. In the past, much of the confusion as well as the strong mixture of successes and failures with involving people has occurred because purposes have not been related to methods. If we examine the successes, we will discover that the continuing educator has been conscious of the purposes for involvement and has developed methods congruent with those purposes.

DISCUSSION QUESTIONS

1 Identify a programming situation that would be most desirable for each of the methods discussed.
2 What are some situations when the use of a given method for involvement would be undesirable?
3 Observe and analyze one or more of the suggested methods.
4 What criteria would you use in deciding on the method of involvement?
5 Discuss whether an involvement method is best for any particular type of program.

Chapter 9

Advisory Committees

The operation of organizations and institutions throughout the country is being increasingly influenced by involvement of people through advisory committees. The value of these committees may be even more significant as the complexity of organizations increases, as demands for accountability become greater, and as the need for communications to achieve effective programs increases. The investment in advisory committees is extensive. The time and energy that members devote to various kinds of advisory committees is significant. The challenge to programmers in program development is to make this investment worthwhile for the institution, the program, and the participant. The terms "advisory committee" and "study group" will be used synonymously throughout this chapter.

PURPOSE OF ADVISORY COMMITTEES
IN PROGRAM DEVELOPMENT

In the identification of any type of advisory committee, the programmer will first need to consider the purpose(s) for having the committee. The involvement of potential clientele through advisory committees may be to achieve several functions. The purpose of a committee will be a major factor in selecting the individuals to serve. Some possible functions are:

- To collect and analyze data for problem identification
- To identify problems, needs, or resources
- To study identified problems and make decisions on priority problems
- To legitimize the program decisions made by the programmer
- To identify alternative problems or need solutions
- To create an awareness among other people of the priority problems or needs

The membership, the roles those members will be expected to perform, the processes to be followed, and the resources needed by the advisory committee will vary according to the functions to be performed.

If the committee is expected to collect and analyze data in the identification of problems, the membership needs to have individuals who are knowledgeable about the situation, who have time to spend on the function, and who are capable and creative in analyzing and interpreting data or information in identifying problems. In the group problem-solving approach, the programmer needs to assume a leadership role in creating an environment and providing the expertise. Group processes involve a considerable amount of time and patience.

The functions of the committee also determine whether the membership shall be knowledgeable of the community or whether they shall be influentials in the clientele group. The role of the committee members varies from expending a great deal of effort in studying and analyzing background materials to legitimizing the decisions made by the programmer. The procedures, too, will vary from a group-solving approach to a diffusion of the background information and priority needs from the planners to the potential clientele.

The role of the programmer will also depend on the functions of the committee. In problem identification, both background information and guidance in search of additional information will need to be provided. In gaining legitimization for decisions about priorities, the programmer will have to be very creative and persuasive.

WHO SHOULD BE INVOLVED?

We can decide who to involve in program development if we know why we want to involve them. These reasons for involvement become the criteria for deciding on persons who can benefit and make a significant contribution.

Research in program development at the University of Wisconsin[1] has tried to determine the extent to which local people contribute to the attainment of the purpose or goals of planning. This research has shown that local people's contributions to the planning process are related to certain of their personal and social characteristics. A direct relationship has been established between quality of performance in program development and characteristics such as educational level, participation in community organizations, occupation, and age. One study,[2] which examined the feasibility of having influential community members serve on planning committees, found that influential people in comparison with the community population as a whole: (1) were more aware of the problems of the community, and (2) were more likely to view themselves as being able to resolve the problems.

Inconclusive as these findings may be, they do point out that if the purpose of involving local people is to identify the problems and concerns of people and the community, then the following characteristics are important for members of the study group:

- Interest in planning for community improvement
- Knowledge of the situation to be analyzed
- Willingness to invest time
- Ability to function in a group

However, if the reason for involving people is to critique and gain acceptance for a program planned essentially by the programmer, these criteria would change. For acceptance, concern should focus on how well the individuals involved represent the subgroups in the community that the program is intended to reach. Thus, the question about who should be involved is answered after the purpose of involvement and the roles to be performed are clearly identified.

IS ORIENTATION OF
STUDY GROUP MEMBERS NECESSARY?

Research[3] has shown that the effectiveness of the involvement effort depends to a considerable extent on the orientation and training of those to be involved. Understanding needs to be developed among people in terms of the following tasks:

[1]Patrick G. Boyle, *The Program Planning Processes with Emphasis on Extension,* NAECAS, Publication no. 24, University of Wisconsin–Madison, 1965.

[2]G. M. Farrell, "Influential Persons' Awareness of Community Problems in Rural Wisconsin," M. S. thesis, University of Wisconsin–Madison, 1964.

[3]M. P. Lacy, "The Effects of Involvement of the Participants in Cooperative Extension Programming Planning in Waupaca County, Wisconsin," Ph.D. dissertation, University of Wisconsin–Madison, 1961.

- The objectives of planning
- The facilities or means available to accomplish the objectives
- Their authority to use means to accomplish objectives
- The importance of planning

It is the role of the programmer to see that these tasks are accomplished.

Another study[4] concluded that two or three meetings with local citizens are not sufficient for them to completely understand the purpose of planning, their role in planning, and to complete the planning activity. Decision making in a group situation is a complex task that takes considerable time.

Whale and Boyle[5] point out that it is more reasonable to expect group decision making to be based on limited rationality rather than on total rationality. They suggest that emotions become involved as various group members are required to alter their views. In view of this, the training of committee heads and members becomes even more crucial in order to minimize irrational decision making.

WHAT ABOUT BACKGROUND INFORMATION?

Studies in the area of small-group problem solving clearly indicate that the quality of decision making is determined primarily by how well the group is able to explore the various dimensions of the problem and consider a wide range of possible solutions. If one defines "quality decision making" in planning groups by how well they are able to identify needs and concerns, then the programmer must attempt to maximize the groups' knowledge and understanding of the situational problem area.

Research has shown that it is not enough to rely entirely on the experience and knowledge of people in defining problems and identifying realistic solutions. Some background information must be provided by the programmer so citizens can use it to analyze situations and identify gaps or imbalances. Research to date indicates that continuing education programmers do not perform this function as well as they might.[6]

Powers[7] suggested three problems that have contributed to the inefficient use of background information by planning groups:

- Background information is not presented in a framework that shows the interrelationships necessary for understanding.

[4]Boyle, op. cit.

[5]W. B. Whale and P. G. Boyle, "Group Decision Making," *Journal of Cooperative Extension*, vol. 4, no. 2, 1966, pp. 109–115.

[6]Boyle, op. cit.

[7]Ronald C. Powers, "Background Information in Planning," *Journal of Cooperative Extension*, vol. 4, no. 1, Spring 1966, pp. 11–22.

- Background information is frequently just presented and not analyzed and interpreted.
- Background information is generally presented all at once rather than developed from the general to the specific during several meetings.

Powers recommends that background information should combine narrative explanation and selected data to illustrate the points. Masses of statistics should be avoided. One approach is to organize data by specific problem areas to provide the study group with a more concrete basis for identifying the gap between "what is" and "what should be."

How specifically the programmer ought to interpret and draw conclusions from background information is a real concern. Studies on influence[8] suggest that the programmer may influence the kind of problems and needs identified by the client.

DO CLIENTELE CONTRIBUTE TO IDENTIFICATION OF NEEDS?

The key question for the programmer is whether the clientele study group should be regarded as a separate source for identifying needs. Obviously, the answer depends somewhat on the purpose for involving people. If programmers are primarily concerned with legitimizing a program, then their purpose is to help the group understand the basis and reasons for the program. If, on the other hand, the programmers' purpose is to use the study group to identify needs and opportunities, then they must minimize their influence on the decisions reached by the group.

This task is difficult. It has already been pointed out that the programmer ought to be involved in selecting, orienting, and training the members of study groups. In addition, it is essential that the programmer provide background information to the group to complement that which is brought to the group by individual members. Obviously, there are many points in the process at which the biases of the programmer may influence the decisions reached by the study group.

A research effort at Wisconsin investigated the extent to which local citizen groups and professional Extension personnel identify similar problems and needs.[9] The results showed only a 17 percent overall agreement between the two sources on all problems identified in four program areas. The findings strongly suggest that when the potential influence of the programmer on study group decisions has been minimized the group will identify needs that the programmers do not identify. In this experiment the planning group members were oriented to the purpose and procedure

---

[8]W. B. Whale, "Appraisal of a Process of Planning for Total Resource Development in a Wisconsin County," Ph.D. dissertation, University of Wisconsin– Madison, 1966.
[9]Ibid.

for planning and provided with background information. It is therefore valuable for a continuing education programmer to employ both sources to identify a broad range of needs from which to establish educational objectives. The challenge is to synthesize data from these two sources to establish program objectives that will be most meaningful to people.

HOW CAN THE PROFESSIONAL ASSIST A GROUP TO IDENTIFY PROBLEMS AND NEEDS?

Experience has shown that identifying problems in a planning effort is a complicated process. Research provides ample evidence that advisory groups are most productive when they follow a definite process in making decisions. Consequently, at the time advisory groups are oriented to their responsibilities, a suggested process is necessary for their use.

A framework for decision making in advisory groups can be somewhat different than the usual process. Such a framework might be thought of as a method of appraisal. This simply means comparing the "what is," based on situational facts, with the "what should be," based on standards arrived at through analysis and judgments about various data. As a result of this comparison, the imbalances are determined. Priorities can then be established, objectives arrived at, and possible courses of action chosen. This method might provide a practical and useful approach to arrive at clearly delineated, relevant problems and needs in a group context. Figure 9.1 illustrates the general and specific steps involved.

ACHIEVING RATIONAL GROUP DECISIONS

A very challenging question for continuing education programmers is whether totally rational decisions are necessarily the outcome of decision making in advisory group activity. Evidence indicates that limited rationality is a more realistic expectation.

Any group situation is likely to require at least some of its members to alter their views if consensus is to be obtained on any matter complex enough to require group decisions. The group may, in effect, be striving for conformity. Factors of cohesion—the degree of closeness and warmth members of the group feel for each other, pride in being members of the group, the desire to work together toward common goals—are highly desirable requisites for effective group functioning. Certainly, participation is necessary for group interaction. Yet, a wide range of studies support the idea that each of these—conformity, cohesiveness, and participation—introduces the prospect of emotional involvement. It may be, therefore, that emotional rather than intellectual influences are responsible for achieving the agreement necessary for reaching decisions in advisory groups, even though a decision-making process is followed. Limited ra-

Figure 9.1   Process for Identifying Problems

General orientation	
1 Orientation information is given concerning the nature, purposes, and responsibilities of the particular group.	2 General situational information is given to fully explain and explore the background of the general topic under discussion.

Identification and clarification of problems	
3 A specific suggestion is made concerning "what should be" in relation to the existing general situation. (This gap or need is interpreted as a problem.) 4 Information is sought concerning the "need" in order to reach some consensus about "what is" and "what should be."	5 Information or opinion is given (or decision made to obtain specific information) to satisfy inquiries made in step 4. 6 Attempts are made to summarize, categorize, interpret, and relate the discussion of the situation, facts, trends, and information. Attempts are also made to establish and examine objectives relating to the specific problems.

Identification and clarification of solutions	
7 Information is sought and given concerning resources available and resources required to facilitate the solution of the problem. 8 Possible techniques and procedures for solution of the problem are suggested, evaluated, modified, discarded, or recommended. Consideration is given to possible consequences of alternative solutions.	9 General recommendations are made concerning the general problems, objectives, and solutions, including priorities.

tionality is more likely to result. How limited it is depends on how the process of decision making is organized and on whether emotionality can be kept from being a major factor in decisions.

Recognizing that group decisions are not often reached on the basis of reason alone puts additional responsibility on those who analyze the problems, opportunities, and recommendations submitted by advisory groups. The advisory group, its activity, and its conclusions need to be analyzed to determine the extent to which nonrational factors may have inhibited the identification of real needs.

CONFLICTS IN INDIVIDUAL VALUES

Another question concerning the problem of identifying relevant needs is whether compromise between competing alternatives is the best approach. Certainly, the consequences of any plan of action in the lives of individual members of a community are manifold. Further, each individual has their own judgments as to the effects of these consequences in their lives, as well as the reasons behind these judgments. But this does not suggest that the real problems can be identified by merely summarizing individual opinions. Rather, the varied and complex factors underlying any problem suggest the need for a more careful consideration of alternatives and weighing of consequences within a system's context.

Two questions then need to be asked: (1) How do individual values affect, and how in turn are they affected by, the group problem-solving process? and (2) Is it more feasible to ignore values or to challenge them in the need identification process?

Values need to be challenged, not so much to override them as to cast them in a new light. Since values do not exist in a vacuum, it becomes imperative for the individual participants, who embody a whole range of values and aspirations, to have the opportunity to share experiences and ideas so new insights and directions can emerge from such interaction. The focus of the group then becomes not one of compromise between different experiences but one of reconstruction of these experiences. The group decision-making process needs to be evaluated to help each member redefine her or his past experiences within the broader context of the group and thereby help reach a more accurate decision.

INDIVIDUAL OR GROUP PROBLEM SOLVING

The issue as to whether individuals or groups are more effective at decision making seems to have been generally resolved in favor of the group, although opinion is not unanimous and the statement requires much qualification.

Shaw,[10] Davis and Restle,[11] and Faust[12] all conclude that groups are generally superior to individuals in coming up with correct solutions to problems. They point out, however, that groups take longer to reach a decision and that the relative advantage of the group over the individual depends somewhat on the degree of complexity of the problem itself.

Other authors, such as Marquart[13] have suggested that a collection of individuals who pool their individual decisions but do not meet face to face will collectively be superior to the interacting group in solving problems.

[10]Nathan C. Shaw (ed.), *Administration of Continuing Education,* National Association for Public School Adult Education, Washington, D.C., 1969.

[11]J. H. Davis and F. Restle, "The Analysis of Problems and Prediction of Group Problem Solving," *Journal of Abnormal and Social Psychology,* vol. 66, 1963, pp. 103–116.

[12]W. L. Faust, "Group vs. Individual Problem Solving," *Journal of Abnormal and Social Psychology,* vol. 59, 1959, pp. 68–72.

[13]D. E. Marquart, "Group Problem Solving," *Journal of Social Psychology,* vol. 41, 1955, pp. 103–113.

To understand what makes groups superior to individuals in solving problems, we must first understand how the individual process differs from the group decision-making process.

Bales and Strodtbeck[14] set forth a phase hypothesis with empirical support to explain the various phases or stages groups go through in decision making. Following is another suggested format to use as the group moves through the phases:

I   Clarify the problem.
    A   Clarify the general problem or solution the group is to work on. If possible, determine the present specific concerns related to the general problem the group is studying and those likely to arise in the future.
    B   Discuss the importance of the specific problem in relationship to the larger society and other problems.
II   Study the problem.
    A   Analyze what has happened, what is happening now, and what is likely to be the trend in the next three to five years. This may be done by personal interview, brief questionnaires, or other contacts with various state and local people. An attempt should be made to record and use factual information.
    B   Analyze the available resources and present programs as they apply to the general problem under study by the group. Also, analyze the resources and activities of other agencies and groups in the immediate community.
III   Evaluate alternatives.
    A   Study the needs and trends relating to the general problem. Be sure the information applies to the immediate community.
    B   Study and discuss several objectives that would help to resolve the problem being studied. Examine each of these objectives very critically.
    C   Study and discuss the resources available and those needed to carry out a program identified by the objectives. What additional resources are needed and where can they be obtained?
IV   Choose alternatives.
    A   Identify objectives a program should aim toward to help resolve the problem studied by the group.
    B   Suggest, if possible, methods and procedures to best meet the objectives.
V   Report decisions.
    Prepare a report for those who will provide funding or other support for the program, giving the present situation, the specific problems, and the group's recommendations for a program.

[14]R. F. Bales and F. L. Strodtbeck, "Phases in Group Problem Solving," in D. Cartwright and A. Zander (eds.), *Group Dynamics Research and Theory*, 3d ed., Harper & Row, Publishers, Inc., New York, 1968, pp. 389–398.

One might argue that the group process of decision making is not very different from the mental phases of individual decision making. The phases discussed so far are essentially task-related and therefore similar for both groups and individuals.

However, when the dimension of interpersonal relationships is added to the group decision-making process, we introduce a series of factors that distinguish it from individual decision making.

Bales and Strodtbeck discuss interpersonal relationships in terms of three sets of problems found concurrent with the task-related phases of group problem solving. The groupings are (1) problems of decision in which group members may be positive or negative in terms of helping to make the decision, agreeing with it, accepting it, and so forth; (2) problems of tension management whereby members may aid in tension reduction or add to it by withdrawing; and (3) problems of integration in which members show antagonism to each other in such a way that group solidarity is endangered. The authors also suggest that the extent of social-emotional problems within the group will increase as the group moves from the orientation phase to the control phase.

Groups involved in problem solving are therefore confronted with two types of problems: (1) those related to the task, and (2) those resulting from the interaction of group members. The latter type is obviously not present when individuals make decisions on their own. It therefore becomes necessary to analyze the interaction of problem-solving groups to understand why the group is generally superior to the individual in solving problems.

FACTORS AFFECTING INTERACTION AMONG MEMBERS OF DECISION-MAKING GROUPS

Many factors that operate within a group ultimately affect the group's decision-making ability. The following items show the variety of forces that may be operative.

Presence of Self-Oriented Goals

Each individual member of the group brings to the group a set of personal goals and needs that may be quite unrelated to the group task and may hinder the group in its problem-solving attempts. Personal needs for recognition, task achievement, and structure are examples. A tendency to attempt to influence the decision making in favor of particular organizations has been seen among members of advisory groups. This lack of identification with the problem-solving group can lead to serious interpersonal problems among group members.

Heterogeneity of the Group

Increasing the heterogeneity of the group in terms of the variety of backgrounds represented by individual members is likely to have two major effects. First, it may increase the potential resources of the group and enhance its ability to solve the problem, and second, it may increase the likelihood of interpersonal problems among members. The critical demands of the task are therefore relevant in determining the optimal degree of heterogeneity in the group. Groups faced with a diversity of viewpoints need to develop norms for tolerance of opinion differences.

Leadership Style

Bales[15] suggests that problem-solving groups have two leadership roles that must be fulfilled. One role focuses on task-related problems, the other is concerned with social-emotional problems. A leadership style that is strongly oriented to solving task problems and that overlooks interpersonal problems may create major obstacles for effective use of group resources. A nonpermissive leadership style also inhibits group creativity by not allowing full expression of ideas and opinions.

Formal Structure

Several studies have indicated that a degree of structure is useful in advisory groups. For example, in leaderless groups, the disproportionate influence of high-status members tends to result in the withdrawal of low-status members, thus cutting off a potential resource for the group. A degree of structure is useful to ensure a hearing for all group members. Structure is also useful to keep the group "on track." Hoffman[16] points out that groups that can be led to be "problem minded" by the leader produce more creative solutions than groups that are "solution minded." However, overstructuring can serve to inhibit interaction and thus be as disfunctional to group problem solving as a lack of structure.

Communication

Communication among group members serves to increase the uniformity of group opinion and therefore is essential to the problem-solving group. The pattern of communication is affected by such group variables as spatial arrangement of members, status hierarchy, feedback on previous attempts at communication, and individual goals and needs. Persons with similar cognitive backgrounds generally achieve superior communication.

[15]R. F. Bales, *Interaction Process Analysis,* University of Chicago Press, Chicago, 1976.

[16]L. R. Hoffman, "Group Problem Solving," in L. Berkowitz (ed.), *Advances in Experimental Social Psychology,* vol. 2, Academic Press, New York, 1964, pp. 99–132.

This may explain why some homogeneous groups are more productive. Through communication, individuals can satisfy various personal needs, thus allowing them to move on to task problems.

Power

The amount and distribution of power in the group is relevant to group interaction in many ways. Most important to problem-solving groups is the amount of power possessed by the total group over individual members. Where group power is high, we can expect a high motivational level among members in terms of productivity, interpersonal attraction that reduces the probability of social-emotional problems, and greater conformity to group norms. If the power of individual members is high, on the other hand, we can expect high-power persons, regardless of the basis of their power, to have a disproportionate influence over other group members. High-power individuals will also initiate and receive more communication. An uneven distribution of power, therefore, has major implications for group interaction. The high-power person, therefore, has a major effect on group interaction; for example, by controlling group procedure and consequently becoming a barrier to a free exchange of ideas.

Cohesiveness

While this factor depends on many of the other factors previously discussed, it nevertheless deserves separate comment in terms of its effect on group interaction. Collins and Guetzkow[17] suggest that cohesiveness depends upon three variables: (1) potential interpersonal attraction among group members; (2) the importance of the task to group members; and (3) the prestige of the group. Cohesiveness is an important determinant of group productivity.

Group Norms

The effect of group norms on interaction may be obvious; however, the presence of norms calling for cooperation, objectivity, tolerance of opinion differences, and the like, are especially important to problem-solving groups. An appeal for adherence to a particular group norm may often be a technique to resolve interpersonal conflict.

Conflict

The Bales and Strodtbeck[18] hypothesis suggests that group problem solving is enhanced when social-emotional reactions are more positive than

[17]B. E. Collins and H. Guetzkow, *A Social Psychology of Group Processes for Decision Making,* John Wiley & Sons, Inc., New York, 1964.
[18]Bales and Strodtbeck, op. cit.

negative. Studies cited by Hoffman[19] caution against overgeneralizing this assumption. He points out that conflict at the cognitive level can serve as a satisfaction reward to the group, but he qualifies this by saying that conflict must be based on different facts or interpretation of facts.

Group Size

For any given task there is an optimum-size group that will be most effective in dealing with it. Any problem-solving group can reach a size in which the addition of more members does not enhance its problem-solving ability. It has been suggested that group size depends on the critical demands of the task, the amount of resources required for its solution, and the degree to which the task requires division of labor. Group size is also relevant in terms of the amount of influence exerted by high-power group members. The disproportionate influence increases with the size of the group. Group size also serves to limit the "air time" of group members. As size increases, the opportunity for individual members to express ideas decreases. A norm of equal air time could serve to limit the contribution of the more creative group members.

No doubt, other factors affect interaction within problem-solving groups. However, the ones discussed are sufficient to make the point that many factors affect the ability of a group to effectively solve problems. By understanding these factors, programmers will be in a much better position to help members achieve both task-related rewards and rewards resulting from satisfying interpersonal relations.

CONSEQUENCES OF GROUP PROBLEM SOLVING

What are the consequences of using groups to solve problems? One could view the following list as advantages and disadvantages, but it seems more useful to discuss them in terms of expected results or consequences and the conditions under which they will most likely occur:

Assembly effect. Complex problems that require a division of labor for solution lend themselves to group problem solving. Problems that do not have this critical demand can probably be solved equally well, if not better, by an individual.

Constructive overlap. Assuming that the task requires members to use some division of labor, we can expect an increase in problem-solving effectiveness when members overlap somewhat in their approach to the various aspects of the problem. They will tend to motivate one another and be mutually stimulating in exploring alternatives and facts.

[19]Hoffman, op. cit.

Creativity. The simple fact that each member brings to the group certain knowledge, values, and interests increases the creative potential of the group and the probability of achieving a good solution by the group approach. However, the interaction process or the group's size may be such that this creative potential is not utilized.

Accuracy. Combining the opinions of group members and exposing them to question and verification serves to reduce the random error of decision, thus increasing accuracy. Again, the extent to which this occurs depends on the degree to which group interaction allows for free and objective discussion.

Conformity. Conformity can serve to enhance or lower the quality of the group product, if the conformity is rational, in that opinions are changed because the opposing opinion is likely to be improved. On the other hand, if conformity is irrational, the quality of the product will be lowered. Irrational conformity may be expected for reasons such as social approval, falsely perceived expertise of another individual, social norms, and the like. A major concern in problem-solving groups is that conformity to a solution will occur before all opinions and alternatives have been explored. This emphasizes the need for the leader to keep the group "problem minded," especially in the early phases of decision making.

Majority rule. Coupled with the expectance of conformity is the expectation that the majority opinion will prevail in decision making. This could have the effect of public but not private conformity among those individuals in the minority. While this may have no bearing on the quality of the decision, it could have some effect on the implementation of the decision, especially if the minority group decides to try to rally public support for their point of view.

Acceptance. In most "real" problem-solving groups there is a concern not only for the quality of the decision but also for the execution of the decision. In this context, how well the decision is accepted by all group members becomes very important. Acceptance reflects the members' feelings about the solution and the way it was reached. Studies have shown that acceptance is related to the freedom of the problem-solving process (the amount of influence individuals feel they have had in reaching the decision) rather than to the quality of the decision itself. This factor strongly supports a permissive style of leadership in problem-solving groups.

Satisfaction. We can expect group-member satisfaction to be determined by two major sources: (1) task-related rewards, and (2) rewards received through interpersonal relationships. Task-related rewards tend to generalize equally to each member of the group, but satisfaction with interpersonal rewards may vary greatly among members. They may or may not be correlated with the quality of the group decision and therefore it may be inaccurate to judge the success of the problem-solving group in terms of member satisfaction.

Motivation. Generally, we can expect the motivation of individuals to increase in the group environment and thus increase productivity. This is probably because most groups reward high productivity and withhold rewards from those who do not contribute their share. Hoffman[20] points out that motivation is often higher in mixed sex groups, perhaps because each sex is role playing with the other.

Perseverance. Davis and Restle[21] indicate that we can expect a group to persevere longer in problem solving than an individual will. This may be because groups take longer to reach a decision or because the obligation to the group inspires perseverance.

Risk-taking. Several studies have shown that decisions evolved through group problem solving involve a greater degree of risk than decisions arrived at individually. Explanations for this may be that the group allows the individual to shift responsibility for the decision to the group; or it may be that risk-taking individuals are more influential in determining group decisions.

These are some of the expected consequences of using groups to make decisions. Although these consequences may not occur individually because of interpersonal problems and the nature of the task environment, collectively they serve to provide some explanation of why individuals interacting as group members achieve more than the most superior group member working alone.

SUMMARY

Advisory committees are one very important method for involving clientele in program development. Several possible functions for the advisory committee were presented. Several concerns in selecting and organizing advisory committees have been discussed in this chapter. Such questions as who should be involved? is orientation necessary? is background information used? do clientele really contribute? can the professional help in problem identification? and are rational group decisions possible? were included. Definitive answers were not provided because the answers depend so much on the programming situation. The last part of the chapter contained a review of ideas about individual versus group decision making and factors affecting the interaction among members of groups.

[20]Ibid.
[21]Davis and Restle, "The Analysis of Problems."

DISCUSSION QUESTIONS

1 Describe a programming situation in which you would decide to have an advisory committee.
2 What function do you believe an advisory committee can perform most effectively?
3 Do you feel an advisory committee can make good decisions?
4 Describe an experience that you had with an advisory committee.
5 Analyze the strengths and weaknesses of individual and group decision making.

SUGGESTED READINGS FOR SECTION III

Berger, Peter L., and Richard Newhaus, *To Empower People,* American Enterprise for Public Policy Research, Washington, D.C., 1977.

Davis, Richard H. (ed.), *Advocacy and Age,* Ethel Percy Andrus Gerontology Center, Los Angeles, 1976.

Maier, Norman, *Problem Solving and Creativity,* Brooks/Cole Publishing Company, Monterey, Calif., 1970.

Simon, R. I., *Developmental Structure of Citizen Involvement,* Institute of Studies on Education, Toronto, Ont., Canada, 1970.

Section IV

Identification of Problems and Needs

Adults do not have to participate in continuing education programs. Thus, it is desirable to have potential participants help design the program. The problems and needs of adults are varied and complex. The analysis and interpretations of situations must provide the basis for establishment of program objectives.

In Chapter 10, the conceptual background for situational analysis is discussed. Consideration is given to individual need identification and analysis of the problems of the communities and environments of people.

Chapter 11 presents the approaches to clientele analysis. A rationale for clientele analysis is discussed. Emphasis is given to the alternative methods for need analysis.

Approaches for community analysis are presented in Chapter 12. A framework for considering all elements in the community is discussed. In Chapter 13, we discuss the task of establishing practices. A framework for priority setting is presented.

Chapter 10

Situational Analysis

The challenge of describing and interpreting situational analysis is complicated by the practical problems of abstractly describing a phenomenon in
constant motion. The processes of planning, implementing, and evaluating continuing education programs are continuous and overlapping. A mechanical process can be stopped and its separate components described
and observed. Unfortunately, this is not the case with social or human
processes. However, even though situational analysis is a part of a continuing programming cycle, we are suggesting that it be separated from the
total program development process in order to be studied and interpreted.
This chapter provides background information for conceptualizing situational analysis as related to the individual and the community.

INTERPRETATION OF SITUATIONAL ANALYSIS

A *situation* is a state of affairs or a combination of circumstances at any
given time. *Analysis* here means a detailed examination of the elements or
components of a situation. Thus, *situational analysis* is the effort to iden-

tify the need, gap, or condition that exists between what is and what should be—or between what is and that which is more desirable.

In the following sections of this chapter, we have provided background information on situational analysis as applied to individual needs and community or situational problems. The procedures for situational analysis are included in later chapters. The assumption is that situational analysis involves the individual and the environment in which that individual exists. This involvement provides the programmer with a much broader basis for analysis and interpretation. For example, if we study the needs of the aged, it may be quite clear that their housing situation or their recreational opportunities are very inadequate. As individuals they do not need to know more about interior design or financing as related to housing but rather about the inadequacy of the housing facility itself. Ideally, the continuing education programmer will utilize both sources, the individual and the environment, in building an effective program. Thus, in developing an effective educational program, the programmer should consider the needs of the individual as well as the conditions or situations in the environment that might reflect problems or needs. In one sense, we are using need and problem synonymously; however, the inference is that *need* is more individual-oriented and *problem* is more community- or situation-based.

THE CONCEPT OF CLIENTELE ANALYSIS

Need is a concept widely used in the literature related to programming in continuing education. Most programming models suggest that one should undertake situation analysis to determine needs that are then used as the basis for identification of objectives. In an analysis of the concept of educational need, Monette[1] identified a number of different definitions of need. He grouped these definitions into four major categories: (1) basic human needs, (2) felt and expressed needs, (3) normative needs, and (4) comparative needs. Each of these will be discussed.

Basic Human Needs

Monette describes this concept of need as indicating:

> . . . a deficient state that initiates a motive on the part of an individual or a non-observable or inferred biopsychological state rather similar to a "drive." This condition may be understood as a tension state of some kind which causes gratification-seeking behavior. Need in this sense denotes an innate, unleashed condition which is "national" to all.[2]

---

[1]Maurice Monette, "The Concept of Educational Need: An Analysis of Selected Literature," *Adult Education,* vol. XXVII, no. 2, 1977, pp. 116–127.
[2]Ibid., p. 117.

Maslow[3] identified five types of needs arranged in a hierarchy. In order of priority, these include physiological, safety, love, esteem, and self-actualization. Maslow theorizes that the emergence of a new need usually depends on the prior satisfaction of a more basic or "prepotent" need. The satisfaction of a more basic need sets up conditions for higher level needs to emerge. Conversely, the deprivation of a basic need causes a person to seek satisfaction of that need before seeking to satisfy higher level needs. In such an approach, people are seen as perpetually wanting, fulfilling needs as they emerge.

The hierarchy-of-needs categories are:

Physiological. Physiological needs, such as thirst, hunger, rest, are those things necessary to maintain life. When a person is extremely hungry or thirsty this need dominates that person's behavior, and gives an untrue picture of most of his or her higher motivations, including social ones.

Security. Security needs are both physical and economic (job tenure, insurance, a home, savings, pension). The common tendency to prefer the familiar and look upon change with skepticism is a manifestation of security needs. This need often becomes dominant during emergencies, such as war, disease, injury, or natural catastrophes.

Social. Love, belongingness, acceptance, and approval are important here. Social needs involve a desire for affectionate relations with people and a place in the group.

Ego. Ego or esteem needs drive people to seek recognition as worthwhile persons. Feelings of confidence, worth, strength, beauty, and usefulness are important.

Self-actualization. The need for self-actualization is the need to become the kind of person one desires to be. Satisfaction of this need is expressed in various ways—becoming a good mother, a good teacher, an athlete, or a musician.

As illustrated in Figure 10.1, these needs come into an individual's consciousness by priority. Individuals cannot be concerned with ego needs, for example, until their physiological, safety, and social needs have been satisfied for a continuous period of time. Continuing educators sometimes overlook the importance of these prior needs in their impatience to move onto the fifth level.

Eckerman has suggested the additional human need of "consistency," which has been defined by research on cognitive dissonance:

> We know of the body's need for homeostasis, the need for physiological integration, balance predictability, and coordination in order for a person to function effectively. In short, consistency. Is there such a thing as homeo-

[3]Abraham H. Maslow, *Motivation and Personality,* 2d ed., Harper & Row, Publishers, Inc., New York, 1970.

Figure 10.1   A Hierarchy of Needs

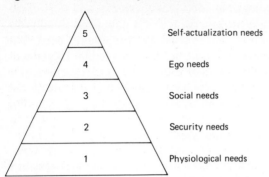

stasis of behavior, a corollary to that of the body? Considerable evidence indicates something of this sort in the nature of a series of interacting psychological processes.[4]

He continues the discussion with the following observations:

> Behavioral consistency can be explained with a model as three links in a strong chain. The links are how one feels, what he knows and how he acts. These constitute the very foundation of individual behavior, a troika as it were, of feelings, knowledge and actions.
>
> No one is going to change his behavior by being told to do so. He will only change if he himself is convinced of a need to change. Training, as with experience, fails unless it can demonstrate an extenuating reason for the individual to alter his behavior in a given direction. This seems to occur best under conditions where the individual can no longer tolerate the discomfort of the results of his own actions.[5]

Maslow was uncertain about the desire to know and understand—the cognitive need—being clearly established in all human beings, as were the others. Although curiosity, exploration, and the desire to acquire knowledge can be readily observed, these characteristics are more evident in persons of higher intelligence and with a stimulating environment than in those of lower intelligence with a dull environment.

Felt and Expressed Needs

This concept of need is probably most common, and it is seen as an individual "want" or "desire." A felt need is something believed necessary

[4]A. C. Eckerman, "A New Look at Need Theory: An Extension of Maslow's Hierarchy," *Training and Development Journal,* November 1968, p. 19. Reproduced by special permission from the November 1968 *Training and Development Journal.* Copyright 1968 by the American Society for Training and Development, Inc.

[5]Ibid., p. 21.

by the individual concerned. McMahon[6] calls these needs "desires." Although felt needs exist they may be neither real nor educational. Real educational needs may not be recognized or "felt" by the individual(s) having the need. McMahon criticizes those who develop programs based on "meeting felt needs," saying that such programming often "results in circumscribing the audience of adult education" who may have real educational needs.[7] Of course, a felt need may also be a real educational need. If that situation exists, the continuing educator does not have the problem of helping the clientele recognize their needs. On a theoretical level, it may be necessary to help adults recognize or "feel" the real educational needs they have in order to motivate them to learn. For example, a client may enroll in a mechanics class in order to achieve the goal of becoming a certified mechanic. Using this concept of need the educator might offer a "cafeteria-type" program based on "felt needs" of clients.

Normative Needs

"A need may be called normative when it constitutes a deficiency or gap between a 'desirable' standard and the standard that actually exists. The individual or group that falls short of the desirable standard is said to be in need."[8] This concept can be applied to an analysis of nutritional standards for low-income families in a given community. If research clearly indicates certain desirable standards for food consumption, and we determine that 85 percent of the families in a low-income community are below the standard, then we have a need. Further, analysis and judgments would have to be made to determine the reason or cause for the gap or need.

Comparative Needs

This concept of need is "comparing the characteristics of those in receipt of a service with others who are not. If these others exhibit the same characteristics and are not receiving the service, they are said to be in need."[9] For example, we might compare the programs of administrators of summer recreational camps or parks in Milwaukee with those of Chicago. If the programs in Milwaukee are involving more youth and aged, then we might say that the administrators in Chicago need some help. Or we might compare scores on a professional competency test administered to engineers in two different areas. If one group scores much lower, it could be said that there is a "need" to raise the competency levels of that group.

---

[6]Ernest E. McMahon, "Needs—of People and Their Communities . . . and the Adult Educator: A Review of Literature of Need Determination," Educational Resources Information Center, Document no. ED038551, Syracuse, N.Y., July 1970, pp. 21–22.

[7]Ibid.

[8]Ibid.

[9]Ibid.

As we examine each of these four concepts of need, it becomes apparent that no one concept of need is adequate in and of itself. Basic human needs or innate needs are rather vague and general. As Monette states: "The mere existence of such a need—in no way lessens the educator's task of goal delineation and selection."[10] Felt needs provide only the perception of individuals who may be limited in their own self-values. Values can be viewed as the bases or standards by which we judge the worth of things. Thus, it is impossible to identify needs without a set of norms.

Normative needs are based on value judgments that may be conflicting. The value orientation of the continuing educator may influence the normative definition of need insofar as the educator must judge the amount of resources to be devoted to meeting the need and whether or not the available resources can solve the problem. Comparative assessments may not represent needs since they do not involve evaluations based on what level is adequate or desirable according to established criteria. The shortcomings of each concept of need suggests that consideration of all types is necessary for effective situation analysis. The concept of need as a gap may be most useful since the other three concepts can be used to help determine a gap that exists.

The interpretation of the concept of need that we are supporting derives from Kurt Lewin's field theory of motivation.[11] Within that theory, tension is the dynamic idea. Weiner states, "The concept of tension is related to that of need: a need is represented as a system in a state of tension."[12] The key assumption of this conception is the acceptance of the physiological theory of homeostasis or equilibrium. Equilibrium is seen as a natural state toward which a person strives, both physiologically and psychologically. In fact, one of the definitions of need provided by Webster describes need as "a physiological or psychological requirement for the maintenance of the homeostasis of an organism."[13]

Within this conception of need, any deviation from equilibrium—a need—prompts a tendency to return to equilibrium by satisfying the need:

> Need is a condition that exists between what is and what should be, or between what is and that which is more desirable. Need is a key instigator of behavior in that it creates a state of disequilibrium. . . . Thus, a need repre-

---

[10]Monette, op. cit., p. 117.

[11]Kurt Lewin, cited in Bernard Weiner, *Theories of Motivation*, Rand McNally & Company, Chicago, 1972, pp. 92–121.

[12]Bernard Weiner, *Theories of Motivation*, Rand McNally & Company, Chicago, 1972, p. 110.

[13]Webster's Third New International Dictionary, G. & C. Merriam Company, Springfield, Mass., 1976, p. 1512. By permission.

sents an imbalance, a lack of adjustment or a gap between a present situation or state of being and a new or changed set of conditions assumed to be more desirable . . ., a need always implies a gap.[14]

Knowles is very specific:

An educational need . . . is something a person ought to learn for his own good, for the good of an organization, or for the good of society. It is the gap between his present level of competencies and a higher level required for effective performance as defined by himself, his organization, or his society.[15]

Work in the field of motivational psychology can be interpreted within the equilibrium-disequilibrium need conceptualization. Cognitive balance theories, such as those proposed by Heider[16] and Festinger,[17] appear to support Eckerman's "consistency" level. As Weiner concludes, "cognitive balance is postulated as a principle of motivation because imbalance corresponds to a state of disequilibrium, is unpleasant, and produces behaviors instrumental to the attainment of a balanced state."[18]

White[19] postulates the existence of an independent energy source for the ego, not connected to libidinal forces, which he calls "effectance." He describes effectance as:

. . . the active tendency to put forth effort to influence the environment. . . . Effectance is a prompting to explore the properties of the environment; it leads to an accumulating knowledge of what can and cannot be done with the environment; its biological significance lies in this very property of developing competence. . . . Competence is the cumulative result of the history of interactions with the environment. Sense of competence is suggested as a suitable term for the subjective side of this, signifying one's consciously or unconsciously felt competence—one's confidence—in dealing with the various aspects of the environment.[20]

[14]Patrick Boyle and Irwin Jahns, "Program Development and Evaluation," in R. M. Smith, G. F. Aker, and J. R. Kid (eds.), *Handbook of Adult Education*, Macmillan Publishing Co., Inc., New York, 1970, p. 61.

[15]Malcolm Knowles, *The Modern Practice of Adult Education*, Follett Publishing Co., Chicago, 1973, p. 85.

[16]F. Heider, "The Gestalt Theory of Motivation," in M. R. Jones (ed.), *Nebraska Symposium on Motivation*, vol. 8, University of Nebraska Press, Lincoln, 1960, pp. 145–172.

[17]L. A. Festinger, *A Theory of Cognitive Dissonance*, Stanford University Press, Stanford, Calif., 1970.

[18]Weiner, op. cit., p. 293.

[19]Robert White, "Ego and Reality in Psychoanalytic Theory," *Psychological Issues*, vol. 3, Monograph 11, 1963.

[20]Ibid., pp. 185–186.

Again this "sense of competence" can be related to the equilibrium-disequilibrium need theory. When a person's environment changes, he or she has a tendency to attempt to influence the new environment, to become competent within it. The difference between prior environment and new environment can represent the gap. White's idea of competence can represent the learning necessary to close the gap. The result is the establishment of a new equilibrium within which the individual feels competent.

It would appear reasonable to approach need determination from the framework of equilibrium-disequilibrium need theory. There are two key problems with this conceptualization. These are (1) helping the clientele to recognize that a gap exists between what they are doing and what they could be doing, and (2) determining what should be. If people do not believe they need to change, or perceive no inconsistency between themselves at present and the desired state proposed, then change is difficult. When people recognize and accept that a need exists, they will try to redress that need.

This leads to the problem of determining what should be. No matter who specifies what should be, if the target clientele do not accept the new conditions described, then no change will be forthcoming. Yet it is necessary to specify "what should be" in order to compare "what is" with the desired new state. This comparison should specify what gap(s) or need(s) exist, if any, and hopefully the extent of the gap(s) or need(s). Boyle and Jahns conclude that after appropriate involvement of the clientele, the continuing educator's responsibility is to determine what the present situation is and what it ideally should be.[21] They continue this line of thought as follows:

> This approach implies that the educator must make some value judgments about "what should be," but these judgments, if based on the best available data, likely will be more realistic and meaningful than if based upon immediate pressures, subjective impressions and tradition.[22]

Although problems of need identification, analysis, and interpretation exist, they can be minimized. The concept of need that is useful for the continuing educator can be defined simply as the gap between what is and what could be.

Values and Need

A discussion of needs is inadequate without a concurrent discussion of values. Much of the literature related to needs ignores the value dimen-

---

[21]Boyle and Jahns, op. cit., p. 62.
[22]Ibid., pp. 62–63.

sion, discussing need as empirically determined through "scientific" analysis of the situation. Worthen and Sanders[23] touch on the importance that value systems play in curriculum development and usage. The product, they say, reflects the value orientations of those involved in programming. Using this argument, it logically follows that the values of people working for change permeate everything they do to promote change regardless of how "scientific" they may be. Whether educators see their role including value judgments or not, their personal values do have an effect. In fact, those who do not see value judgments as a part of programming may have more problems with personal bias affecting their programming process simply because they are not aware of their values. Those who consciously deal with value judgments are more likely to examine their personal values in the process.

Bennis et al.[24] recognize the complicated role values can play in programming. Value considerations present themselves intertwined with cognitive and technical considerations, making it difficult to sort out the value component of decisions and judgments from other components. Warwick and Kelman say that "values may influence the choice of goals not only in explicit, conscious ways, but also in a covert way." They continue: "Our assessment of the consequences of an intervention depends on what values we are willing or unwilling to sacrifice in the interest of social change."[25]

Paolo Freire[26] would agree with this point of view. He believes that education cannot be neutral. The fact that a person chooses a topic or subject from the infinite possibilities is in itself biased. Freire's attitude is that it is impossible to do purely "objective" programming because the educator cannot be purely objective. He suggests that the educational process begins with the felt need of the learners and follows with interactions between the educator and the learner.

One recognizes a real dilemma in that as programmers and through the manipulation of human behavior within an educational experience, we impose our values on the clientele. The dilemma violates a fundamental value of the freedom and opportunity to choose. However, there exists no formula for structuring an effective change situation where such manipulation is totally absent. In order to mitigate the dehumanizing effects and

[23]Blaine Worthen and James Sanders, *Educational Evaluation: Theory and Practice,* Charles A. Jones Publishing Company, Worthington, Ohio, 1973.

[24]Warren Bennis, Kenneth Benne, Robert Chin, and Kenneth Corey (eds.), *The Planning of Change,* 3d ed., Holt, Rinehart and Winston, Inc., New York, 1969.

[25]Donald Warwick and Herbert Kelman, in Gerald Zaltman (ed.), *Processes and Phenomena of Social Change,* Robert E. Krieger Publishing Co., Inc., Huntington, N.Y., 1978, p. 379.

[26]Paolo Freire, *Pedagogy of the Oppressed,* Herder and Herder, New York, 1972, p. 55.

to deal with this dilemma in a positive way, programmers and clientele need to be conscious or aware of the values held and involved in the situation.

Getting back more specifically to needs assessment, it is not a question of who can best determine needs (i.e., individuals through "felt" needs versus others who define "real" needs). The perspectives of both the adult learner and others can help identify the gap. Since the programmer's values have a great influence on what is defined as the critical need, personal values must be made explicit. Programmers must become aware of their own values, make these values known to the clientele, and do all that is possible to maximize the input of (consider values of) the clientele. In most cases, the programmer's values can and should be put to stringent tests by comparison with the values of the clientele, the program administrators, the funding agency, and others involved. The programmer should do everything possible to consider the values of all parties involved. However, the ultimate decision of need should be based on the programmer's own values.

It is the responsibility of the educator to broaden his or her own base as well as to help clients and colleagues do the same for themselves. Bloom supports this point:

> Although it is recognized that an individual is, on many grounds, entitled to his own opinion as well as his own judgments about the value of specific ideas, objects or activities, one major purpose of education is to broaden the foundation on which judgments are based. Thus, it is anticipated that as a result of educational procedures individuals will take into consideration the greater variety of facets of the phenomena to be evaluated and that they will have in mind a clearer view of the criteria and forms of reference being used in the evaluation.[27]

Value judgments are an implicit part of needs assessment and should be obtained from all parties involved in the process. As Freire[28] suggests, the role of dialogue between educators and clientele is critical while needs are assessed. The notion of value-free needs assessment is a denial of the role values perform. Values affect needs assessment and should not be ignored.

THE CONCEPT OF COMMUNITY ANALYSIS

This concept of situational analysis involves every aspect of community life. All the activities that help people meet their needs for educational,

[27]Benjamin Bloom et al. (eds.), *Taxonomy of Educational Objectives: The Classification of Educational Goals, Handbook*, vol. 1, *Cognitive Domain*, David McKay Co., Inc., New York, 1956–1964, p. 186.

[28]Freire, op. cit.

economic, social, political, aesthetic, and moral well-being require some degree of analysis. But the common conception of analysis and planning as a technical process to be undertaken only by professionals to meet specific problems or needs has led to many false expectations for the people and communities concerned.

To illustrate the diverse and interdependent issues involved in any analysis activity, let us take the case of poverty. Any planning in this area must begin by identifying, first, who the poor are and how many there are. Is there a movement in and out of poverty from year to year? A complete demographic study of the various population groups is needed to determine, for instance, whether there are racial inequalities as well as class inequalities and whether the aged poor have different problems. The economic questions involve problems of unemployment, conditions for economic growth, and the effect of taxation on the poor. The question of taxation leads to a consideration of the community's legal structure which, in turn, reflects upon the political process. How does participation of the poor in the political process, or lack of it, affect their conditions and the community as a whole? In the social dimension questions of family planning, crime, youth culture, and the culture of poverty need to be considered. How does such a culture affect learning? How does poverty affect land use and what implications does it have on the ecology as well as on the social welfare of the community? The physical dimension includes questions of design, convenience, efficiency, and aesthetics. Also involved are some basic ethical questions related to such problems as family planning.

There are questions of how conditions in one community affect other communities. Are the problems of the poor similar? In what way does change in one community affect people in neighboring communities? What are the implications of attracting new industry for the region as a whole? Would this affect migration patterns? Would it affect the rural areas? How does family planning affect total population growth? What are the implications for the values of different population groups? Other questions relate to how the work of agencies at various levels may overlap, and how agencies can coordinate their activities within a community and between communities.

It is apparent that developing a program for a community is complex and has many aspects. Three major sets of relationships are involved.

The first set of relationships involves the various interactions within a community with respect to its economic, social, psychological, political, physical, and technological aspects. The second set relates to the various interactions that cut across communities and how change in one affects conditions in the others. The third involves the relationship between the process of analysis and planning for community improvement and the growth and development of individuals, involved groups, and the community.

The goal of a holistic planning effort aimed at poverty is to reduce or eliminate poverty. Yet the means to that end may be the learning achieved by people, their groups, and the community. Only through conceptualizing and using such relationships can we really come close to effective holistic analysis and planning.

Analyzing the community as a system does not help clarify what directions or problems need to be focused upon nor how to proceed in planning for the community's growth and development. Rather, the system helps provide a framework for analyzing the various segments of the community in a much more comprehensive way than if each segment were considered alone. In any system analysis, one must be able to perceive the structure not as isolated facts and figures but as a network of interacting social forces that have given rise to the existing situation. The total community as a framework is valuable not only in identifying problems or formulating goals but also as a framework for analyzing facts, values, and other relevant information. The various economic, educational, environmental, and social elements of the community system serve as inputs to the framework.

The concept of community is most important to this concept of planning because the community is a viable social environment within which change takes place. A community in this context is the social interdependence that arises from the association of people. Depending on the magnitude of the problems and, therefore, the extent of interdependence, a community may refer to anything from a neighborhood to the entire world.

The concept of community as a system of relationships implies a patterned aggregation of individuals and objects operating as an interdependent whole with some degree of regularity. Miller defines system as "bounded regions in space-time, involving energy interchange among their parts, which are associated in functional relationships, and with their environments."[29] The activity of planning thus becomes primarily the reorganization of the mechanisms of human and environmental interchange within a community. It aims to alter the pattern of interdependencies within the system by establishing new elements or relationships, for example, the relationships that are established through joint economic and environmental consideration of a new factory in a community. This goal is achievable through planned educational activities. A new element or relationship becomes significant only when and how it functions differently from the old; this difference depends not only on the new element itself but also on the system within which it functions.

The systems or total community approach allows for the analysis of

---

[29]James G. Miller, "Toward a General Theory for the Behavioral Sciences," *The American Psychologist*, 1955, p. 514.

mutually interdependent variables functioning in and related to a total social situation. These variables include individuals and their motives, their development, their attitudes, the physical setting, the institutions in the system, and many more. They are woven into an overall pattern of interdependency. The focus of planning shifts from the component parts and is refocused on the system of interrelationships among the parts.

Change is dynamic. Although it is usually viewed at a particular level of society, the ramifications of any given change may extend throughout the various levels of societal institutions. Regardless of its level of existence or the institutional category in which it occurs, a social system possesses certain elements that determine its character. It is these elements that are affected by change. They provide a systematic way of looking at a given social system. By assessing its elements, a programmer may be in a better position to help determine what changes are needed, to make judgments about the capability of a system to make changes, and, of course, to assess the stresses that a given type of change might place on a system. We believe that the continuing education programmer can use the concept of social system as a general overall basis for analysis, interpretation, and judgments about the setting within which more specific problems and concerns will be analyzed. The social forces provide a conceptual framework for identifying the problems and needs for a continuing education program. This conceptual framework can be applied to the numerous subsystems in a community such as low-income families, farmers, people with small businesses, food service employees, or professional groups. The concept can also be applied to professional associations, agencies, or institutions, such as the professional physical associations, medical societies, farm bureaus, labor unions, or a commercial industry or company. In each case, the use of the forces in the social system will provide a general overall understanding of the system or setting within which specific need/problems analysis will be completed.

Loomis describes a social system as:

> . . . composed of the patterned interaction of members. It is constituted of the interactions of a plurality of individual actors whose relations to each other are mutually oriented through the definition and mediations of a pattern or structural and shared symbols and expectations.[30]

The elements are usually defined as follows:

- *Ends or objectives*. These are the things that members of the social system expect to accomplish or gain from their membership in the

[30]C. P. Loomis, *Social Systems: Essays on Their Persistance and Change,* 1960 by Charles P. Loomis. Printed by permission of D. Van Nostrand Company, Inc., Princeton, N.J.

system. For example, a farmer may wish to derive higher milk prices through membership in a farmer's organization. A citizen may desire certain legislation by becoming active in a political organization. A family may have the objective of providing its members with a particular level of living that is compatible with its standards.

- *Norms*. Those rules (written or unwritten) that prescribe what is socially acceptable and what is not. In fact, one may say that norms define the appropriate ways for attaining the ends of the social system.

- *Status roles*. These include the expectations members of a system have for the various positions that exist in the system. For example, in most societies the father is expected to be a provider for the family. In some situations, social change has caused him to be unable to fulfill this expectation, thereby creating a sense of alienation from the system and, in some instances, a breakdown of the social system itself (in this case, the family).

- *Power*. Power refers to control over others. We may think of it as having two dimensions—authority, which is the right to control and the sanctions that are available to control, and influence, which is nonauthoritative, depending upon such things as human relations skills, knowledge, certain types of wealth, etc. Generally, a person's position in a social system (i.e., one's status role) defines one's authority. A person's influence is related to his or her performance of that role.

- *Social rank*. Members of a social system are ranked according to what is rated high or low in the system. It results from an overall rating of the individual's worth. In our society this usually considers such things as wealth, education, work ethic, and the like. Subsystems within the larger social system are accorded social rank, as are individuals; for example, the country club set and hippies.

- *Sanction*. Social systems have at their disposal certain rewards and sanctions that may be used to gain the compliance of members to the ends and norms of the system.

- *Facilities*. The means available to a system for use in attaining its ends constitute the facilities of the social system. A farm family, for example, has property and equipment; a school has buildings, libraries, and laboratory equipment.

- *Territoriality*. Territoriality involves the physical space required by the social system. Obviously, this can be a major influence on many of the other elements.

Continuing education programmers are generally concerned with initiating concrete changes in social systems. For example, the local dairy herd association, the labor union, or the physician's association. It is at this level that the elements just discussed are most easily identified.

So we have discussed only the specific aspects of social systems that are affected by change—the elements. We should also know something of the process through which change is brought about, or resisted, in social systems. Briefly, they are as follows:

Communication. The process by which information is diffused through a social system is termed the communication process. It is through this process that opinions and attitudes are developed or modified. In our society communications is a multichannel process, ranging from mass involvement via television to person-to-person communication over the backyard fence or telephone.

Decision making. Simply stated, decision making is the process through which the resources of a social system are allocated, usually for the purpose of attaining the goals of the system. It involves the selection of a course of action among several alternatives. The process is influenced by such systemic elements as norms and sanctions. The right of certain persons within the system to influence decision making is determined by such systemic elements as status, power, and social rank.

Boundary maintenance. The efforts of a social system to maintain its identity and its existing pattern of interaction is termed boundary maintenance. The tendency of a social system to coalesce and resist an outside force that threatens its values is an example of the process of boundary maintenance.

Systemic linkages. When the elements of two or more social systems become integrated to the point at which the systems involved can function as a unit, systemic linkage has occurred. For example, when the county agent works with farmers' organizations on a particular program the values and goals of the Extension system and those of the organizations are temporarily synonymous and linkage is said to have occurred.

At this point, the change system, represented by the county agent, is initiating the linkage with the target system (i.e., the farm organizations). Once this has been achieved, the linkage must then be made "rightful" within the membership of the target system. This is why the programmer is wise to initiate linkage with the power structure of the target system, since successful legitimation is usually dependent upon their support. Once legitimation has occurred, systemic linkage can occur and the program put into effect.

SUMMARY

Situational analysis is an essential part of any effective program development process. The tasks of thoroughly analyzing data and information from and about the learner will lead to programs that do contribute to the real educational needs. Also, the analysis of the situation in which the learner lives, works, and plays will reveal the bases for very significant programs. In this chapter, we have presented conceptual frameworks for situational analysis. Information on how to implement situational analysis is given in Chapters 11 and 12. It is our feeling that the continuing education programmer will benefit from a strong understanding of the bases or the conceptualization of situational analysis.

DISCUSSION QUESTIONS

1 What does situational analysis mean to you?
2 How would you relate need and community analysis in a programming situation?
3 What factors relating to community analysis in rural areas do not seem to be as appropriate for the urban areas?
4 Describe an experience you had with clientele analysis.
5 What dimensions of the community would you include in your analysis of problems or needs?

Chapter 11

Approaches to Clientele Analysis

Need is a complex concept, yet significant and far-reaching in its implications for the continuing education programmer. The interpretation of need that we accepted in Chapter 10 assumes that equilibrium is a natural state toward which people strive. Need is a condition between what is and what should be, or between what is and what is more desirable. Need is a key instigator of behavior in that it creates a state of disequilibrium. People are motivated to fulfill the need or find a substitute to restore the equilibrium. Thus, a need represents an imbalance, a lack of adjustment, or a gap between a present situation or state of being and a new or changed set of conditions assumed to be more desirable.

This interpretation, portrayed in Figure 11.1, provides a framework useful to the development of a continuing education program. In using this framework, it is necessary to be able to compare what is—the present situation—with what should be—the more desirable condition. The result of this comparison will be a description of the gap or the need. In clientele analysis, need can be expressed in terms of a person's level of knowledge, present attitude, skills, or the practices or behaviors a person needs to follow.

Figure 11.1   A Framework for Needs Analysis

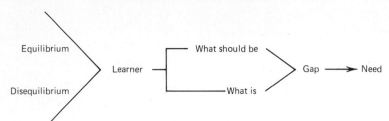

The continuing educator's challenge and responsibility is to have an adequate basis for determining what the present situation is and what it ideally should be. The continuing educator must become aware of and identify the changes that should take place in the learner in order to reach the objectives desired in the educational program. Tyler[1] identified three sources of information helpful in determining need and developing educational objectives. These sources are the potential learners, contemporary society, and the subject specialist or discipline. They can all be related to the individual in clientele analysis. It should be recognized that no single source of information is adequate in itself to provide a basis for wise and comprehensive decisions about educational objectives. Each source has its own part to contribute in providing potential educational objectives. Involving the potential learners as a source for need identification often requires the continuing educator to help the learner develop the skills to recognize her or his own needs.

In many cases, clientele analysis will result in the identification of needs that cannot be satisfied or met through an educational program. A real educational need has various characteristics, as discussed throughout the previous text. An educational need has the capacity to be met by the participation in a learning experience providing required knowledge, attitudes, and/or skills. It is necessary for a desired state or change. An educational need may represent an absence, deficiency, and/or a quest.

Figure 11.2 presents a framework for analysis of a nutritional situation. As was previously indicated, the responsibility of the programmer is to identify and obtain the necessary data or information for the comparison of present situations with some norm also identified through an objective analysis. In this example, the programmer is working with low-income families on their nutritional situation. In determining the present situation, the following factors need to be analyzed: (1) the families' present level of knowledge, attitudes about nutrition, and food preparation skills; (2) nutritional practices followed by the families; (3) economic

[1]Ralph Tyler, *Basic Principles of Curriculum and Instruction,* University of Chicago Press, Chicago, 1974.

status of the families; (4) nutritional characteristics peculiar to their cultural heritage; and (5) their judgments about nutritional practices. These are a few of the factors necessary for an effective understanding of the present situation. This information must be obtained from a variety of sources, by different approaches.

The other information necessary for effective analysis is what the desired situation should be. Evidence about the desirable nutrition for low-income families should come from (1) research findings about nutritional requirements; (2) value judgments of professionals and others; (3) alternatives based on economic status, geographical location, cultural beliefs, and so forth; and (4) opportunities through government programs, legislation, and the like.

The challenge is to compare the present situation with the desired situation using the components derived from the analysis. These judgments should show what causes the present situation so that alternatives for changing it to the desired situation can be recommended. Judgments must also be made about what should be focused on in the educational program. The professional change educator should make these judgments in consultation with the people to be affected by the change.

Figure 11.2   Analysis, Interpretation, Judgment

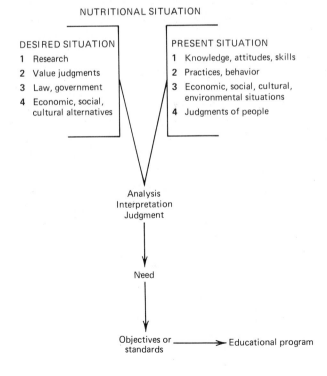

NUTRITIONAL SITUATION

DESIRED SITUATION
1 Research
2 Value judgments
3 Law, government
4 Economic, social,
   cultural alternatives

PRESENT SITUATION
1 Knowledge, attitudes, skills
2 Practices, behavior
3 Economic, social, cultural,
   environmental situations
4 Judgments of people

Analysis
Interpretation
Judgment

Need

Objectives or ————————➤ Educational program
standards

APPROACHES TO FORMAL NEEDS ASSESSMENT

There are several formal approaches that the continuing education programmer can use in the assessment of clientele needs. The approach that is used will depend on such factors as (1) the type of program being developed, (2) the nature of the target clientele to be served, (3) the availability of the learner for involvement, and (4) the resources available to the programmer. Several short descriptions of formal approaches are provided below.

Surveys

The survey or poll is a popular method of determining needs as expressed by the clientele. This procedure is often used where information is to be gathered from many and widely dispersed clients. It provides similar information from respondents that can be tabulated and discussed numerically and can be easily acquired in a systematic way. It can provide various kinds of information related to such things as (1) conditions and situations; (2) opinions, beliefs, attitudes, practices, knowledge, or performance; and (3) resources available to meet needs.

Surveys or polls may be carried out using (1) a questionnaire or (2) an interview schedule. A questionnaire is a set of questions answered by respondents with little or no direct contact with a questioner. They may be mailed out or distributed at a meeting. Interviews are carried out in face-to-face situations or by phone, with a questioner asking the respondent questions.

Steele[2] suggests the following steps in carrying out a survey:

- *Decide if a survey is necessary.* Is the information really needed? What do you need to know? Is the information already available? If not, what is the best way to get it? Would it be more efficient to use a different source, such as an expert, a leader, or other key people?
- *Define the purpose and identify essential information.* Start with the decisions that need to be made. Who will make the decision? What is difficult about making the decisions? How can information help? What information is crucial to that decision? Be sure to get all the information you need and be careful not to collect information that is interesting but not essential.
- *Develop a basic plan.* The list provides a basis from which to develop the survey. Compare the survey questions with the original list to identify gaps and overlap.
- *Look through the respondents' eyes.* If possible, involve respon-

[2]Sara M. Steele, "Developing a Questionnaire—Information Gathering Series," Division of Program and Staff Development, University of Wisconsin-Extension, Madison, 1974.

dents in sponsoring and developing the survey. Be sure the appropriate key power people are aware of the survey. Consider your relationship to the respondents. You not only want information now but also cooperation in the future. Consider whether the respondents can give you the information being asked for.

• *Decide how to get information.* Are interviews or questionnaires most appropriate? Interviews may be desirable if (1) you want descriptive detail, (2) information and instructions are complex, (3) interviewer can determine accuracy of response, (4) respondents cannot or will not use written forms, (5) high response rate is essential. Written questionnaires may be most appropriate if (1) resources are short, (2) many respondents are desired, (3) respondents are cooperative and well educated. Survey questions should be easy to answer, and should (1) have clear instructions, (2) be nonthreatening, (3) be short and concise, (4) have a clear format, (5) be organized in logical manner, and (6) require little writing.

• *Design instrument for accuracy.* This includes making sure questions can be interpreted only one way, avoiding an indication of the type of answer expected, checking for consistency in answers when possible, making questionnaire easy to tabulate, and keeping the survey small.

• *Test and revise.* Have colleagues critically review the questionnaire. Always pretest the questionnaire. Make appropriate changes. Double check to see if it meets the purpose.

• *Prepare the questionnaire.* Develop the message carefully, being sure to keep it short, to indicate confidentiality, to help the respondent feel comfortable and motivated, and to set a deadline for return of the mailed questionnaire.

• *Plan for use of results.* Know before you get the information how it will be analyzed so appropriate statistical or other analysis can be used. Make sure adequate resources are available to follow through.

While surveys can be valuable for needs assessment, it should be kept in mind that an opinion expressed on a survey is only an opinion at one moment in time. It is not necessarily a commitment to act. Many people may express a positive attitude about a general issue but may be opposed to a particular plan. Questions should be as specific as possible.

Critical Incident Approach

This technique is generally used to assess needs as a basis for developing educational programs for clientele that have a specific job or profession. For example, Goyen[3] investigated the critical components of the work environment of County Extension Youth Agents in fourteen states to establish a clear definition of the job of a youth agent. Flanagan describes this technique as follows:

---

[3]Loren F. Goyen, "Critical Components of the Work Environment of County Extension Youth Agents," Ph.D. dissertation, University of Wisconsin–Madison, 1968.

The critical incident technique, rather than collecting opinions, hunches and estimates, obtains a record of specific behaviors from those in the best position to make the necessary observations and evaluations. The collection and tabulation of these observations make it possible to formulate the critical requirements of an activity. A list of critical behaviors provides a sound basis for making inferences as to requirements in terms of aptitudes, training, and other characteristics.[4]

Keregero lists the following basic steps necessary for carrying out needs assessment using the critical incidents technique:

1 Determining the population to be studied, i.e., the particular job and its location
2 Selecting the observer group
3 Collecting an adequate and representative sample of critical incidents
4 Examining all incidents and rejecting those not meeting specified criteria
5 Determining a frame of reference for categorizing behavior
6 Isolating the critical behaviors contained in the critical incidents
7 Placing incidents with similar behaviors into broad categories
8 Writing a descriptive title for each broad category of related behaviors
9 Subcategorizing groups of behaviors within the original broad categories, writing subtitles, and restudying and recategorizing behaviors as required
10 Having an independent analyst make consistency checks by categorizing random samples of incidents.
11 Determining and writing critical requirements based on the final grouping of critical behaviors
12 Determining the relationship between the critical incidents and control variables[5]

The advantages of this technique are that it provides specific data rather than mere impressions and opinions and provides a relatively precise and comprehensive definition of effectiveness on a job in terms of the behavior implied. The technique also has several possible limitations, including:

1 The observer group that selects the critical incidents is subject to such limitations as errors in recalling incidents; different ecological, geographical, and seasonal conditions; different judgments on whether an in-

[4]John C. Flanagan, "The Critical Incident Technique," *Psychological Bulletin,* vol. 51, no. 4, 1954, p. 355.
[5]Keregero Keregero, unpublished Master's thesis, University of Wisconsin–Madison, 1977.

cident led to effective perceptions. This suggests that different critical incidents might be obtained under different circumstances and/or using different observers.

2   Categorization and classification of critical behaviors proceed inductively. The procedures tend to be more subjective than objective and could greatly affect the validity and reliability of the data despite the use of consistency checks.

3   Not all behaviors are likely to be identified, and not all are easily attributable to specific skills, concepts, or values.

The data used in the critical incident technique can be obtained by utilizing several procedures, including (1) individual interviews of observers; (2) group interviews (including orientation and briefing followed by reporting of critical incidents in writing); and (3) mailed questionnaires.

Individual Profile

The individual profile is a procedure used to individually determine and record needs. Many different assessment materials are available to various professions and in various subjects or content areas. An excellent example of the individual profile was developed by the Wisconsin Department of Post Graduate Medical Education. Sivertson et al. describe the profile as follows:

> Planning for continuing medical education of physicians involves many variables. The Individual Physician Profile is one method bringing these variables into focus. Problems patients bring to a physician are codified; the physician is tested on those problems; and, with additional personal information, consultation leads to a tailor-made educational program. To expedite this method, it was necessary to develop computerized techniques for storage and retrieval of practice, data relevant test questions, and learning resources. The Individual Physician Profile permits better investment of a busy physician's time and energy for education to meet the needs of his practice. It points to the need for a new arena in continuing medical education, an educational consulting service (or consultant) for the physician.[6]

This individual-profile approach to need analysis is very similar to approaches described as task analysis or job analysis.

Competency Analysis

Competency-based approaches to need analysis are often carried out as a basis for designing continuing education programs for professionals. This approach uses information from experts in the field to identify the desir-

---

[6]Sigurd E. Sivertson et al., "Individual Physician Profile: Continuing Education Related to Medical Practice," *Journal of Medical Education,* vol. 48, November 1973, p. 1006.

able or minimum competency that professionals should possess. The target clientele are then tested to determine their level of competency. The difference between what experts identify as necessary and the determined level of competency is the basis for selecting content and developing an instructional design.[7]

INFORMAL ASSESSMENT METHODS

The approaches to analysis previously discussed are all rather formal and require considerable planning time and resources. While these approaches provide a firm foundation for programming, there are often situations where such lengthy and resource-consuming approaches are impossible. An effective continuing education programmer is constantly evaluating and assessing needs of the clientele as part of her or his ongoing responsibilities. Other professionals and clients also carry on needs assessment in their informal day-to-day contacts with situations and people. These informal assessments are valid and valuable inputs to program situation analysis and play an important role in ongoing needs analysis. Two informal assessment techniques will be discussed.

Informal Conversations

As the continuing education programmer goes about daily activities, numerous contacts are made with clients and colleagues. Such contacts can provide inputs regarding needs. Needs identified in such a way can be clarified and specified by talking to specific people such as community leaders and other involved individuals. The educator or others may locate themselves at "listening posts" in a community (taverns, churches, stores, etc.) where people congregate and discuss issues and problems. Advisory committees are often used for the same purpose.

More deliberate actions can also contribute to informal needs assessment. For example, postmeeting reactions from participants, suggestion boxes, and questions raised at meetings are attempts to elicit reactions that can reflect needs.

Unobtrusive Measures

Webb et al.[8] suggest that there are considerable data available that are not obtained by interview or questionnaire techniques. Such data can be valuable in needs assessment. Since such data can be from almost any observ-

---

[7]For a model and discussion of needs assessment directed toward professional competence, see: Carl Lindsay, James Morrison, and E. James Kelley, "Professional Obsolescence: Implications for Continuing Professional Education," *Adult Education*, vol. XXV, no. 1, 1974, pp. 3–22.

[8]E. J. Webb et al., *Unobtrusive Measures*, Rand McNally & Company, Skokie, Ill., 1966.

able source, it is impossible to spell out how to go about collecting the information. Perhaps the best way to explain this approach is to list a number of unobtrusive measures suggested by Webb et al. They group such measures into three categories: (1) physical traces, (2) archives, and (3) observations.

I Physical traces surveying past behavior
A Paths worn across lawns suggest a need for a sidewalk.
B Tiles worn in front of a check display at a museum suggest its popularity.
C Wear on library books suggests interest in certain topics.
D Polluted streams suggest a need for environmental programs.
II Archives
A The city or county budget that shows no money spent on parks may indicate a need.
B The record of the number of people who voted in the last election may indicate lack of interest or lack of good candidates.
C Birth records may indicate the need to plan for new schools and other facilities.
III Observation
A Clustering of blacks and whites may indicate a need for developing better relationships.
B Observing looks of boredom, fatigue, etc., may indicate a need for recreational activities.

While these examples may not always be relevant to continuing education programming, they do point out the possibility of using such measures as indicators of need. They can be especially useful where questionnaires or interviews are inappropriate or impossible.

SUMMARY

In this chapter several different approaches to needs assessment and analysis have been identified. Each approach has strengths and weaknesses. The programming situation should have an influence on the approach utilized. A framework was suggested for analyzing, interpreting and judging potential needs.

DISCUSSION QUESTIONS

1 Which of the formal approaches to needs assessment and analysis would be most appropriate for the following situations:
a Farmers in a farm organization
b Welfare families in low-income communities
c Lawyers in a large urban center

    d Teachers in a school district
    e Families in a small rural community
2 How is needs analysis different when the target clientele are "poor" people?
3 Describe a formal clientele analysis approach that you have used. Why was it effective or ineffective?
4 What informal approach have you used and found worthwhile?
5 How would you describe the role of the programmer in clientele analysis?

Chapter 12

Approaches to Community Analysis

The features of today's community life present much less of a common pattern than those of some years ago. Analysis and planning for balanced and desirable development cannot adequately be done without an open system of reciprocity. Such a system is one in which all people are allowed to exert their influence to the fullest. In Chapter 10, we suggested that the social system framework was a useful approach to obtaining a general understanding of a community. This would involve an analysis of the various subsystems that are functioning within the overall system. The major difficulty in achieving this, however, involves the relationship of one dimension, or subsystem, with another. The tremendous amount of autonomy and the corresponding lack of reciprocity between subsystems may be adequate only for a limited range of activities. Since planning often entails varied implications in different parts of the system, the importance of establishing this link between subsystems cannot be overemphasized.

THE COMMUNITY FRAMEWORK

Before identifying and discussing the major elements for analysis in a community, it should be emphasized that all such elements operate within an environment that reflects the people's values and standards. The value dimension is reflected in the criteria or standards used in making decisions about goals. For example, such economic data as employment statistics might reflect the need for an industrial park in a community. The criteria or standards by which a community would make decisions might include a strong feeling about preserving the environment and a "no-growth" variable. In such a situation this economic goal would be given low priority. The value-oriented approach to decision making is causal or functional when the relationships are directly interdependent and act upon the whole community.

Situational analysis is concerned not only with the conscious selection of goals but also with the conscious selection among approaches to achieve those goals. The value question in planning arises simply because people have to choose among alternatives.

Facts and other background information always involve value judgments, so rational decisions among alternative courses of action cannot be based on consideration of "facts" alone. Particularly in the economic dimension, the tendency has been to treat economic variables as impersonal and self-explanatory while ignoring or deemphasizing the other dimensions, since they are assumed to involve only personal values that conflict with the "factual situation."

But is not efficiency a value judgment? And according to what standards should cultural bonds be weakened to promote efficiency? Another interesting question is whether "acceptance of innovations" is strictly economic. Or can "changes in the products grown" be considered strictly economic? Much of the failure of planning in the past may be traced to a lack of explicit judgment as a logical justification for social action. Holistic planning for a community requires that we make explicit the value premises from which our goals derive and that we formulate our plans to consider their effect on the whole array of values and institutions.

Since the various aspects of life in a community are so interdependent, we can inflict much harm by failing to carefully analyze and anticipate the consequences of our actions on the whole community. Insofar as planning aims to accomplish a desirable state of affairs in a community, the planning activity must seek to create conditions for the people themselves to express their thoughts, grow, and develop in achieving their goals. When a person or a community perceives a problem and the possibility of solving it, this recognition sets in motion the actions that lead to the desired changes. The concrete forms such changes may take are determined by those factors that make up environmental conditions, as well as those that have shaped the character and values of the participants. Holistic planning for a community recognizes that explanations, as well as predictions of such changes, can be adequately undertaken only with full awareness of these varied influences.

The following is an interpretation of the major elements in a community:

1 *The cultural elements.* The body of culture is the environment from which individuals learn about the world around them. Behavior, thought, and character are greatly influenced by this learning. The effects of culture on individuals are seen through such factors as primary groups, which help the individuals give meaning to their environment; language, which is the vehicle for communication with, and interpretation of the environment; and roles and statuses that define performances and expectations in the various groups constituting the community. A culture influences the value judgments of all its members. Judgments are based upon value structures that have evolved out of the experiences of the individuals and groups concerned. Responding to these values, whether consciously or unconsciously, individuals constantly modify and create the cultural situations within which they live.

2 *The social elements.* Examining the composition of groups and group life reveals many important dynamics of social behavior. The composition of a population, its distribution, its social classes, and many other characteristics become important in identifying community needs and problems. The social processes of interaction and communication play a vital role in influencing how people relate to each other and perceive the problems and needs of their community. Such elements as conformity to group norms are becoming more and more important in understanding resistance to change. The concept of social change itself includes such elements as continuity, leadership, and individuals that constantly interact to shape the course of events in any social action program.

3 *The psychological elements.* A group is constituted of its individual members. Every individual is unique and different from every other individual. Individuals are moved in varying degrees not only by cognitions but equally by emotions as they respond to situations in their private or public lives. Such factors as motivation, need, and self-concept have a tremendous bearing on the individual's actions. Perceptions and attitudes help us understand and explain the implications of programs for the total life of the individual.

4 *The economic elements.* Analyzing economic factors as they affect a certain course of action becomes essential, not only in terms of the means for realizing change, but also in terms of their effects on the total conditions in the community. Elements of production and service enter into every phase of planning for a community's development. Social and political institutions as well as people's values and attitudes have played major roles in shaping the economic life of every community.

5 *The political elements.* The influence of politics in programs of change is very evident when we see how the value premises of many political groups are reflected in change programs and enacted into law. We must understand that planning is directly influenced by the power structure of the community if we are to understand the many impediments to change. Decision making, management, and the legal system also have direct influence on the way programs are planned and their goals specified.

6 *The environmental elements.* All planning is carried out within a physical environment. The physical elements include not only such factors as land and space but also the environment's technological factors, such as mechanization. Aesthetic considerations are always involved when people plan their future environment. With the adverse effects of technology, more and more attention has been directed toward ecological balance and preservation of resources. Such problems as housing, health, and transportation also reflect the important role of environment in satisfying the needs of each community.

Figure 12.1 illustrates how this framework can be superimposed on the social system and used as the basis for analyzing each subsystem. In this example, all farmers and agribusiness professionals in a geographical area are viewed as a social system. This broad clientele group can be used as the basis for situational analysis, using the economic, social, cultural, psychological, political, and environmental elements of the framework. Examples are given in Figure 12.1. This illustration emphasizes the need to analyze each subsystem in terms of all the elements—economic, social, cultural, psychological, political, and environmental—since changes in any one element might affect the functioning of the whole system. Thus, problems may not simply be identified as "social problems" or "economic problems," except for very limited purposes. Likewise, solutions

Figure 12.1   Elements for Situational Analysis

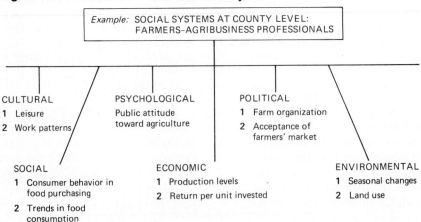

Figure 12.2 Potential Change Situations

Environmental changes	Social-psychological changes
Reducing water pollution	Reducing school dropouts
Rezoning land	Reducing bias against minority groups
Building recreational facilities	Decreasing unemployment
Cleaning up and beautifying the land-scape	Improving parent-child relationships
Increasing the comfort and attractive-ness of homes	Developing leadership potential for youth
	Voting in every election

Economic changes	Political changes
Suiting fertilizer application to soil	Increasing the number of people voting
Using credit wisely	People taking advantage of government programs
Changing a cost-accounting procedure	
Attracting new industry	

Cultural changes
Recreational opportunities
Knowledge of minority group heritage

to problems should not be expected from one specialist or one knowledge base. Solutions must be integrated into the community if they are to be accepted and useful. There are many examples of outside specialists offering viable solutions, but they were unacceptable because they were from outside the system and represented only one element of the system.

If a geographical area, such as a county or city, is identified as a social system, Figure 12.2 illustrates the kinds of potential change situations that might be studied.

Since the features of today's community life present much less of a common pattern than those of some years ago, centralized planning by technicians becomes futile. Instead, we must now identify and analyze the system's elements and their interrelationships as they affect the total community and modify them according to the people's projections and expectations. We must plan in light of the relationships and consequences that will occur either directly or indirectly as outcomes of our actions. Thus, our most urgent need is not for a master plan for communities but for projected views and plans that are continually modified and updated. These views must be obtained from the people and the plans developed by people.

THE PLANNING FRAMEWORK

Planning for balanced and desirable change cannot adequately be done without an open system of reciprocity. Such a system is one in which all people are allowed to exert their influence to the fullest.

The planning activity begins with certain value assumptions and proceeds through analyzing the system, setting goals, and selecting means to achieve those goals. The activity entails certain consequences. These may be planned consequences that follow a conscious and rational course of action even though they may have been modified throughout the process; or they may be unplanned consequences in that there is little relationship between two or more sequences, a lack of reciprocity between one element and another that results in inconsistent or even incompatible patterns of change.

The framework suggested in Figure 12.3 stresses the importance of seeing things in a total perception and helps bring together the elements discussed above.

Change comes about as a consequence of certain actions taken by individuals and groups. Where one planned course of action is clearly motivated by economic values, another course is motivated primarily by social values, customs, politics, and so forth. In each case, certain values thought to be desirable by one group or another are brought to the fore. In terms of planning, the patterns of change that will emerge represent the interplay of all the values as they influence and balance each other.

In Figure 12.3, three planned action sequences are charted to illustrate this process of interplay leading to the various consequences (though there may well be more than three groupings making an input into any phase of the planning process). Different patterns of action result from the interplay of forces that tend to modify original positions. Such modifica-

Figure 12.3   Interactions in Planning

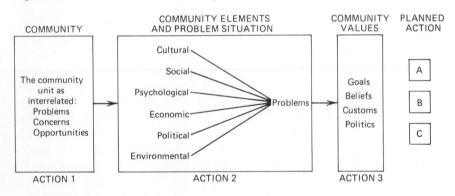

- *Action 1.* The community as a unit and with its people will interact on the problems, concerns, and opportunities.
- *Action 2.* The various elements in the community are interacting with the problem situation and the alternative solutions.
- *Action 3.* The alternative solutions are screened and interact with the goals, beliefs, customs, and politics of the community and its people. The desired planned action results.

tions may occur at each phase of the planning process. Each action sequence produces consequences that affect the total pattern of change in the system. In Figure 12.3, points A, B, and C represent the points of equilibrium after all elements have exerted their influence. The different points represent different levels of interdependency and therefore lead to different consequences. This kind of broadened perspective suggests the need for more research in the area of interrelationships among various elements in the system and the further need to identify relevant value dimensions for more balanced community planning.

SUMMARY

There is the need for a broad perspective in analyzing the problems and needs of people in a community. This chapter focused on an integrated approach through which the economic, psychological, social, cultural, political, and environmental elements can be considered in the total analysis process.

DISCUSSION QUESTIONS

1 What dimensions of the community would you include in your framework for analysis and decisions on program efforts?
2 Describe an experience you had in analyzing the problems of a community.
3 Do you feel that the analysis of a community will lead to relevant programs? Why or why not?
4 Compare differences and similarities in community and clientele analysis.
5 What people in a community should be involved in community analysis?

Chapter 13

A Framework for Establishing Priorities

Continuing educators usually face the dilemma of too many problems to work on, too much content to teach, and too many clientele groups to reach with the time and resources available. So, we must make decisions about program priorities. Priority setting is a continuous process of decision making that takes place during all phases of programming including delineating needs, specifying goals, identifying target audiences, defining available resources, and determining necessary actions.

There are several major difficulties in making decisions about program priorities.

First, priority setting is not an individual nor even a group decision-making process, but rather a multigroup decision-making process. The challenge for the programmer is to use decisions from many individuals and groups in the final decisions about program priorities. For example, many different individuals and groups are involved in deciding on a broad-based community program provided through Extension.

Second, group decision making is very difficult. Boyle[1] suggests that

---

[1]Patrick G. Boyle, *The Program Planning Process with Emphasis on Extension*, NAECAS, Publication no. 24, University of Wisconsin–Madison, 1965.

rational decisions by groups in program development are difficult. They are difficult because the group characteristics of conformity, cohesiveness, and participation introduce emotional involvement among the group members and may be influential in the ultimate decisions reached by the group. Thus, a totally rational outcome can become the ideal to work toward rather than the assumption around which group decision-making efforts are organized.

Third, it is often very difficult to obtain the necessary data to clearly identify alternatives for decision making. Also, we sometimes lack the time and skill to effectively analyze and interpret data for use in decisions.

Fourth, in making decisions about program priorities, several categories of criteria must be used as the standards or bases for decisions. Thus, the real challenge is to precisely identify the criteria and then interrelate them in decision making.

THE PRIORITY-SETTING SITUATION

As suggested earlier, the situation in which priorities are made is very complex, involving many sources of influence, information, criteria alternatives, resources, and cooperation. Following are six broad categories that provide the basis for specific criteria and evidence for the decision-making process.

1 Society-Community

The larger society, with its institutions, governmental units, pressure groups, trends, goals, and values, provides a broad framework within which programming must be carried out. Also to be considered is the specific community, with its economic, social, environmental, and cultural needs and desires; its formal and informal power and social structures; the linkages among its various organizations; its potential for change based on past traditions and values. This category provides the most general level of inputs as we make decisions about priorities.

2 Clientele

Continuing education has a long tradition of basing programs on clientele needs. We all believe in and support this tradition. However, the question is: What clientele and what clientele needs? We need to look at clientele in terms of subgroups within a community. For example, farmers, senior citizens, low-income families, people in business, and neighborhoods are specific clientele groups with various needs, resources, and priorities. They can provide more direct information about priorities, but will often be in conflict with one another. In some cases, the program budget will determine the clientele.

3 Politics

Programming decisions are made within political structures. We recognize the influence of government at the town, county, state, and federal levels in establishing program priorities. The perceptions of governmental units should be utilized in our decision-making process. However, it is important that the political category does not become such a constraining force that it overbalances all the other categories. There are times when program decisions are not politically attractive, but we need to take risks and accept responsibility for influencing the political structure at various levels so that more rational decisions can be made. However, the question "Is it politically feasible?" is always relevant.

4 Organization

Organizational statements of philosophy and mission provide insights to many questions about priorities for programs and clientele. For example: Does the organization support innovations? What is the organization's programming position with such controversial issues as family planning? What kinds of programs does the organization reward? How much flexibility and personal input does the individual staff member have? What is the organization's position on programming with and for institutions and agencies that affect families versus programming with individuals or groups of individuals? Many other questions like these are addressed through organizational statements of missions and philosophy. They are important as criteria for decision making about program priorities, and they are important in conflict situations within the organization that cause frustrations, inhibit objectivity, and stifle innovation in programming.

5 Resources

Many questions about resources must be answered in setting priorities: Do we have the quality and quantity of resources necessary to affect change through a program? Are they the right kinds of resources? Are there adequate financial resources? Are we employing new personnel to coincide with changing program priorities?

It is recognized that the most important resources are the available subject matter expertise and teaching skills and that these quite frequently need updating and redirection. Studies show that a community agent will set priorities based on the kind and quality of specialist assistance available.

We often spread our resources so thin that we do not have a major impact on a problem. We often use a Band-Aid instead of major surgery. Questions about availability of a variety of resources—budget, personnel, materials, staff assistance, and so forth—become extremely important criteria.

6 Personnel

We are interested in helping staff members see themselves as educational leaders. If we support this concept, provisions for use of personal value and perceptions must be allowed in the decision-making process. Continuing educators are individual human beings with their own experiences, education, personalities, value systems, and perceptions about what is important and what should be done. Their different philosophies of education, whether they are self-directed or other-directed, how they feel about clientele groups, how they view their roles as educators or technicians, are all important considerations. The challenge is to provide opportunities in our programming structure and staffing patterns so that individual values and beliefs can become another important influence on decisions about programming.

IDENTIFYING CRITERIA FOR SELECTING PRIORITIES

The critical step in priority setting is establishing the criteria upon which decisions will be made. How do we decide which criteria are important? Ultimately the programmer must make the decision, but it will be based on inputs from the six sources of influence that were just presented. It is important to utilize these sources so that the final criteria selected reflect a balanced set that will be acceptable, considering each source. For example, a client group might want a program that is also a high priority for the programmer. However, if the programmer's organization does not see that concern fitting in with its philosophy or goals, the program will be thwarted. Or suppose the programmer, client group, and organization set criteria that are politically unfeasible within the community. Such an oversight would result in a blockage of the program even though it is a high priority for several categories. These examples point out the critical nature of considering all aspects in setting priorities.

Several ideas about the six categories may help further clarify their use in establishing criteria for priority setting.

First, the interrrelationship of the categories. For example, the political feasibilities must be considered along with personal desires and needs of clientele, in making a specific decision about programming with a low-income group. Figure 13.1 illustrates this idea.

Second, these categories can be seen as constraining and driving forces interacting against each other in the decision-making process. Figure 13.2 shows how driving forces within a community, personal feelings, and clientele needs are restrained by criteria related to resources, organizational, and political needs.

The third way of using these categories is as screens, at which point a decision may be made to go or not to go with a program because of a

Figure 13.1   Interrelationships of Categories for Priority Setting

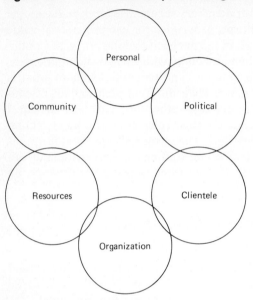

judgment based on criteria within one of the categories. Figure 13.3 illustrates this idea.

PRIORITY-SETTING FRAMEWORK

Forest and Mulcahy[2] suggest six steps for priority setting. Each step involves decisions on what needs to be done and an order of what should be accomplished first to get results. The steps they suggest are:

[2]Laverne Forest and Sheila Mulcahy, *First Things First: A Handbook of Priority-Setting in Extension,* Division of Program and Staff Development, University of Wisconsin-Extension, Madison, 1976.

Figure 13.2   Interaction of Driving and Constraining Forces in Priority Setting

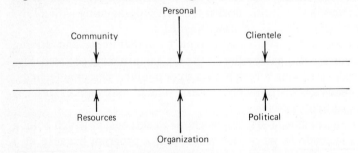

Figure 13.3   Screening the Priorities

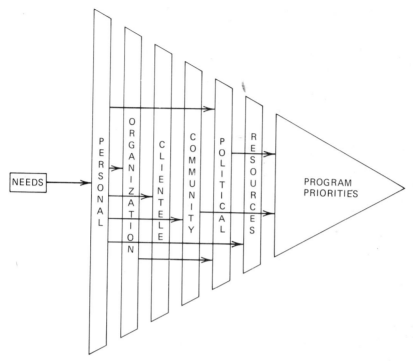

1 Understanding the priority-setting situation
2 Identifying the possible priorities
3 Identifying criteria for selecting priorities
4 Determining the relative importance of priorities
5 Reflecting on priorities: consequences and timing
6 Commitment to action on priorities

A community resource development agent's experience in programming illustrates the above process. She described working with a planning
group concerned with lack of total community commitment to the city's
problems. Most concerns were dealt with by splinter groups. The committee was concerned about providing an educational forum for the community. But, as she stated, first the group needed to understand their role
and set priorities before they could even deal with the complex situation.

Through various sources (surveys, community government, newspa-
per articles, and the like) the committee members recognized and described numerous problems. At the beginning each one wanted to have
their idea dealt with in a program. They listed drug problems, divorce

rate, teen-age pregnancies, child abuse, teen-age crime, misuse of property, heart attacks and other medical problems, among others. Realizing that they needed to focus their efforts, questions were raised to help direct them. What problem was mentioned most frequently by local citizens? Could they consider a larger category that encompassed several of the problems listed? What resources could they organize and obtain that might help?

After discussion of various criteria, they decided that several alternative priorities could be grouped under "stress on the family." A structure was established to deal with social, ethical, and legal concerns. It was decided that other alternatives listed at the beginning, such as medical problems, were beyond the program's scope.

The committee proceeded to ask questions on timing: What would they achieve? Who would be most dynamic in helping the community as a whole focus on the priority set? Has needed information been included? After decisions on program design, action was taken in two phases. One phase was an awareness, understanding phase. The second phase was programming that would be over a more extended time and include various activities.

In this chapter, the identification of criteria for priority setting has been focused upon. Steps 1, 2, and 4 have also been discussed in several other chapters in this text.

Priorities are what is important or valuable at the present time. Programming situations often have a number of priorities at any given time, so it is necessary to decide which priorities are most important. Although scientific facts can help us decide on priorities, the personal values of the programmer and others involved in programming determine their relative importance. Thus, conclusions about priorities are based on certain human assumptions. Forest and Mulcahy[3] also suggest that we will need more information about two things:

- *The probability of the priority alternative actually happening, if selected.* Is the alternative acceptable to people with the most influence on our jobs? Are barriers, people, lack of time or interest, conflicts with other ongoing programs, or lack of resources likely to prevent it, even if it is very important?
- *The consequences of the priority alternative, if selected.* We need to know what will happen to the people we work with, to ourselves, and to the community if we choose a particular priority. On the other hand, what will happen if other possibilities receive higher priority? Will neglecting a possibility bring dire consequences in the future? Answers to these questions are not easy to obtain. The programmer will have to rely on personal judgment along with facts and inputs from others involved.

[3]Ibid., p. 21.

Obtaining information as a basis for making decisions on priorities is not always easy. A number of appropriate methods and techniques discussed earlier in Chapter 10 are also applicable for priority setting. Methods such as the critical incident, surveys, advisory committees, and group techniques, such as brainstorming, nominal group techniques, and discussion, are all appropriate for obtaining information and ideas relevant for priority setting.

Such techniques are important not only for information but also for legitimization and support of the priorities arrived at. It is essential for the programmer to involve the people and groups that can influence the effectiveness of the program. If they have input into the priority-setting process, their support is much more likely.

REFLECTING ON
THE CONSEQUENCES AND TIMING OF PRIORITIES

Once criteria and priorities have been examined, it is important to explore the future consequences of the decisions. Two aspects must be explored according to Forest and Mulcahy: (1) What must be done first? and (2) How much time should be blocked out during the upcoming week, month, or year to get the job done adequately? They suggest the following examples:[4]

1 Readiness of people (knowledge, attitudes, enthusiasm)
2 Calendars and accessibility of backup resources
3 Interrelationship with other programs at some time or other
4 What part of the problem needs to be solved first
5 The complexity of the problem and how much time it needs
6 Potential payoff and future consequences of undertaking or neglecting a priority
7 What other activities are needed to precede the major activity

Once time has been allotted to the priorities, the timing and sequence of activities must be considered in order to achieve the priorities. One way of determining sequence and timing is to work backward from the perceived goal.

COMMITMENT TO ACTION ON PRIORITIES

An idea outlined by Forest and Mulcahy[5] includes several critical concepts related to committing ourselves on the priorities identified:

[4]Ibid., pp. 37–38.
[5]Ibid., pp. 41–43.

1 *Commitment.* The programmer must be committed to the priority goals set. Without this commitment the program is unlikely to succeed.

2 *Communication.* The programmer must make clear her or his priority commitments to others who have an interest in the program or in other programs. A public statement about goals is a sign of commitment.

3 *Resources.* One way of getting commitment to priority goals is to get resources allocated to them. These might include money, resource people, meeting places, schedules of events, and the like.

4 *Action.* Actions taken in connection with a priority item suggest a commitment to that priority. The involvement of other people in the priority program, arrangements for facilities, and resource people and others are all actions that indicate commitment to priority goals.

5 *Flexibility.* Flexibility is an important concept, especially for creating priorities for programs built on problems in need. Emergency situations often arise that need immediate attention. The programmer must be able to respond to these needs if they are within the scope of her or his mission and that of the institution. Some time must always be left in a schedule for such emergencies. Some priority needs cannot be seen or do not exist at the time major program priorities are being set. Flexibility allows for unexpected priorities.

SUMMARY

This chapter emphasized the need for a systematic approach to priority setting. The materials developed by Forest and Mulcahy are excellent and can be used in any programming situation. The basis for establishing criteria was focused on. Six general categories were suggested as being relevant in the decision-making process.

DISCUSSION QUESTIONS

1 Describe your framework for analysis and decisions on program priorities. What criteria and why?
2 Personal values of the professional educator are more important than the philosophy and mission of the organization in establishing priorities for programs. Agree or disagree and why?
3 Describe a conflict that you may have experienced in priority setting.
4 Why is setting program priorities difficult?
5 Discuss the relative importance of each criterion suggested for priority setting.

Section V

Providing Learning Opportunities

The most widely accepted definition of learning is acquiring new patterns of behavior through experience. In this definition, behavior includes ways of thinking and feeling as well as of acting. If the learner obtains satisfaction from a new pattern of behavior, and if the learner continues to derive satisfaction from it, practice will continue until it becomes part of her or his repertoire of behavior. Then, we say, learning has taken place.

This view of learning is a useful guide for the programmer in planning educational opportunities. In this approach, the programmer must identify situations that are available for the students to carry on the desired behavior, and that they are impelled to try it. Ample opportunity must also be provided for the students to practice until the new behavior becomes part of their normal repertoire.

Chapter 14 illustrates the differences between program and instructional designs. In Chapter 15, the concept of educational objectives is presented and illustrated. Planning effective learning experiences are focused on in Chapter 16.

Program Development
and Instructional Design

Program development is an effort to affect the economic, social, environmental, and cultural health of a community. It is a deliberate series of acts and decisions through which representatives of the people are involved with professional staff to plan an educational program that will contribute to improving the community and its people. This chapter will attempt to illustrate the differences in program development and instructional design. In the program development process outlined in Chapter 4, we have included phases related to the design of instruction. Obviously we are not using program development and instructional design synonymously. Our interpretation is that instructional design is a part of every effective program development process. Design of instruction is planning the interactions between the learner and the instructor and resource materials. Assume the other phases in a program development process are completed and that they resulted in the decision to have a three-day workshop. The answer to the question of what will be done at the workshop is instructional design.

In implementing a program, whether it is for two days or spread out over two years, the programmer and other instructors must design what they are going to teach in the various learning opportunities. The opportunity may be a two-day workshop, a three-hour meeting, a two-week institute, or a fifteen-minute radio program. In each case, the programmer must face key decisions about content, methods, and resources.

In order to illustrate the relationship between program development and instructional design, we present a format for a major program. Included as part of the major program is a format for the design of specific instructional activities. These formats are illustrated with a program in family financial affairs, appropriate for a small rural county or a specific community in a larger populated area.

BUILDING IMPACT THROUGH A MAJOR PROGRAM

A major educational program is an effort to structure numerous and varied educational opportunities to help people better their lives by helping them to change their present knowledge, skills, attitudes, or behavior. A major program is not just an isolated workshop or institute or course; it is not just a smattering of educational offerings presented cafeteria-style; it is not just ad hoc responses to the continuous bombardment of urgent requests and clamorous needs. Rather, it is a total concentrated effort initiated by the professional programmer to deal with one major problem that needs such attention. A major educational program has a specific and major focus. It is developmental in nature and requires a series of specific decisions as the major program emerges and develops over a period of time. Although the development of the program proceeds in a systematic manner, each phase in its development depends on the others. With the key problem or major focus as a guide, one immediate problem may lead to another, one decision becomes another decision, one action creates other action, and so on. Also, a major program demands an interdisciplinary approach and intensive staff effort by the professional, by other staff members, and appropriate resource persons who are chosen for involvement, or who choose to involve themselves in the major program.

In short, the lives of people cannot be bettered overnight nor can they be significantly changed in a two-hour meeting or a half-day institute. Such ultimate goals can only be attained when programming efforts are focused on a major problem or need. A major program needs time and the intensive efforts not only of the programmer but also of a variety of resource persons. A major program is hard work, but it usually has guaranteed impact on the life of the clientele group.

Figure 14.1 identifies nine phases for developing and carrying out a major program. Each phase requires specific actions by the programmer. In phase 6, instructional design is developed or planned, to be imple-

Figure 14.1   Phases for a Major Program

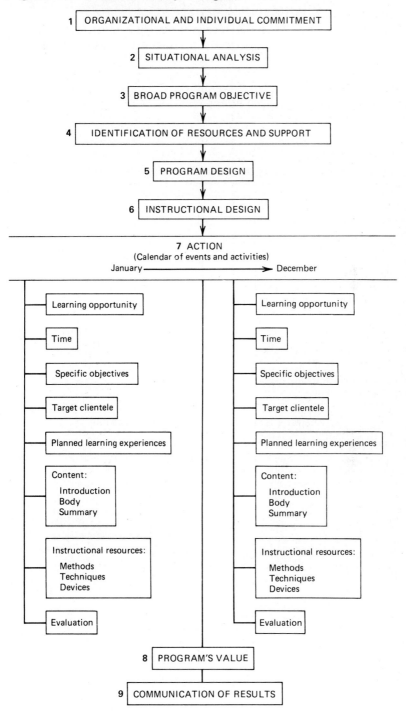

1 ORGANIZATIONAL AND INDIVIDUAL COMMITMENT

2 SITUATIONAL ANALYSIS

3 BROAD PROGRAM OBJECTIVE

4 IDENTIFICATION OF RESOURCES AND SUPPORT

5 PROGRAM DESIGN

6 INSTRUCTIONAL DESIGN

7 ACTION
(Calendar of events and activities)
January ⟶ December

Learning opportunity

Time

Specific objectives

Target clientele

Planned learning experiences

Content:
  Introduction
  Body
  Summary

Instructional resources:
  Methods
  Techniques
  Devices

Evaluation

Learning opportunity

Time

Specific objectives

Target clientele

Planned learning experiences

Content:
  Introduction
  Body
  Summary

Instructional resources:
  Methods
  Techniques
  Devices

Evaluation

8 PROGRAM'S VALUE

9 COMMUNICATION OF RESULTS

mented in phase 7 by action. The program design is illustrated in Figure 14.2, where a program in family financial affairs is used as the case example. Figure 14.3 outlines a specific instructional plan for the case example.

Figure 14.2 Phases of a Major Program
Case Example: Family Financial Affairs

Suggested phases	Example of family financial management
1 Establish organizational and individual commitment.	
• The organization's philosophy and procedures for program development should influence each professional's behavior on the job. They also affect the role and involvement of people in your programs. The organizational philosophy and procedures become the framework within which specific actions will take place. Before developing a major program, understand your role and responsibilities, the role of local persons involved in your programs, the organization's program focus, and the relationships with other agencies, groups, and institutions.	• A statement from the annual program or budget will reveal the organizational commitment: "Programs to help 1500 families develop more effective situations regarding family financial affairs."
2 Analyze the situation of community and clients.	
• Start with some basic information about the people and community. This situational analysis will reveal the need for the program, the potential barriers and sources of support, and your own ability to handle it.	• Present inflationary trends make the need for planning family financial security extremely important. • In last year's program, emphasis was given to wise use of credit, money management, and record keeping. Evidence was obtained at various meetings that there is a lack of understanding by people of all facets of financial security including investments, social security, insurance, plans for property transfer, and wills; and lack of communication among family members about the money facets of the family business relating to financial security. • A study of older families showed little understanding of, and planning for, financial security, especially of property transfer, health insurance, and emergencies.

Figure 14.2 *(Continued)*

Suggested phases	Example of family financial management
	• Considerable interest in wills, property transfer, and insurance was expressed in a statewide study. • The State and County Bar Associations estimate that only 3 percent of the families have wills and half of those are outdated. Few families have property-transfer plans. • There are only ten known father-son written agreements among farm families in the county. • Fifty percent of the families with children have no life insurance and few farm families have adequate liability, property, and health insurance. • Less than 1 percent of the families store their important records in a safe-deposit box and a survey by the Bar Association shows that in 90 percent of the families, the location of records and the amount of insurance is not known by all members of the family.

3   Identify broad program objectives.

• State the expected results from your program: What will be changed or improved in the economic, social, cultural, or environmental situation and what evidence will help you identify those results? Also consider the expected impact of each objective on different types and numbers of people affected by the problem. More specific objectives will come in the program design and instructional plan phases.	• Families in county to have a will. • All farms and businesses to have plan for businesslike transfer of property. • Families to have adequate insurance. • Families to keep financial assets in safe place known to family members.

4   Determine needed resources and support.

• Major programs usually need resources (people, time, money, materials) and support from several professionals, citizen leaders, and other agencies and groups. Find out what resources you will need to carry out your program; make sure they will be available when you need them.	• Three professional staffs are available to work on program. • $9500 is available for program. • Instructional materials, such as slide-tapes, transparancies, and bulletins, are needed. • Promotional fliers are needed.

Figure 14.2 *(Continued)*

Suggested phases	Example of family financial management
Communicate with advisory groups, administrators, colleagues, resource people, professionals, media representatives, and others who can help you. Specify the exact resources and support you need, from whom, and how you will get them. Plan enough in advance so they are ready when you are.	

5   Design program.

• Unite your broad program objectives with the specific audiences you want to reach and decide how to approach them. Define the general content (appropriate to the problem or need) that best fits the needs of the audiences. Choose methods to fit each audience type's learning style and build combinations of these methods in a logical sequence so one learning experience builds on another.	• The program is planned to extend over 24 months. The materials in phase 7—action—reveal what will be done during the first 12 months. Each activity can be related back to a broad objective.

6   Prepare instructional plan.

• Instructional plans are developed for each specific activity or event. They include: learning opportunity, time, specific objectives, target clientele, planned learning experiences, content outline, instructional resources, and evaluation.	• An instructional plan is illustrated in Figure 14.3.

7   Take action.

• Your most challenging effort will be to promote and actually carry out the program and its related activities. It requires good program communication, promotion, time and resource management, and checking to see whether things are going as planned. Make sure that the different activities and events are in proper sequence and integrated; change them if they are not.	• Hold a meeting with the president of the County Bar Association when this program is being developed in order to (1) develop an understanding of and cooperation with the program, and (2) solicit support and participation in various parts of the program. Also, hold a meeting of the citizens and other interested professionals most closely associated with the area to outline the program.

Figure 14.2 *(Continued)*

Suggested phases	Example of family financial management
	Learning opportunities (activities and events) to provide desirable experiences
January	• Have three meetings with professional people such as bankers, insurance agents, etc., who work with financial security problems. The purpose of these meetings is to provide information about the program, solicit cooperation, and secure unity of and through topics in the program.
February	• Meeting with County Bar Association. The purpose of this meeting is to solicit cooperation and familiarize the association with the topics in the program. Also, to make arrangements for their participation in the program.
February	• Meet with other professional educators in the county to discuss the program on family financial security and solicit their cooperation. Suggest that this subject be included in their programs and be willing to provide materials.
February– April	• Meeting with several different women's groups: (a) planning for family financial security; (b) social security in the family financial security plan; (c) wills and property transfers.
January– May	• Township meetings with farm organizations and community groups. There are fourteen such organizations in the county and they meet monthly. Give illustrated talks on social security, wills, and property transfers. Use case examples to illustrate the importance of financial security.
January– December	• Meetings with civic groups. There are about twenty-five such groups in the county. They include Lion's Club, PTAs, Sportsman's Clubs. Send each group a brochure describing the program and telling them how to get literature, exhibits, and speakers. Give illustrated presentations on social security, wills, and property transfers.

Figure 14.2 (Continued)

Suggested phases	Example of family financial management
Through the year	• At every meeting where space is available, display special exhibits and literature, and make announcements relative to this educational program.
October– December	• General special-interest meetings will be held in four areas of the county. Topics to consider are insurance— health, accident, life, property, and liability. Emphasize types of policies and provisions, with special attention on planning an insurance program.
	• At the series of three area leader training meetings for youth organizations, give an explanation of the family security educational program. Encourage the county youth organization to develop exhibits for booths at the county fair, window displays, and floats on such topics as property-transfer plan, father-son agreements, social security, wills, and insurance.
	• Encourage members to use these topics in the speaking contests. Suggest the best ones to civic and community groups as potentials for their programs, and use them on radio.
April–May; October– November	• Small group meetings with families. A five-meeting series with two groups of five to eight families will be devoted to the topics: (1) property transfers; (2) social security; (3) insurance; (4) investments; and (5) making a will. Have families set forth on paper their present situation and the desired situation according to their current family status.
January– December	• Radio—used to publicize meetings and activities. Also, to create a feeling among the families of the importance of the topics in this program. Interviews with families with successful social security plans, with parents about father-son agreements, guests such as the president of the County Bar Association and specialists from the university.

Figure 14.2 (Continued)

Suggested phases	Example of family financial management
January – December	• Newspapers—used to publicize meetings and activities and to create interest in the program. Feature stories on successful property-transfer plans, question-answer columns on social security and insurance questions, and releases from university specialists and local members of the Bar Association will be provided throughout the year.
January – December	• Television—have several programs through the year in which the topics of social security, property transfer, and insurance are presented.

8   Determine the program's value.

• The value is judged by participants and others whom the results affect, no matter what personal judgment you make about its success. You will need evidence such as participants' reactions, actions taken, objectives met, problems solved, and needs satisfied. Its value to you can be judged by the program's implications for your future programs.

• There are two different approaches to the evaluation of this program: the immediate evaluations of the input to learning opportunities provided; and an attempt to determine the results or changes in practices by people.

Input

• Kinds of evidence: (1) extent of participation in the various learning opportunities; (2) value judgments from the participants regarding the effectiveness of the learning opportunities; (3) value judgments from the individuals making presentations.

• The procedure used in collecting this evidence is end-of-meeting reaction surveys.

Results

• Kinds of evidence are number of families in selected township with wills, plans for property transfer, and appropriate insurance plans.

•The procedures used to collect this evidence are (1) questionnaires in two selected townships; (2) interviews administered to selected individuals who participated in the program.

Figure 14.2 *(Continued)*

Suggested phases	Example of family financial management
9 Communicate results.	
• Report the program's results to key resource people, participants, leaders, advisory groups, colleagues, administrators, and the public. Such reports may take different forms for different audiences—from word of mouth to formal documents. No matter what form they take, reports should include: the need for the project; an explanation of what was done; agency's role; major results, benefits, action; and reactions of people and participants.	• Distribute a printed document showing the results of program to local elected officials, leaders, administrators, and participants. Discuss it with the programmer's supervisor.

SUMMARY

In this chapter, the relationship between the development of a program and the instructional design for a learning opportunity was illustrated. A specific program was used as an example. Obviously, the program was not completely identified. The continuing education programmer can use both the program and instructional designs, depending on the programming situation.

DISCUSSION QUESTIONS

1 Discuss the similarities and differences in program and instructional designs.
2 Illustrate and discuss a program that you have designed.
3 Discuss and compare learning experiences and learning opportunities.
4 How flexible do you think a design for a learning opportunity should be?
5 What are the difficulties in developing a program design?

Figure 14.3   A Specific Instructional Plan

Learning opportunity	• A series of three meetings with eight to ten families.
Time	• Each meeting two hours, 7:30–9:30; September, October, November.
Specific objectives	• Families to understand the importance of developing and keeping up-to-date a plan for family financial security. • Adults to understand all facets of planning for family financial security, including social security, investments, and insurance. • Adults to know the legal aspects of property transfer and making a will. • Families to know how to make a will. • Families to know how to prepare a plan for property transfer. • Families to understand the various types of insurance, how to evaluate policies, and what is adequate coverage.
Target clientele	• Families in 35–50 age group.
Planned learning experiences (for families)	• Hear people who have benefited from various kinds of insurance talk about their situations. • See a "will" and a "property-transfer plan." • See exhibits about the preparation of a will, social security, and property transfer. • Hear local professional people and university specialists talk about social security, property transfer, and insurance.
Content outline (Introduction, body, summary)	• Develop a content outline for each of the three meetings.
Instructional resources (Methods, devices, techniques, evaluation)	• Five copies of examples of a will and a property-transfer plan. • Slide-tape set on preparation of a will. • Printed materials on social security and insurance. • Plans for use of small discussion techniques. • End-of-meeting reaction surveys to determine the participants' judgments about the value of the learning opportunity.

Chapter 15

The Concept of Educational Objectives

Programs produce more important results if directed to clear and precise targets. These targets need to be identified so that they are on course with the mission of your organization and the responsibilities of your position. The targets are the results expected from your program activities. Such targets are called desired results or objectives. They indicate what is supposed to occur because of the program.

Much confusion exists over the terminology used in describing and using the concept of objectives. Different words, such as "objectives," "goals," "aims," "targets," "purposes," and "ends" are used interchangeably by some and mean different things to others. The basic meaning of all these terms is the same and it is not worthwhile to make distinctions among them. It is necessary, however, to clearly define the term "objective" before we consider its various dimensions. According to Dewey,[1] an objective is a foreseen end that gives direction to the activity.

[1]John Dewey, *Democracy and Education,* The Macmillan Company, New York, 1977, p. 102.

Krech et al.[2] define goals as sought after terminal actions with respect to both approach and avoidance objects. For our purposes, we will define an *objective* as an end toward which action is oriented, a condition or state of being to be reached. An objective reflects how the situation is to be changed, improved, or maintained.

PURPOSES OF EDUCATIONAL OBJECTIVES

Objectives should be selected and organized so they (1) provide direction, (2) are useful in selecting learning experiences, (3) provide the basis for evaluation, and (4) cause decisions and predictions.

Provide Direction

It is impossible to teach when a teacher is not clear about objectives. It is the same as trying to reach a certain destination when you are not sure of where you are headed. In each case, the direction and the route must be known and planned in advance. In most situations, several routes may lead to the same destination, but we must still know the route we will take. An educational objective tells us what the clientele want to achieve through our program.

Provide Basis for Selection of Learning Experiences

The achievement of educational objectives is difficult. The critical challenge is to select and provide those experiences that will allow the learner to grow and develop. This growth and development will contribute to achieving the social and economic changes discussed in previous chapters. Without clearly defined objectives, the learning experiences become fuzzy and hit or miss. Objectives need to be not only clearly defined but also clearly understood by all who participate in the program.

Provide Basis for Evaluation

Statements of objectives can be very general or quite specific. Regardless of their level of generality, objectives must be used as the basis for determining the value, results, or impact of a program. The approaches to assessing program results may be changes among the participants or changes in the physical, political, economic, or social situations.

Provide for Decisions and Predictions

Understanding why you may have trouble setting objectives is helpful. Developing objectives is much more than just writing words. The words

---

[2]David Krech et al., *Individual in Society,* McGraw-Hill Book Company, New York, 1962, p. 69.

you write express decisions you have made and publicly commit you to those decisions. You have to decide on the clientele, how many clientele, the results, and how many results you expect before you can state objectives.

You have to choose among alternatives. Most programs could be done with one of several clientele groups and could take any number of focuses. The set of objectives that would fit one clientele group and one focus would be considerably different from the objectives for another focus and clientele group. You have to consider the potential of the different alternatives and choose the most important and feasible.

SOURCES OF EDUCATIONAL OBJECTIVES

In order to develop an educational program that will be adequate, realistic, and effective, one must have some notion of the real needs of the potential learner. The programmer must be aware of and identify the changes that must take place in the situation to reach the desired end. To analyze the community and clientele situation and determine needs and problems, which in turn lead to the development of objectives, Tyler[3] and many others agree on three sources of objectives to be examined and studied:

- The learners themselves
- The contemporary life or society
- The subject specialist and discipline

In Chapters 10, 11, and 12, detailed presentations were given on the background and procedures for situational analysis. Here, materials are presented in a different context; however, they still focus on the learner, society, and the discipline as sources of objectives.

Study of Learners

The programmer needs to focus attention upon the learner's present needs and interests. It is necessary to compare the information obtained from the learners with some desirable norms or standards in order to identify the gaps or needs that can be transformed into objectives. Many methods can be used in studying learners as a source of educational objectives. Tyler suggests the following methods: (1) observations of the learners by the teachers; (2) interviews with the learners; (3) questionnaires to the learners; and (4) tests to ascertain their present status in

---

[3]Ralph Tyler, *Basic Principles of Curriculum and Instruction,* University of Chicago Press, Chicago, 1974.

skills, knowledge, attitudes, and in problem-solving abilities. Tyler also indicates that the learners themselves can be actively involved in the investigation.

Study of Contemporary Life or Society

Society is the second important source from which to obtain objectives. It reveals the status of the situation in which the learner exists and it identifies immediate problems, issues, or trends that are prevalent. This, in turn, identifies the demands that society has on individuals with implications for educational experiences to adequately prepare them to meet the needs, carry on their activities more effectively, and live successfully in society. The main arguments for using contemporary life as a source of objectives are (1) it is necessary to focus educational efforts upon the real needs of the contemporary society if education is to have a pragmatic approach, and (2) the learners are more likely to benefit in retention and transfer if education is related to real-life situations. While studying contemporary life, it will be desirable to divide the study into various areas such as health, family, recreation, and vocations, so as to have manageable units for investigation. Information about contemporary life only reveals the present status of the learners, or the conditions of life within the community. It does not provide the educational objectives. Data have to be interpreted to provide the needed objectives.

Discipline

The discipline is the third important source of educational objectives. An expert resource person representing a discipline can analyze and review data and situations to suggest what could be the most desirable situation. In some respects, the expert is suggesting norms or standards to be attained. The expert's role is to suggest the changes that should take place to improve the situation or to reach a level that reduces or eliminates need. Suggesting knowledge or skills from the expert's discipline that are appropriate and will bring about the desired changes is an important contribution the expert can make in this regard.

Screening Objectives

There is an important role for the programmer after objectives are identified. The three sources almost always provide more objectives than any agency can incorporate in its educational program. Tyler recommends two screens for this task. The first is the screen of the educational and social philosophy to which the agency is committed. If there is incompatibility between some potential objectives and the educational and social philosophy, those objectives are eliminated. For example, if some of the potential objectives are concerned with controversial issues in planned parenthood, abortion, divorce, energy, or use of land, it is possible that the institution would prefer not to focus on them. Therefore, they would not be included in the program.

The second screen relates to the programmer's beliefs about learning. Tyler suggests that each professional should have her or his own theory of learning, which includes the nature of the learning process, how it takes place, and under what conditions. For example, if the potential objective being considered is one that requires the learner to have very close guidance to carry on the new behavior she or he is to learn, and if the professional feels it is not possible to provide that close guidance, then that potential objective would very likely be eliminated.

After the professional uses these two screens to analyze the potential educational objectives and eliminate those that are not compatible with the educational and social philosophy of the institution, or with her or his beliefs about learning, a priority scale must be developed among those objectives that remain. This in itself is another challenging task.

LEVELS OF OBJECTIVES

If we study the various educational program documents at national, state, and community levels, it will be clear that educational objectives are stated at various levels. Broad, general statements of objectives are appropriate for general programs of an organization, clientele group, or problem or program area. More specific statements are desirable for a specific program such as for one meeting or a three-day conference. A close look at these will help us identify them as being located on different points on what might be called a "generality-specificity" continuum. Figure 15.1 illustrates this idea.

Although it is possible to prepare statements of objectives at the var-

Figure 15.1   Generality-Specificity Continuum of Educational Objectives

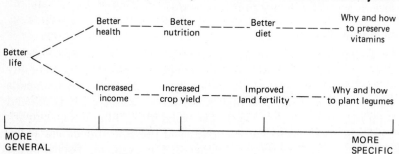

Figure 15.2   Three Levels of Objectives

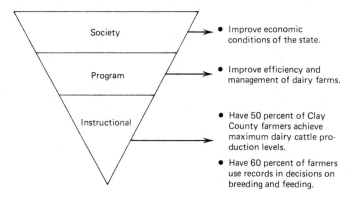

ious levels of this generality-specificity continuum, the three levels identified in Figure 15.2 are probably adequate for most programming.

Society Level

These statements are very general. They are philosophical in nature and reveal the general goals of a society. Some examples might relate to better living conditions for all people; improved social-economic status for people; better health care for all citizens. Societal objectives are statements often used to reflect the mission or general purpose of a governmental agency or an educational institution.

Program Level

This level of objective is characterized by statements about specific situations that are in need of improvement through educational programs. Examples would include: (1) have people with small businesses improve their efficiency through improvement in the management of such operations as record keeping, cash flow, advertising, forecasting, pricing, planning, and inventory management; (2) educational programs to help inmates and administrators of mental, correctional, and other institutions understand their legal rights and responsibilities; and (3) educational programs to provide hospital and nursing home administrators, governmental agency personnel, and those involved in health with information concerning innovative management techniques and regulatory changes.

This level of objective may be stated so as to apply for a two- to three-year period of time or for a particular learning opportunity, such as a two-week institute, a three-week course, or a two-day meeting. They focus on what is to be gotten from the program.

Instructional Level

These are more specific statements that focus on the learner. The instructional-level objective provides specific guidance regarding the particular actions that are to result from participation. Again, these statements may be very specific or more general depending on the particular program and the desires of the programmer. An example of a very specific objective for a two-hour meeting might be: Have all people with small businesses in the community understand all new social security regulations. A major program with several learning opportunities could have as an instructional objective: Have fifty families understand efficient family budgeting procedures. The important consideration is that the programmer be comfortable with the statements and that he or she finds them useful in programming.

TYPES OF OBJECTIVES

A programmer may find the task of stating objectives for an educational program simplified if a distinction is made between organizational and educational objectives. In the previous section on levels, educational objectives were focused upon. In general, educational objectives should state results in terms of what happens to people and/or the benefits to those people. In addition, each programmer and agency or institution will have organizational objectives for program maintenance. Some examples might include: reaching fifty new clients; obtaining $500,000 through student fees; having 2 million people participating in the programs; hold fifty meetings during the year; coordinate twenty-five institutes. Organizational objectives are important to the programmer in providing guidance as to what must be done by the organization in order to be able to provide the educational program.

There is a great deal of controversy in the literature about behavioral objectives. However, the literature will not be reviewed here. In behavioral objectives, clarity is more important than specificity. You do not need highly specific objectives, but you need to be clear about what you mean. One of Tyler's last statements on behavioral objectives reinforces this thought:

> So I agree that if by behavioral objectives we have come to mean highly specific, only observable outcomes, then, in that sense, behavioral objectives do a disservice. But if you think of behavior as including thinking and feeling and acting, and you're talking about such things as what will help learners understand certain concepts—what principles they can follow; what

kinds of problem-solving skills they can develop—then I think that the clarification of objectives can be really helpful to an adult educator.[4]

Again, the main consideration should be usefulness in teaching and learning in the program.

Meaningful Objectives

There are many and conflicting views about the exact way in which objectives should be stated. Each programmer has to use her or his own professional judgment in deciding on the exact wording of objectives. First and foremost, the wording must be useful and used in the programming situation. Second, it should clearly communicate to any others who will be involved in or who are interested in the program. The exact form is not as important as is whether the objectives are meaningful and used. Guidelines that may be useful in stating objectives are:

- Specifies the type of participant who is expected to secure results.
- Indicates the minimum number or proportion of the target clientele that are expected to show results.
- Indicates what the participants are expected to achieve through the program.
- Deals with things important and valuable to the prospective clientele.
- Shows a clear relationship to the problem statement. Achieving the objective will, in fact, cope with the problem or need.
- Is attainable with the amount of input you and the participants in the program can muster. Be realistic.
- Can be attained within the time frame specified in the program.
- Is clear and specific enough that it is possible to determine whether or not the objective has been attained. The result expected is something tangible or clearly identifiable.
- Focuses on the most crucial parts of the program.
- Makes a significant contribution to the carrying out of the fundamental responsibilities of your position.

Measurable Objectives

The desired results of a program should be so specifically and tangibly described that it is possible to determine whether or not the objective has been attained. It is possible, for example, to find out whether people are

---

[4] G. L. Carter (ed.), *Facilitating Learning With Adults: What Ralph Tyler Says,* Division of Program and Staff Development, University of Wisconsin-Extension, Madison, 1976, p. 31.

eating more iron-rich foods. It is also possible to get their perception of whether they feel stronger. This is what people mean when they say that objectives should be measurable. Measurement is the means of determining whether or not the objective has been attained. It is not important that things are measured, but that measurement gives quantitative evidence that indicates quantity and scope of achievement.

Often it is possible to translate the intangible objective to important concrete results if you keep analyzing it. For example, the objective of developing leadership is a common one in Extension programming. As stated, it is intangible and very difficult to determine when it has been accomplished. It can be translated into a variety of specific actions that can be observed and counted, depending upon what is meant by leadership. For example, if the type of leadership meant is taking more responsibility for a group's activities, the objective could be worded "to increase leadership" as shown by (1) becoming an officer of an organization, (2) being considered a good officer by group members, (3) accepting committee chair positions, (4) getting the task of the committee completed smoothly and rapidly, and the like.

The focus must be on the question: What definite action or product will indicate that this objective has been attained? In most instances, you can change intangible to tangible targets that are both important and discernible.

Should you express targets in terms of numbers of clientele in your objectives? By doing so, you bring activities into bounds and are better able to concentrate your efforts. The number targeted for achieving specific action is usually considerably less than the number you are expecting to reach through the program. You may reach 1000 people with information on iron-rich foods, but only 300 will be sufficiently motivated to keep the right foods in the diet week in and week out. The other 700 probably got some benefit from the information but not as much as those that really took complete action.

TAXONOMY OF EDUCATIONAL OBJECTIVES

Three broad classifications of behavior—the cognitive, affective, and psychomotor—were identified several years ago by a group of educational psychologists, and taxonomies were developed for each area. These classifications were initially developed to assist in the development of appropriate measurement instruments. The behavior categories are very useful in deciding on the extensiveness of different experiences necessary to achieve the desired level of behavior. The desired level can be reflected in the objective. For example, if the learners need to be able to analyze and synthesize content about family financial management, then a variety of different experiences over a period of time would need to be provided.

Cognitive Domain

The cognitive domain[5] deals with those behaviors that are concerned with the recall or recognition of knowledge and the development of intellectual skills and abilities.

Within the cognitive domain, six major areas have been developed within two broad classifications. Under the classification of knowledge, one area is identified, that of knowledge. *Knowledge* includes those behaviors that emphasize the remembering, either by recognition or recall, of ideas, material, or phenomena. Basically, this type of behavior prescribes that the student store the information and, when called upon, reproduce the material as it was presented. This remembering is described as the least complex of the cognitive behaviors.

The second broad classification of cognitive behavior contains those areas pertaining to the development of intellectual skills and abilities. These areas include comprehension, application, analysis, synthesis, and evaluation. These behaviors are described as increasing in complexity as one moves from comprehension to evaluation.

The simplest and the broadest of the intellectual skills and abilities, *comprehension*, refers to the behavior that is exhibited when the student understands the literal message contained in a communication and is able to make some use of the material or ideas contained in it. This understanding takes three forms: translation, interpretation, and extrapolation.

Beyond knowledge and comprehension, application is the third major area in the cognitive domain. Under comprehension, students must understand an abstraction well enough so that they can correctly demonstrate its use when asked to do so. *Application*, however, requires the student to go one step beyond this: When faced with a new problem, the student applies the appropriate abstraction without being prompted.

The next area in the cognitive domain is analysis. Under *analysis*, the behavior that is called for emphasizes the breakdown of the material or abstraction into its constituent parts and the detection of relationships of the parts and the manner in which they are organized. To differentiate, in comprehension the emphasis is on grasping the meaning and intent. In application, the emphasis is on remembering and bringing to bear upon the material the appropriate idea or abstraction. In analysis, however, the student can be expected to be able to identify or classify elements involved in a communication, to make explicit the relationships among the

[5]Benjamin Bloom et al. (eds.), *Taxonomy of Educational Objectives: The Classification of Educational Goals, Handbook,* vol. 1, *Cognitive Domain,* David McKay Co., Inc., New York, 1956–1964.

elements, and to recognize the organizational principles and structure that hold them together.

Synthesis is the fifth of the six areas in the cognitive domain. *Synthesis* is defined as the putting together of elements and parts to form a whole. This process involves fundamentally the ability to combine parts and elements together in such a manner as to constitute a pattern or structure not clearly there before. Three categories are involved in synthesis, basically: the production of a unique communication, the development of a plan or proposed set of operations, and the production of a set of abstract relations.

The final area of the cognitive domain, evaluation, is considered the most complex intellectual behavior because it involves the other five behaviors. *Evaluation* is defined as the making of judgments about the value of ideas, works, solutions, methods, materials, and the like, for some purpose, using criteria or standards as the basis for judgment.

Affective Domain

The affective domain[6] is divided into five broad areas: (1) receiving (attending); (2) responding; (3) valuing; (4) organization; and (5) characterization by a value or value complex. The first area, receiving (attending), suggests that the learner be sensitized to the existence of certain phenomena or stimuli. Responding, the second level or area, indicates that the student is committed in a small measure to the phenomenon involved. The third level is called valuing. At this point, the phenomenon or behavior is perceived as having worth, indicating that it is internalized or accepted by the student. Organization, the fourth level, implies that a student encounters situations for which more than one value is relevant, thus creating a situation where values must be organized into some sort of system within the mind. Some values, of necessity, will become dominant and pervasive. At the fifth level, the characterization by a value or value complex, the values already have a niche in the individual's value hierarchy. They are organized into some kind of internally consistent system, and have controlled the behavior of an individual for a sufficient time so that the individual has adapted to behaving in this way.

Psychomotor Domain

The third domain, the psychomotor,[7] is concerned with the manipulative or motor-skill area of behaviors. There are five areas of identified behav-

[6]David R. Krathwohl, Benjamin Bloom, and Bertram Masia, *Taxonomy of Educational Objectives: The Classification of Educational Goals,* vol. 2, *Affective Domain,* David McKay, Co., Inc., New York, 1972–1973.

[7]Gryphon House, *The Psychomotor Domain,* National Special Media Institute, Washington, D.C., 1972.

ior in this domain. The first area is perception, which suggests that the learner becomes aware through sense organs and recognizes cues, makes choices, and relates to actions. The second area is referred to as set. The learner has a mental, physical, or emotional readiness for learning. The third area is guided response, which is interpreted as overt action by trial and error under supervision. The fourth area is the habitual response and is referred to as a mechanism. The fifth area is the complex overt response. It is action performed without hesitation, leading to automatic performance.

SUMMARY

The concept of educational objectives has been described from several viewpoints. Purposes, sources, levels, and types of objectives have been discussed. Also included were some ideas about meaningful and measurable objectives. The last section of the chapter described the taxonomies of educational objectives for the cognitive, affective, and psychomotor domains. It was suggested that the taxonomies serve as a useful guide in (1) stating and interpreting an objective, (2) deciding on the number and kind of learning experiences, and (3) developing the evaluation approaches.

DISCUSSION QUESTIONS

1   How do you interpret the idea of levels of objectives?
2   The notion of studying the learner as a source of educational objectives does not apply when developing a community-oriented program. Agree or disagree?
3   Illustrate the usefulness of the taxonomies in designing the instruction for a two-day institute.
4   Describe and illustrate the relationship of organizational and educational objectives.
5   Prepare statements of objectives for organizational, program, and instructional levels.

Chapter 16

Planning
Learning Opportunities

Once the educational objectives have been identified, the continuing education programmer can concentrate on how to help learners attain them. Emphasizing the intended educational outcomes for a clientele group with certain known attributes or needs puts the primary focus on the learner as the chief component of the educational effort. The programmer must analyze the present competencies of the learner in relation to intended educational ends and consider what experiences will result in maximum attainment of the desired attributes or behaviors. In this light, the continuing education programmer is less an information giver than a strategist who designs situations, events, and activities so that learners can experience certain effects. It is the active interaction between the learner and the event—on a mental and/or physical level—that results in learning. Thus, a learning experience is not what the instructor does; it is not a content outline for an event or activity; it is not a facility, device, or technique. It is the learner actively interacting in the educational process. The programmer's role is to structure the educational opportunities. A distinction is made between a learning opportunity and a learning experience. A

Figure 16.1   Learning Opportunities

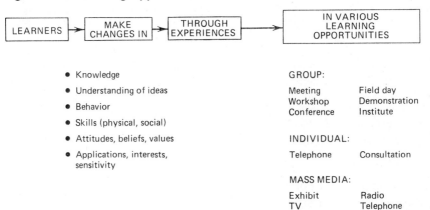

learning opportunity is an activity or event provided as a workshop, conference, meeting, or individual consultation. Figure 16.1 illustrates the relationship between a learning opportunity and a learning experience.

TWO THEORIES OF LEARNING

A discussion of learning experiences must, it seems, begin with very basic questions, such as: What is learning? How does it occur? How can it be promoted? These questions have been asked by interested philosophers, psychologists, and educators for many years. While there have been many theories, models, and concepts devised over the years attempting to answer these questions, there remains today a wide variety of views regarding learning and learning experiences. Two major theories or models of learning are widely discussed. They are (1) the behaviorist orientation—also known as stimulus response, associationism, and connectionist; and (2) the phenomenological orientation—sometimes called Gestalt-field theory. These two orientations have a long history of development, but their historical antecedents will not be presented. Instead, these two major views of learning will be presented to show the diversity of thought and to illustrate their implications for continuing education programming.

Milhollan and Forisha explore the two positions and their implications by comparing contemporary writers B. F. Skinner and Carl R. Rogers. They describe the central conflict between the two orientations as follows:

The behaviorist orientation considers man to be a passive organism governed by stimuli supplied by the external environment. Man can be manipulated, that is, his behavior controlled, through proper control of environmental stimuli. Furthermore, the laws that govern man are primarily the same as the universal laws that govern all natural phenomena. Therefore, the scientific method, as evolved by the physical sciences, is appropriate as well for the study of the human organism.

The phenomenological orientation considers man to be the source of all acts. Man is essentially free to make choices in each situation. The focal point of this freedom is human consciousness. Behavior is, thus, only the observable expression and consequence of an essentially private, internal world of being. Therefore, only a science of man which begins with experience, as it is immediately given in this world of being, can ever be adequate for a study of the human organism.[1]

Milhollan and Forisha point out that it may not be useful to consider these two orientations as being mutually exclusive, since actions and self-awareness are both necessary in descriptions of human learning. There are, however, many contradictions between the two models. The behaviorist view is that people are predictable and live in an objective, reliable, natural, and measurable world. People are viewed as an element in the world, having the capacity to transmit information but not alter it. People exist as complex machines, with intelligence being only that which is fed into the human system. Thus, in the behaviorist view human intelligence can be measured and controlled and behavior reflecting this input can be predicted.

In contrast, the phenomenological view of people is subjective. Phenomenologists hold that people have a private world of feelings with emotions, perceptions, and a capacity not only to transmit information, but also a capacity to ask new questions, to make decisions on actions never contemplated before, and to generate new information. This view sees each human being as unique. Thus, descriptions of behavior must be in relative terms. The behaviorist would say that behavior is not possible because everything is contingent upon something else.

Acceptance of one of these positions over the other has implications for approaching the design and implementation of learning experiences.

Bigge describes the behaviorist or neobehaviorist view of learning as follows:

In the eyes of neobehaviorists, learning is more or less permanent change of behavior which occurs as a result of practice. Thus, the learning process consists of impressions of new reaction patterns on pliable, passive organisms. Since learning arises, in some way, from an interplay of organisms and their environments, the key concepts of neobehaviorists are stimulus

[1] Frank Milhollan and Bill Forisha, *From Skinner to Rogers: Contrasting Approaches to Education,* Professional Educators Publications, Inc., Lincoln, Nebr., 1972, p. 13.

(that excitement which is provided by an environment) and response (that reaction which is made by an organism). Consequently, the problem of the nature of the learning process is centered in a study of the relationships of processions of stimuli and responses and what occurs between them. Since the focus always is upon behavior, in practical application, a neobehavioristically-oriented teacher strives to change behaviors of his students in the desired direction by providing the right stimuli at the proper time.[2]

The behaviorist orientation uses such terms as conditioning or reinforcement when discussing the learning process. Bigge explains this position as follows:

> For behaviorists or conditioning theorists, learning is a change in behavior. It occurs through stimuli and responses becoming related according to mechanistic principles. Thus, it involves the formation of relations of some sort between series of stimuli and responses. Stimuli—the causes of learning—are environmental agents that act upon an organism so as either to cause it to respond to or increase the probability of a response of a certain class or kind. Responses—effects—are physical reactions of an organism to either external or internal stimulation.[3]

The phenomenological orientation has a quite different view of learning. Learning is viewed as gaining new insights and/or modifying existing ones. Insights are gained through individuals being highly sensitive and aware of the environment and their relationship to it. In this awareness, new meanings and utilizations occur through the individual seeing different ways of putting elements together. The phenomenological orientation views learning as a purposive, an explorative, an imaginative, and a creative enterprise. Such a view is much different than the behaviorist view that learning consists of linking one thing with another. Instead, learning is identified with thought or conceptualization; it is a nonmechanical development or change of insight.

What implications do these views of learning have for developing learning experiences? Skinner[4] believes teaching is the arrangement of contingencies of reinforcement under which students learn. He suggests that to become competent in a subject matter, the material must be divided into very small steps, Reinforcement must be contingent upon the completion of each step satisfactorily. Teachers who adopt this approach to learning decide specifically what behaviors they want their students to manifest and proceed in such a way as to evoke and fix those behaviors.

[2] Morris Bigge, *Learning Theories for Teachers,* 3d ed., Harper & Row, Publishers, Inc., New York, 1976, pp. 86–87.

[3] Ibid., p. 11.

[4] B. F. Skinner, *Beyond Freedom and Dignity,* Alfred A. Knopf, Inc., New York, 1971.

Rogers's[5] approach is much different. He assumes a person has the ability to adapt and to grow in a direction that enhances that person's existence. Formal principles regarding human behavior have been identified by Rogers. These principles concern (1) the development of an individual's own sense of reality, (2) the internal forces that cause the individual to act, and (3) the development of the individual's own self-concept. Rogers would devise learning experiences designed to help learners gain insight. This would involve pointing out patterns of the whole rather than focusing on isolated facts.

These two orientations underscore the difficulties in designing learning experiences. Neither theory provides an adequate basis for designing all learning experiences. The learner and the learning situation should be used in determining the approach or orientation of the learning experience. The two theories provide a background understanding that is useful in planning for the involvement of the learner.

PRINCIPLES OF LEARNING

There are several principles of learning that are acceptable to the proponents of the two major theory orientations to learning. Since the principles are general guidelines, the programmer must interpret and use them according to her or his philosophy and values. The principles have been found to be useful criteria in analyzing learning opportunities that are being planned:

Learning environment. The learning environment must be physically and psychologically comfortable for the learners. It should be characterized by physical comfort, mutual trust and respect, mutual helpfulness, freedom of expression, and acceptance of differences. If learning is to proceed creatively, the learner must be adjusted emotionally to the learning situation, the teacher, and to the other students.

Need to learn. The learner must feel a need to learn. Learners must perceive the goals of the learning opportunity as their goals. A problem-centered learning situation helps to motivate the learner to seek some kind of solution or to better understand the need to learn.

Previous experiences. Learning experiences must relate to previous experiences. The learner must be capable of carrying on or participating in the behavior. The learner must have the necessary resources so that effective use can be made of the learning opportunity provided.

Learners involved. Learners should be involved in planning and implementing learning experiences. If the goals of the learning opportunity are to relate to the needs and problems of the learner, then the search for

---

[5] Carl R. Rogers, *Freedom to Learn*, Charles Merrill Publishing Co., Columbus, Ohio, 1969.

solutions must be undertaken with the learners. In the process, the learner will be able to influence the goals and learn the process of problem solving.

Learning and practice. Learning must be experience centered. For learning to occur, the learner must be an active participant in the experience. Whenever there is any involvement of the ego in the problem, the individual develops vested interests in certain solutions when they affect her or him. Learners must be able to make use of experiences or practice behavior suggested by the learning experience. This must be built into every learning opportunity.

Feedback. Learners should get feedback so they can evaluate their success in reaching their goals. Success in reaching goals is necessary to maintaining the learners' motivation in learning.

While these principles are by no means exhaustive, they do provide the continuing education programmer with some general guidelines in the design of effective learning opportunities. These principles are suggestions for stimulating and maintaining the learner's motivations. They can be used as standards in analyzing the various experiences being provided through a learning opportunity.

ORGANIZING LEARNING OPPORTUNITIES

To effectively plan and implement learning opportunities, one must consider a number of important factors. First, the learning experience is what the learner experiences through the learning opportunity. Second, the aim of this aspect of programming is to design and carry out a series of activities that will provide the learner with the opportunity to achieve the objectives decided upon. Following is a discussion of nine major factors to consider when organizing learning opportunities.

1 Major Goals of the Learning Opportunity

What are the goals of each learning activity? In selecting and providing learning experiences, we can think of levels in developing knowledge, attitudes, and skills. Bloom and several others[6] have described taxonomies for educational objectives.

Three broad classifications of behavior—the cognitive, affective, and psychomotor—have been identified. The cognitive domain deals with those behaviors that are concerned with the recall or recognition of knowledge, and the development of intellectual skills and abilities. The affective domain includes those behaviors that describe changes in inter-

[6]Benjamin Bloom et al. (eds.), *Taxonomy of Educational Objectives: The Classification of Educational Goals, Handbook,* vol. 1, *Cognitive Domain,* David McKay Co., Inc., New York, 1956–1964.

est, attitudes, and values, and the development of intellectual skills and abilities, appreciation, and adequate adjustment. The third domain, the psychomotor, is concerned with the manipulative or motor-skill area of behavior. Within each domain there are levels of objectives or desired behavior. For example, in the cognitive domain the six major areas are knowledge, comprehension, application, analysis, synthesis, and evaluation. In planning a continuing education program the challenge is to determine the desired level of behavior and then to select and organize learning opportunities to achieve that desired level. An example would be a three-day conference on cost accounting for people with small businesses. If the desired level of behavior is application, then the programmer must design appropriate experiences.

Taxonomies are valuable to guide the continuing educator in selecting and providing learning experiences to meet and expand the levels of the learner's development in knowledge, attitudes, or skills. For example, if we are concerned with the cognitive domain at the knowledge level, we must help learners acquire facts or be aware of ideas. Consequently, the learning experiences might include listening, watching, and reading. At the synthesis level, we are concerned that the learner be able to apply and use the new understanding or knowledge. Learners must be able to take what they have acquired and put it into a form that is usable to them. This level requires much more active involvement on the part of the learner. The taxonomies have been discussed in Chapter 15.

Figure 16.2 summarizes the need for greater internalization by the learner at the higher levels of the taxonomy. The programmer will need to provide more extensive opportunities for the learner to interact with the content and feelings of the proposed change in knowledge, attitude, or skill.

It is suggested that consideration of the objective of a learning opportunity in relation to the levels of the taxonomy can be beneficial. If the objective is to help the learner to grow and develop to the synthesis level, then appropriate experiences will have to be provided through the conference, workshop, or individual consultation.

2 Methods and Techniques

The continuing educator can provide information for hours, but learning will not take place unless the learner does something. What the learner does through a learning experience is often more important than what the educator does. In the effective planning of any learning opportunity the continuing educator must consider the methods, techniques, and devices that will be utilized. Definitions of these terms are as follows:

Method. A way of doing something, a systematic mode or approach used to reach people (group contact, individual contact, or mass media).

Figure 16.2 Objectives and Learning Experiences

Objective level	Learning experiences
Lower level	
Attitude: Be aware	Listening
Knowledge: Acquire facts	Watching
	Examining
Skill: Know what to do	Reading
	Questioning
Higher levels	
Knowledge:	Discussing
• Understand	Answering
• Apply	Practicing
• Reconstruct	Experimenting
	Relating
Attitude:	Demonstrating
• Interest	Diagramming
• Value	Reconstructing
• Integrate	Comparing
Skill:	Illustrating
• Some skill	Applying
• Adequate skill	Analyzing
• Adapt skill	Clarifying

Technique. The form used to present material to be learned (lecture, panel, group discussion, or farm walk).

Device. The mechanical items and conditions used to facilitate learning (film, radio, slides, or telephone).

Figure 16.3 illustrates the relationships between a learning opportunity, method, technique, device, and learning experiences. A three-day workshop for fifty business executives would probably utilize the group-contact method with perhaps limited individual contact. The programmer may plan to use the lecture, small-group discussion, game simulation, and a panel as techniques. The devices or instructional materials available include films, slide-tapes, materials for game simulation, and a group of charts. The real challenge for the educator is to provide experiences through which the learner can interact with the content, feelings, and skills. These experiences need to be sequential over the three days so that the learners might achieve their desired objectives.

Kemp suggests three major approaches to teaching: (1) teachers present information to students through lecturing, talking informally, writing on the chalkboard, demonstrating, and showing audio-visual materials, such as films, filmstrips, slides, and transparencies; (2) students

Figure 16.3   Learning Experiences, Methods, Techniques, and Devices

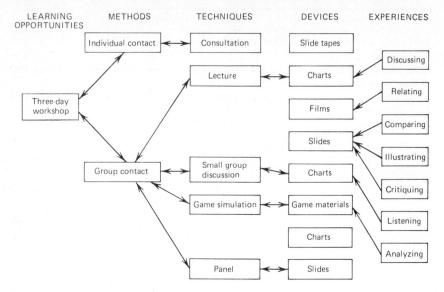

work independently by reading, solving problems, writing reports, and doing research; and (3) interaction occurs between teacher and student and among students.[7] Each of these approaches provides opportunities for interacting through such experiences as listening, analyzing, or critiquing. Kemp also warns that there is no formula for identifying the right experiences for a given set of objectives. What may work with a particular group of participants or for a particular teacher may be unsatisfactory for another.

Interaction is especially important for adults and should be provided for whenever possible. Interaction implies a two-way process between two or more individuals. A variety of techniques are available for the continuing educator to use. Some examples are listed below:

• *The "huddle" method.* The division of a group into small groups of four to six members for discussion purposes.
• *The "buzz-group" method.* The breaking of a group into two-person discussion groups.
• *The symposium.* A group of talks, speeches, or lectures presented by several individuals on the various phases of a single subject or problem.

[7] Jerrold Kemp, *Instructional Design,* Fearon-Pitman Publishers, Inc., Belmont, Calif., 1971, p. 55.

- *The panel discussion.* A discussion before an audience by a selected group of persons (three to six) under a moderator.
- *The dialogue.* A discussion carried on in front of a group by two knowledgeable people on a specific subject.
- *Brainstorming.* A type of small-group interaction designed to encourage the free introduction of ideas on an unrestricted basis without any limitations as to feasibility.
- *Role playing.* The dramatization of a problem or situation through acting out of various roles.

These and similar interactive techniques are especially useful for promoting learning:

> Through the give-and-take of discussions, students can be motivated and helped to sharpen their judgments and disseminations, to deal with new and novel situations and unpredictable happenings, and to approach attitudinal objectives, which we find so hard to define and state in carefully measurable terms.[8]

Given an understanding of the various methods and techniques available, the critical job for the educator is to select the most effective method and technique for achieving the desired experience. While this decision is often difficult, Knowles[9] suggests two guidelines: (1) match the technique to the objectives, and (2) when given a choice, choose the method or technique involving students in the most active participation.

3 Instructional Resources and Materials

An effective learning opportunity requires adequate instructional resources and materials. The two areas that the continuing education programmer needs to plan for are (1) staffing or human resources and (2) instructional resources.

The quality of any learning opportunity is achieved through the staff or instructor. A programmer may do an effective job of identifying needs and establishing objectives, but the program will not be successful if poor-quality instruction is provided. The ideal situation is to have instructors who (1) understand and are sympathetic to the needs of students, (2) know their subject matter, (3) have practical experience, and (4) have the ability to stimulate and maintain interest through effective teaching.

An effective instructor is one who is prompt, patient, understanding, kind, and who has enthusiasm for the subject being taught.

---

[8] Ibid., p. 54.

[9] Malcolm Knowles, *Modern Practice of Adult Education,* Association Press, New York, 1970.

In planning learning opportunities, the programmer should use every caution possible when selecting instructors. For example, Rindt[10] suggests that when a recommendation is made, ask for more details, such as:

Does the instructor use visual aids?
Is the instructor dynamic? Enthusiastic?
Does the instructor read from copy?
Does the instructor involve the students?
Does the instructor give practical examples?

Rindt also has some worthwhile suggestions about unreliable criteria for screening instructors:

Years of experience
Articles the instructor has written
Formal education
Desire to appear on a program
Impressions given over the phone or in person
Past experience in speaking engagements
Appearances on other programs
Recommendations by a subordinate, boss, or colleague

An in-depth interview with the proposed instructor is probably the most reliable means of determining whether your standards of performance are likely to be met.

Instructional materials such as films, charts, slide-tapes, printed documents, game simulations, and transparencies are useful aids in effective teaching. They are useful in adding variety, clarifying ideas, and arousing interest. It is extremely important that instructional materials are used to aid instruction and are not used as a substitute. In selecting and utilizing instructional materials, the programmer might benefit from considering three questions that Kemp[11] raises:

1 Which teaching/learning pattern—presentation, individualized learning, or small-group interaction—is selected or is most appropriate for the objective and the nature of the student group?
2 What category of learning experience—direct realistic experiences, verbal or printed experience—is most suitable for the objective and instructional activity in terms of the selected teaching/learning pattern?

---

[10]Kenneth E. Rindt, *Handbook for Coordinators of Management and Other Adult Education Programs,* University of Wisconsin-Extension, Madison, 1968.
[11]Kemp, op. cit.

3 If sensory experience is indicated or selected, which attributes of the communications media are necessary or desirable?

4   Physical Facilities

It is often very tempting to plan a quality program, yet omit the important logistical considerations. In many cases, the programmer has little choice or control over facilities. If alternatives are available, the following should be considered:

- Accessibility of meeting location to transportation
- Adequate parking
- Rooms of varying size and flexible arrangement
- Good lighting and acoustics
- Comfortable chairs
- Adequate restroom facilities
- No distractions
- Proper audio-visual equipment
- Adequate floor space for desired classroom arrangement
- Relaxing atmosphere

All dimensions of a program must be well coordinated to make sure that logistical problems do not reduce the program's effectiveness.

5   Financial Considerations

The budget available for each learning opportunity is likely a part of an overall program budget. An adequate budget for promotion, instructors, instructional materials, and evaluative feedback is necessary for effective development of an educational opportunity. It is recognized that continuing education programmers often operate on very limited budgets. However, the budget, regardless of the sources, is an important consideration in planning for any educational opportunity.

6   Responsibilities of Teacher

In Chapter 6, the roles of a programmer in the development of a program were discussed. In planning and organizing an individual learning opportunity, such as a conference or workshop, it is important to identify what the instructor will do as part of the instructional process.

The instructor has the dual responsibility of facilitating learning related to the identified task of the program and also related to maintaining group process. The learners may perform these functions, but the instructor is responsible for seeing that someone performs them when necessary. Within these two responsibilities are aspects of an administrative nature and aspects of a more cognitive nature. First, there are the functions related to the identified task:

- *Administrative nature*. Developing an agenda, initiating and coordinating learning experiences, setting up communications media needs, etc.
- *Cognitive nature*. Seeking and giving information, elaborating on materials, structuring learning materials, evaluating and giving opinions, etc.

Second, there are the functions related to the group process:

- *Administrative nature*. Making room arrangements, seeking consensus, timing, etc.
- *Cognitive nature*. Giving and receiving feedback, assessing how the group is progressing, encouraging, being sensitive to all group members' opportunities for contributions, etc.

In order for the learner to achieve in any learning situation, the instructor needs to consider several actions. These actions are usually external to the learner and are provided by the teacher or other instructional resources with which the learner interacts. Kidd[12] suggests the following actions as relevant:

- Animating or inspiring attention and commitment
- Presenting information or demonstrating processes
- Raising relevant questions, developing habits of self-questioning
- Clarifying difficulties or obscurities
- Drawing parallels or finding relationships
- Reflecting feelings
- Expressing agreement and support
- Evaluating or developing the learner's capacity for self-evaluation

In continuing education, teaching and learning are difficult to separate. The process should be both interactive and cooperative, so that the teacher and learner work together. The instructor needs to structure this interactive process in a way that learners experience certain effects. The instructor facilitates this process by performing the above actions whenever necessary and appropriate.

7 Responsibilities of Learners

The central figure in any learning opportunity is the learner. This statement suggests that the major focus in designing learning opportunities should be on the responsibilities and activities of the learners.

The teacher must have a well-developed idea of her or his responsibilities in the learning experience, but must also spell out what is expected

[12]J. R. Kidd, *How Adults Learn*, Association Press, New York, 1973.

Figure 16.4   Teacher and Learner Responsibilities as Related to Content and Process Goals

Learning opportunity	Teacher activity and responsibility	Learner activity and responsibility
Content goals		
Understand food additives.	Discusses three types. Asks for illustrations from students. Shows slides.	Relates what is being said to personal needs. Cites illustrations. Analyzes slides.
Process goals		
Stimulate interest.	Asks questions.	Asks questions.
Establish trust and atmosphere of open communication.	Supports and reinforces those who speak.	Gives opinions or experiences.

of the learners. One way of exploring learner responsibilities is to examine the points made in previous sections in terms of learner expectations. Do we expect the learners to be responsible for any of the tasks or maintenance functions? What kind of activities do we expect the learners to carry out?

Figure 16.4 suggests a framework that can be used as an aid in thinking about teacher and learner activities as they relate to content and process goals of a particular learning opportunity. The main point of this illustration is to stress the importance of considering both teacher and learner activities and processes as well as content goals.

8   Relationship of Various Learning Experiences

It is important to keep in mind that each learning experience must be closely tied to the other experiences of the program. Tyler[13] suggests three major criteria to be met in building an effectively organized group of learning experiences: continuity, sequence, and integration. He explains each as follows:

Continuity. This refers to the vertical reiteration of major program elements. That is, ideas, concepts, and skills introduced early in the program must be dealt with again and again so that students can recall, practice, and tie them to each new learning experience.

Sequence. This is related to continuity but goes beyond it. Sequence

[13]Ralph Tyler, *Basic Principles of Curriculum and Instruction,* University of Chicago Press, 1974.

emphasizes the importance of having each successive experience build upon the preceding one, but to go more broadly and deeply into the matters involved.

Integration. This refers to the horizontal relationships of program experiences. The organization of these experiences should be such that they help the learner get an increasingly unified view and to unify behavior in relation to the elements dealt with.

These three criteria offer a guide for relating learning experiences. As each experience is being planned, these three criteria should be considered. As the experiences are actually being carried out, the criteria should be reevaluated and the learning experiences adjusted as necessary.

9   Evaluation of Learning Activity

The concept of evaluation is discussed in Chapter 17. In planning an educational opportunity, it is important to recognize that the evaluation approaches must be planned. The programmer needs to consider what decisions can be improved by using evaluation and what kind of evaluative data are needed in the particular decision situation. In general, a program can and perhaps should be evaluated at three different stages:

Design. The completed plan or program design should be evaluated when it is still being planned and before implementation. Evaluation at this point focuses on the soundness of the objectives and the quality of the program that should occur if the design is properly implemented.

Process. Programs should also be evaluated while they are in process and conclusions fed back into the planning of the remainder of the program. Major changes in program content or procedures should be considered when the final evaluation is made.

Completion. Programs also should be evaluated at the completion or wrap-up of a given program phase. Such an evaluation points to desirable next steps and provides information about the actual effectiveness of the original program design.

Although the judgments involved in completing the evaluation are made after the program is through, the process of such an evaluation actually starts with the identification of need for the program. It must be planned into the total programming process. The design for completing evaluation should be developed at the same time the program is designed.

SUMMARY

The planning of learning opportunities is one of the most complex yet important responsibilities of the continuing education programmer. In this chapter, a distinction has been made between learning opportunities and learning experiences. A review of the two theoretical approaches to learning was followed by a discussion of principles of learning. Nine major factors that are extremely important in organizing learning opportunities were presented. They are useful in planning and analyzing the effectiveness of learning opportunities.

DISCUSSION QUESTIONS

1 What are your beliefs about learning?
2 Design a set of learning experiences for a two-day institute. You suggest the topic and audience.
3 Illustrate the relationship of learning opportunities and learning experiences.
4 Why are instructional materials often misused?
5 What was the most significant idea for you in this chapter?

SUGGESTED READINGS FOR SECTION V

De Bono, Edward, *Lateral Thinking,* Harper/Colophon Books, New York, 1973.
Klevins, Chester (ed.), *Materials and Methods in Continuing Education,* Klevins Publication, New York, 1976.
McClusky, Howard Y., "An Approach to a Differential Psychology," in Malcolm Knowles (ed.), *The Adult Learner: A Neglected Species,* Gulf Publishing Company, Houston, Tex., 1973, pp. 142–159.
Patton, Michael, *Alternative Evaluation Research Paradigm,* University of North Dakota Press, Grand Forks, 1975.
Willis, G. (ed.), *Qualitative Education,* McCutchan Publishing Corporation, Berkeley, Calif., 1978.

Section VI

Determining and Communicating Program Value

What are the central goals of continuing education programs? To preserve certain cultural characteristics from one generation to another? To transmit certain skills so that each individual is equipped for a profitable role in the economy? To help people "live a good life" or "fulfill themselves as persons?" To improve or otherwise change society by the installation of certain attitudes and values that will impel new generations in desired directions?

Regardless of how these goals are perceived and utilized in continuing education, the programmer must develop appropriate approaches for determining the effectiveness of the program. The judgments about the value of the program must then be communicated to a variety of audiences.

In Chapter 17, the concept of evaluation will be reviewed. Emphasis will be given to the use of evaluative data for decision making in program development. A framework for relating the structure of evaluation to problems in programming will be presented.

Chapter 18 will present some ideas about communicating the value of a program to various audiences. Guidelines for preparation and use of reports will be discussed.

Chapter 17

Determining
Program Effectiveness

A continuing education programmer has to develop a concept of evaluation and then make the proper application to her or his particular programming situation. Systematic evaluation is difficult and costly. Informal evaluation is often questioned. Thus, the decisions about the application of evaluation concepts are difficult, yet extremely important.

A CONCEPT OF EVALUATION

Some recent literature on educational evaluation presents the main purpose of such evaluation as that of improving decision making. The main use made of evaluative data is as input into the decision-making process. Steele suggests that:

> Program evaluation is the process of judging the worth or value of a program. This judgment is formed by comparing evidence as to what the program is with criteria as to what the program should be.[1]

[1] Sara Steele, "Program Evaluation—A Broader Definition," *Journal of Extension,* Summer 1970, p. 8.

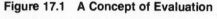

Figure 17.1　A Concept of Evaluation

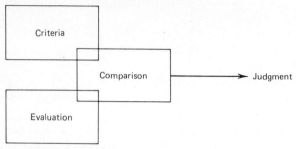

Thus, evaluation is a process of deciding that involves (1) establishing standards or criteria, (2) gathering evidence about the criteria, and (3) making judgments about what this comparison revealed. Figure 17.1 illustrates this concept.

Criteria

The evaluator must first have a clear picture of what "should" be. The evaluator must have some standards, norms, or descriptive statements called criteria. Criteria should be selected that apply to the kind of decisions the evaluator has to make. Steele and Moss say that criteria are:

> . . . measures against which something can be judged. They may be rules, standards, norms, objects, or conditions of behavior which are considered to be "good" or "ideal." They provide a description or image of what a valuable program is like, thereby assigning value to a given phenomenon related to the program.[2]

The criteria identify what needs to be found out about the actual program. The criteria are then used to determine what kinds of evidence must be gathered and examined. Then the evidence of the actual program, or its product, is compared with the criteria to arrive at the program. This is the basic framework for a concept of evaluation. It is applicable whether one is evaluating a learning opportunity or the total program. It is applicable both to the results and processes and to the various characteristics of the program.

Evidence

The second important part of the concept is that of evidence. Evidence is an indication, or an outward sign. In evaluation, evidence is composed of:

[2] Sara Steele and Gwenna Moss, Paper presented at the 1970 Adult Education Research Conference, Minneapolis, Minn., February 1970, p. 2.

1   Acts, words, numbers, or things that provide a sign or indication
2   That which provides proof of the extent to which the quality we are examining is present in a program
3   That which, when accumulated into a pattern, provides a picture adequate for judging the extent to which criteria have been met.

Criteria of what should be direct our collection of evidence about what is. That does not mean that we collect only evidence that indicates that we are meeting the criteria. It means that we use criteria to tell us the kind of evidence that should be collected, and then we try to get objective evidence.

Evidence can be what people say, such as the perception of participants or of experts or their actual behavior. It can be what actually occurs or what people think occurs. Evidence about quality is often taken directly while the program is in process, by a means of rating scales filled out by skilled judges, or it may be taken in retrospect, by getting participant's judgments of quality. The perceptions of participants and/or of experts are the major sources of evidence related to such characteristics as effort, contact, and quality.

Records of behavior are the usually accepted evidence about the accomplishments of a program. Such records include scores on knowledge tests when the objectives have cognitive goals; ratings on attitude scales when the program deals with the affective domain; or records of actual practices or of skill when these are the aims of the program.

Evidence of change in the actual situation is required when the objectives of a program are stated in terms of changes in income or the physical, social, or cultural environment.

Judgment

Judgment is the part of the evaluation process in which alternative conclusions are considered, a decision is made, and worth or value is assigned to that which is being judged. Program judgments are decisions about how well the program actually has met the specified criteria and, as a result, how valuable it has been.

Judgments are made by people and are dependent upon them. Judgments are influenced by the past experiences and beliefs of the individuals making them. They may be reliable, valid, and objective, or highly biased, depending upon how well the individual is able to control her or his own mental activity and screen out biasing factors.

Accurate program judgments are enhanced when sound criteria and reliable evidence are used. However, even then many alternative conclusions may be reached. The programmer must consider these alternatives carefully before reaching a final conclusion.

Evaluation does not occur unless judgment occurs, no matter how detailed the description of the criteria or of the evidence. Some individuals feel that they have made an evaluation by just describing what happened during or as a result of a program. Descriptions become evaluation only if the programmer presents definite conclusions as to the value of the program.

Decisions in the Evaluation Process

The five kinds of decisions that make up the process are as follows:

1 *Initial decisions about evaluation*. What is its purpose? How will it be used? What are the resources? When will it be done? What characteristics will be evaluated?

2 *Decisions about criteria*. Selecting and developing criteria against which the program will be judged; determining what "should" be.

3 *Decisions about evidence*. Developing the description of those characteristics of the program that are to be judged. Deciding the kind of evidence to be collected; determining how it can best be secured; securing and analyzing it.

4 *Judgmental decisions*. Making judgments by comparing the evidence with the criteria. Arriving at a summary statement as to the value of the program.

5 *Feedback decisions*. Putting the evaluation into a usable form, using it in further programming operations, and sharing it with others.

PROGRAM CHARACTERISTICS TO EVALUATE

Steele, in describing a broad definition of evaluation, indicates that many different characteristics can be evaluated:

There are at least five program characteristics that are sometimes evaluated. These characteristics have been called different things and aren't completely separate. Each contributes to the other.

• *Quality:* How good was it? What was the quality of the content, learning activities, media, teacher's performance? How did people react to it?

• *Suitability:* Did it meet the needs and expectations of the participants? Was it at the appropriate level of difficulty? Did it meet the expectations of the community? Was it within the mission of the programming unit?

• *Effectiveness:* What did it accomplish? How well did it accomplish its objectives?

• *Efficiency:* Were the accomplishments sufficient for the amount of resources required from the agency and the participants? Was this the best use of resources?

- *Importance:* How valuable was it to those who participated and to society? Was its importance sufficient to the resources that were involved?

Our old concept of evaluation focuses primarily on program effectiveness or how well the objectives were accomplished. Actually, however, much of our evaluation has been in terms of quality and suitability of program as judged by participant response to end-of-meeting sheets which explore such things as how the participant would rate the program, whether he thought he understood the content, whether the program was timed well, etc. Those holding to a definition of evaluation that includes only examining behavioral results, have in effect, said over the years that these end-of-meeting reactions weren't evaluation. However, if one accepts the fact that a program may be judged in terms of more than one characteristic, then these sheets contribute to evaluation, but explore different characteristics (quality and suitability) of the program.

There is value in making judgments about the quality and suitability of the program, and its effectiveness. It is also essential that contemporary educational programs be judged on still other characteristics.

When resources are limited, perhaps the most important characteristics for examination are those of efficiency and importance. Both depend on the program's effectiveness, but consider more than effectiveness. We need to give more consideration to whether we're using our resources to best advantage and to the relative importance of its many program opportunities.

Judgments as to potential importance must be made about the program design before it's actually implemented. We need more evaluation of programs when they're in the design state, but our traditional concept of evaluation focuses on the extent to which an objective has been reached. It doesn't challenge the objectives. Sometimes those objectives should have been evaluated and altered before the program was launched. Achievement of a poor objective doesn't result in a good program.

Regardless of the point in programming at which a program is evaluated or the characteristics of the program being examined, the basic structure of evaluation—criteria, evidence, and judgment—applies. We need to: (1) develop criteria related to the different characteristics and understand what characteristics of a program we're actually using as the basis of judgment when we use a particular kind of criteria, (2) identify which criteria are most important in which situations, and (3) increase our experience in making judgments of various characteristics and the quality of those judgments. Evaluation isn't necessarily easy, but a broad understanding can make it easier.[3]

Bennett[4] developed seven broad categories of criteria that can be useful in formally evaluating the effectiveness of continuing education programs

[3] Steele, op. cit., pp. 13–14.
[4] Claude Bennett, *Analyzing Impacts of Extension Programs,* Extension Service, U.S. Department of Agriculture, ESC–575, Washington, D.C., 1976.

Figure 17.2 Examples of "Hard" and "Soft" Data in a Hierarchy of Evidence for Program Evaluation

	"Hard" data	"Soft" data
7 End results	Trends in profit-loss statements, life expectancies, and pollution indexes	Casual perceptions of changes in quality of health, economy, and environment
6 Practice change	Direct observation of use of recommended practices over a series of years	Retrospective reports by people of their use of recommended farm practices
5 KASA change	Changes in scores on validated measures of knowledge, attitudes, skills, and aspirations	Opinions on extent of change in participants' knowledge, attitudes, skills, and aspirations
4 Reactions	Extent to which random sample of viewers can be distracted from watching a demonstration	Recording the views of only those who volunteer to express feelings about demonstration
3 People involvement	Use of social participation scales based on recorded observations of attendance, holding of leadership positions, etc.	Causal observation of attendance and leadership by participants
2 Activities	Prestructured observation of activities and social processes through partipant observation, use of video and audio tapes, etc.	Staff recall of how activities were conducted and the extent to which they were completed
1 Inputs	Special observations of staff time expenditures, as in "time and motion" study	Staff's subjective reports regarding time allocation

and attempts to provide guidance in choosing evidence regarding these categories. Figure 17.2 shows examples of hard and soft data in a hierarchy of evidence for the seven categories. This framework has been found to be very useful in making decisions about criteria and evidence.

REASONS FOR EVALUATION

Program evaluation, the process of determining the value of a program, is considered an essential part of the educational process by tradition and by experts. It should be something that you want to do—not something that you are forced to do by tradition or by administrative assignment.

For evaluation to attain its greatest value, we must be very clear in terms of what we are doing and why we are doing it. We must be able to distinguish our goal and/or purpose from the roles that we are expecting the evaluation to fulfill and the values that we expect to attain from it.

Following are some reasons for evaluating:

Affords a feeling of accomplishment. Most human beings need a feeling that they are accomplishing something worthwhile. Continuing educators are no exception. Even the most confident often have an uneasy feeling about whether or not they have actually accomplished something.

Provides information. Most of us are faced with questions in programming. In most cases, we take the best guess that we can without being absolutely certain that it is the right one. Evaluation can help you answer questions.

Helps focus on goals. We function in a constantly changing programming situation. We are apt to become engrossed in certain traditional programs and procedures. It is not easy to adapt to the changes that are taking place around us. Evaluation can help.

Can be a learning opportunity. We can learn about clientele and their situations from evaluation.

KINDS OF DECISIONS WHERE EVALUATIVE DATA ARE USED

Education evaluation is defined as the process of delineation, obtaining, and providing information useful in decision alternatives. The model presented here is based on the concept of evaluation as a process to acquire and use information for problem solving. Program development itself is based on the idea of improving decisions about possible courses of action. Thus, there is a direct relationship between data or information and various courses of action. This relationship is depicted through a time flow from past to present to future as illustrated in Figure 17.3. The main idea presented is that data are available about the past and present and must be used to develop action plans for the future.

Figure 17.3   A Time-Flow Relationship between Data and Possibilities for Action

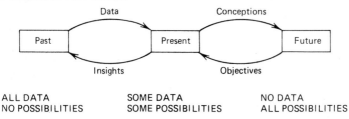

Within such a time flow, both past data and ideas about the future, formulated as objectives, will be vital inputs into programming. On the other hand, new insights will further generate new data. Thus, evaluation becomes the process that points to future possibilities for action from the analysis of accumulated data. The movement, however, is not a one-step movement from past to present to future. Rather, it is a continuous flow process. As a result, evaluation may focus on the same segment of a program from three time perspectives as the program proceeds.

The above picture is only the basic structure upon which the following evaluation framework is built. The model is adapted from the CIPP model developed by Stufflebeam, et al.[5] It involves four basic types of evaluation corresponding to four basic problem categories. The four types of evaluation are context, input, process, and product evaluations; while the four categories of problems are planning, structuring, implementing, and recycling. The distinction among the types of problems and relationships involved will be briefly discussed below.

Problems of Planning

This type of problem relates to what goals are in a program and how they are formulated. Questions include: What goals do we need to formulate? Should our priority needs be rearranged? What sort of problems must we solve to meet those priority needs? Who should be involved in determining these questions? How can clientele be more effectively involved? Answers to these questions can come through context evaluation. Context evaluation serves to define the relevant environmental situation and the rationale for determining objectives, identifying needs, and specifying involvement strategies. For example, all of those questions that are related to involvement and determining objectives would need to be considered in planning a nutrition program for twenty-five disadvantaged families.

Problems of Structuring

These problems involve questions about what goals are in a program and how they are determined. Relevant areas of concern include: What alternative resources and means are available? Can available resources limit the achievement of objectives? Who should be involved in the decision to allocate resources? What are the limitations on the use of these resources for the designated objectives? What problems must we solve to improve the quality of resources, especially human resources? The solutions to these and similar problems rest on input evaluation. Accordingly, input evaluation serves to define the appropriate design for achieving program

[5]D. L. Stufflebeam et al., *Educational Evaluation and Decision Making,* F. E. Peacock Publishers, Inc., Itasca, Ill., 1971.

objectives in terms of potential costs and benefits, where costs and benefits are defined in both monetary and social terms. Again, if a nutrition program is being planned, questions about the methods to use, instructional materials, and other materials would need attention. It is being suggested that by using the concept of evaluation, better analysis and decisions will result.

Problems of Implementing

This category of problems specifies what processes and procedures are needed and how to operationalize them in carrying through the action plan. For instance, what level of staff development is needed for the program? What new procedures are called for and how are they to be instituted? How can the schedule of activities be modified without major changes in the plan? Are responsibilities well defined? Making decisions on these and similar questions is the job of process evaluation. Process evaluation identifies defects in the procedural design of the program or its implementation by continuously monitoring activities to learn that objectives are achieved. A continuing educator is more likely to provide effective educational programs if feedback is obtained while the program is being conducted. An example is an end-of-meeting reaction sheet that gets at how useful the program has been.

Problems of Recycling

This last category of problems relates to the question of when to continue, modify, or terminate the program. Questions that need to be answered include these: Are the participants' needs being met? Has the problem been solved as intended? Were the results worth the investment in time, money, and effort? How much satisfaction or dissatisfaction did the participants experience and why? Was the program better than the preceding one? In what way? Answers to these questions constitute product evaluation. Product evaluation measures and interprets results at the conclusion of a program as well as at each successive stage during its implementation in order to provide a yardstick for future programming efforts. Also, more attention should be given to getting feedback about the effectiveness of the program and what additional needs exist.

In Figure 17.4, the total evaluation model is illustrated as a flow process through time. The evaluation process is illustrated as four major subprocesses: context, input, process, and product. Each of these subprocesses deals with a different set of problems: planning, structuring, implementing, and recycling. These are the basic components of people, activity, and change in each subprocess. The evaluation process culminates in a comparison of actual results with those originally intended. The discrepancy is identified and fed back into the system through a rede-

Figure 17.4   An Evaluation Model

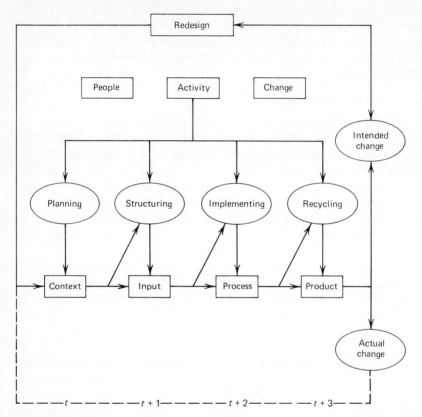

signed program that may be thought of as the ability of the system to redirect itself or learn from past mistakes and improve system performance. In the financial planning program discussed earlier, these four parts of the evaluation model were actually applied. It would be desirable to review Chapter 14 and identify the many different efforts to use evaluation in establishing objectives, identifying the methods, and determining the value or effectiveness of the program.

SUMMARY

This chapter has developed a concept of evaluation. The usefulness of evaluative data was emphasized in the many decisions that are involved in program development.

The concept of evaluation that was developed was very broad. This is reflected in the identified framework. It involves four basic types of evaluation corresponding to four major dimensions of program development.

DISCUSSION QUESTIONS

1 What is your concept of evaluation?
2 Compare the sources of criteria and evidence as used in the evaluation process.
3 Why are judgments so important in the evaluation process?
4 Describe the use that you made of an evaluation in subsequent programming.
5 How often should you evaluate a program?

Chapter 18

Communicating
Program Value

One of the important functions of evaluation is to contribute to the many decisions that are a part of program development. These decisions vary from determining priorities to making judgments about the value of the program. It is suggested that a task often neglected by the continuing education programmer is communicating the value of the program. As educators we make the assumption that all education is good or worthwhile. We also assume that others feel that education is always valuable and worthy of public support. In this era of technology and accountability, we must question our assumptions and systematically analyze our effectiveness in communicating the values of our programming efforts. Some general ideas about communicating program values will be reviewed in this chapter. Communicating to a specific audience will not be focused upon.

FUNCTIONS OF COMMUNICATING

Communicating or reporting the values of a program is very important for the programmer, the clientele, and the institution sponsoring the program.

In the previous chapter, it was emphasized that the purpose of evaluation was not only to defend and support the program but also to further the growth of the learner and the programmer. Thus, the following functions of reporting are broad and comprehensive:

- Provides a basis for further program development and improvement. Reporting the effectiveness of a program will allow various clientele and support groups to suggest new directions for programs, new topics, and needed changes in format, promotion, and methodology.
- Provides the necessary information or data for support and defense for continuing or expanding programs where such action is appropriate. Individuals who hold financial decision-making responsibilities are supportive of quality or success. They want continuous evidence that they are making correct decisions.
- Provides the basis for promotion and public relations. Findings and conclusions of evaluations are useful in creating a positive image for the institution and in the promotion of future program efforts. A strong promotional effort is essential for maintaining the interests and commitment to continuing education.

CONTENT OF REPORTS

There are many different kinds of information or data about a program that can be included in a report. Bennett's seven broad categories[1] for evaluation evidence can serve as a useful framework for decisions on what to include in a report:

- *End results*. The changes or actions by people and communities. Emphasis would probably be on the economy, environment, or social and cultural adjustments and improvements.
- *Practice change*. The focus would be on specific actions that the learner is now doing, such as accounting practices, farm practices, business procedures, nutritional practices, or relationships within a family.
- *KASA change*. This category refers to changes in knowledge, attitudes, skills, and aspirations. The measurements may be validated or they may simply be opinions on the extent of change.
- *Reactions*. The views of the participants of a program often are very useful in a report. These views often can reveal real feelings about the value of a program.
- *People involvement*. Data on the number of people participating in a program can be used in a variety of ways in a report. Numbers can be described in terms of student-contact hours, as percentage of the total population, of social-economic groups, or of professional groups.

[1] Claude Bennett, *Analyzing Impacts of Extension Programs,* Extension Service, U.S. Department of Agriculture, ESC–575, Washington, D.C., 1976.

- *Activities*. The inclusion of information about what was made available through various learning opportunities is useful in a report. This type of information illustrates the efforts of the programmer to assist people through educational opportunities.
- *Inputs*. This category includes the staff and other resources that are put into the program.

Reporting provides an opportunity for the programmer to summarize, interpret, and record the effectiveness of a program. It is necessary to take advantage of this opportunity and achieve the benefits from effective reporting.

GUIDELINES FOR REPORTS

Some institutions have rigid reporting requirements and procedures. Rigidity can often discourage creativity and innovation in reporting. If your institution or agency allows for flexibility, you may want to consider the following ideas:

- *Purpose*. Clarify the purpose of the report. What do you want to communicate?
- *Audience*. Identify a primary audience for the report. It may be used with other audiences, but should be prepared with a specific audience in mind.
- *Brief*. Reports should be brief, concise, and well organized. The main ideas must be clearly identified and emphasized.
- *Appeal*. Reports must have appeal in order to be useful. The style and layout are important whether you are doing a very inexpensive, simple report or an elaborate total-agency report.
- *Treatment of results and values*. Steele has suggested several ways of treating results:

Descriptive statements with or without support—Be sure to use sharp and clear narrative statements about general results and benefits from the program. Although support from one or more of the following can be useful, don't sell the program short just because you don't have testimony or findings. Make a statement if you feel you can muster support later if challenged.

Support from case examples—Real or illustrative case examples can be used for support.

Real testimony support—Individuals telling what they did as a result of your program and the value it had to them.

Findings from surveys—Case examples and testimony make results real and human to a reader, but the reader can't tell if most of the participants benefited or only a few. Surveys provide the framework for knowing how many achieved what things.[2]

• *Presentation.* It has been inferred that the report is always printed, but you may not find reporting through a printed document the most appropriate medium. Instead, you may communicate through one-to-one contact, at group sessions, through newspapers, radio, television, or indirectly through associations and groups. The main ideas that have been included will apply regardless of the medium used.

SUMMARY

This last chapter has focused on the need to communicate the effectiveness and value of your program. Several functions for a report were suggested and seven categories of potential content were identified. These categories vary from reporting the impact of a program to identification of the time and resource input of the programmer and the institution. Several general guidelines for effective reports were discussed.

DISCUSSION QUESTIONS

1 Do you think reporting is a part of the job of a programmer? Why?
2 Analyze and describe an effective report that you have prepared or seen.
3 Identify a plan for reporting for your institution.
4 Visit with several financial decision makers and determine what they look for in a report.
5 Analyze the different ways of reporting the effectiveness and value of a program to the learner. Is there one best way?

[2] Sara Steele, "Ideas Behind Program Reports," Division of Program and Staff Development, University of Wisconsin-Extension, Madison, 1977, p. 5.

Index

Accreditation, 33
Advisory committees:
  consequences of, 132 – 134
  definition of, 118
  interpersonal dynamics in,
    129 – 132
  members' contributions to,
    124 – 125
  orientation of members, 122 – 123
  problem solving, 127 – 129
  purpose of, 120 – 121
  rational decisions in, 125 – 126
Advocacy planning, 114 – 115
Affective domain of behavior,
  28, 204
Alinsky, Saul, 116 – 117
Alport, Gordon, 151
Apps, Jerold W., 22 – 23
Arnstein, Sherry, 116, 121

Beliefs:
  about learning and the learner,
    23 – 26
  about program development,
    29 – 34, 61, 63 – 68
  about purpose of education, 20 – 23
  about teaching and the programmer,
    26 – 29
Bennett, Claude, 229 – 230, 237 – 238
Bennis, W. G., 21, 29, 39
Biddle, Loureide, 76 – 77
Biddle, William, 76 – 77
Bigge, Morris, 208 – 209
Bloom, Benjamin, 148, 203
Boyle, P. G., 122 – 123
Brainstorming, 150

CEU (continuing education unit), 67

Change (*see* Social change)
Clientele analysis (*see* Need; Needs
    assessment)
Clientele involvement:
    assumptions about, 109–110
    concept of, 91–94
    definition of, 29, 45, 94, 108
    justification of, 95–97
    methods of, 113–118
    nature of task and, 97–102
    planning ideologies for, 104–106
    reasons for, 94–95, 109–113
    roles in, 103–104
Cognitive domain of behavior,
        203–204
Community:
    major elements of, 167–169
    social system and, 151–153
Community analysis:
    approaches to: community
            framework, 166–169
        planning framework, 169–171
    concept of, 148–153
Content analysis, 117
Continuing education unit (CEU), 67

Decision making, 31
    (*See also* Program; Program
            development; Social change)
Delbecq, A. G., 117–118
Developmental programs:
    definition of, 7–10
    phases of, 51–54
Devices, identifying instructional
        design with, 49
Dewey, John, 20–21, 25

Eckerman, A. C., 141–142
Education:
    behavioral view of, 20–21
    experiential view of, 20
    for government officials and
            personnel, 67
    mandatory fees for, 31–32
    for minority groups, 32–33, 66

Education (*cont.*):
    purpose of, 20–23
    right to, 65–66
    subject-matter view of, 20
    (*See also* Program; Program
            development)
Educational objectives:
    definition of, 194–195
    levels of, 198–200
    purposes of, 195–196
    sources of, 196–198
    taxonomy of, 202–204
    types of, 200–202
Evaluation:
    decisions in, 228
    effectiveness of, 225–228
    program characteristics for,
            228–230
    reasons for, 31, 230–231
    (*See also* Reports)
Evaluative data, uses of, 231–234

Formal hearing, 115
Franklin, Richard, 75–76
Freire, Paolo, 21, 26, 29

Gallaher, A., 74
Government officials and personnel,
        education for, 67
Growth process:
    affective domain, 28, 204
    learning, 27
    rote memory, 27
    teaching, 27

Hoffman, L. R., 130, 132

Informational programs:
    definition, 7, 11–12
    phases, 57
Institutional programs:
    definition, 7, 10–11
    phases of, 55–56

Instructional design, 48 – 49, 53
  and program development,
    183 – 193
Involvement (*see* Clientele
  involvement)

Keregero, Keregero, 160
Knowles, Malcolm, 80 – 82

Last, Donald, 99 – 100
Learning, 27
  factors in, 211 – 221
  and the learner, beliefs about,
    23 – 26
  principles of, 210 – 211
  theories of, 207 – 210
Legitimation in program development,
  47 – 48
Lippitt, Ronald, 39, 77 – 79

Methods, identifying instructional
  design with, 49
Milhollan, Frank, 208
Minority groups, education for,
  32 – 33, 66
Monette, Maurice, 140 – 144

Need(s):
  basic human, 140 – 142
  comparative, 143
  felt and expressed, 142 – 143
  normative, 143
  values and, 146 – 148
Needs assessment:
  community (*see* Community
    analysis)
  definition of, 29 – 30, 155 – 157
  formal, 158 – 162
    competency analysis, 161 – 162
    critical incident approach,
      159 – 161
    individual profile, 161
    surveys, 158 – 159

Needs assessment (*cont.*):
  informal, 162 – 163
    informal conversations, 162
    unobtrusive measures, 162 – 163
  situational, 52, 139 – 140
Nominal groups process, for
    involvement, 117 – 118

Objectives (*see* Educational objectives)
Ombudsman, 114
Osborn, A. F., 116

Planning, advocacy, 144 – 115
Powers, R. C., 123 – 124
Priorities, establishing (*see* Program
    priorities)
Problem solving (*see* Advisory
    committees; Program; Program
    development; Social change)
Professional certification, 66 – 67
Program(s):
  balanced, 30 – 31
  developmental, 7 – 10, 51 – 54
  focus of, 32
  informational, 7, 11 – 12, 57
  institutional, 7, 10 – 11, 55 – 56
  levels of, 15 – 16
  major, 14, 184
    phases for, 185 – 193
  quality of, 33 – 34
  relationship between, and
    organization, 12 – 13
  types of, 6 – 11, 51 – 57
Program development:
  assumptions for, 65 – 67
  beliefs about, 29 – 34, 61, 63 – 68
  concepts of, 43 – 51
  constraints in, 46
  definition of, 5, 42
  guidelines for, 64 – 65
  instructional design and, 183 – 193
  legitimation in, 47 – 48
  promotion in, 49
  rigidity or flexibility in, 47
  supportive resources in, 50

Program priorities:
  consequences of, 179—180
  criteria for, 173—176
  definition of, 46—47
  framework for, 176—179
Programmer:
  personal attributes of, 71—72
  philosophical concerns of (see
    Beliefs)
  responsibilities of, 13—15
  role of:
    aimed at program goals, 73—84
    in change, 70
    in community, 70—71
    conflict in, 85—86
    in educational process, 28—29
    organizational factors and, 71, 82
    orientations of, 86
    set, 84—85
  teaching and, beliefs about,
    26—29
Psychomotor domain of behavior,
  204—205

Reports:
  content of, 237—238
  functions of, 236—237
  guidelines for, 238—239
Rindt, Kenneth E., 216
Robinson, Jerry W., 73-74
Rogers, Carl, 24, 210
Rote memory, 27
Rothman, Jack, 70—72, 84—86

Situational analysis, 52, 139—140
  (See also Community analysis;
    Need; Needs assessment)
Skinner, B. F., 209
Social change:
  conflict strategy for, 91—93
  definition of, 38, 195, 196
  functional approach to, 93
  institutional building model approach
    to, 93—94
  planned, 39—41
  types of, 36—37
Steele, Sara, 158—159, 228—229,
  238—239
Stufflebeam, D., 111—112
Surveys, involving people through, 118

Task force, 113—114
Teaching and the programmer, beliefs
  about, 26—29
Techniques, identifying instructional
  design with, 49
Thelen, Herbert A., 29, 39
Tyler, Ralph, 19, 219—220

Unobtrusive measures, gathering
  information through, 116

Warwick, Donald, 147
Webb, E. J., 116, 162
Whale, W. B., 97, 123, 124